Excel 98 For Macs® For Dummies®

COMPUTER BOOK SERIES FROM IDG

The Excel Worksheet Window

- Close Box
- Formula Bar
- Menu Bar
- Title Bar
- Formatting Toolbar
- Standard Toolbar
- Vertical Scroll Bar
- Collapse Box
- Zoom Box

- Horizontal Scroll Bar with Tab Sheets
- Workbook Window
- Status Bar

The Standard Toolbar

- New
- Save
- Spelling
- Cut
- Paste
- Undo
- Web Toolbar
- Paste Function
- Drawing
- Zoom
- Office Assistant

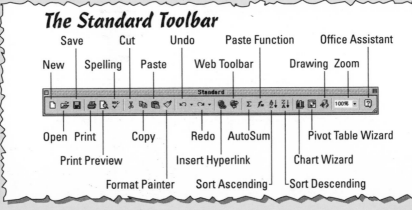

- Open
- Print
- Print Preview
- Copy
- Format Painter
- Redo
- Insert Hyperlink
- Sort Ascending
- AutoSum
- Sort Descending
- Chart Wizard
- Pivot Table Wizard

...For Dummies: #1 Computer Book Series for Beginners

COMPUTER BOOK SERIES FROM IDG

Excel 98 For Macs® For Dummies®

Cheat Sheet

Function Keys in Excel 98

Function Keys	Alone	Shift	Control	Option	Control+Shift
F1	Undo	What's This?			
F2	Cut	Edit comment			
F3	Copy	Paste Function (dialog box)	Define Name		
F4	Paste	Repeat Find	Close window		
F5	Go To	Find	Restore window		
F6	Next pane	Previous pane	Next workbook		Previous workbook
F7	Spelling		Move window		
F8	Extend selection	Add to selection	Resize window	Macro (dialog box)	
F9	Calculate active worksheet				
F10	Activate menu bar	Display shortcut menu			
F11	Create a chart	Insert new worksheet	Excel 4 macro sheet	Visual Basic Editor	
F12	Save As	Save	Open		Print (dialog box)

The Formatting Toolbar

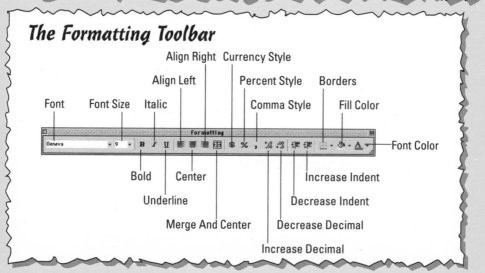

Align Right — Currency Style — Align Left — Percent Style — Borders — Font — Font Size — Italic — Comma Style — Fill Color — Geneva — 9 — Font Color — Bold — Center — Increase Indent — Underline — Decrease Indent — Merge And Center — Decrease Decimal — Increase Decimal

IDG BOOKS WORLDWIDE

...For Dummies: #1 Computer Book Series for Beginners

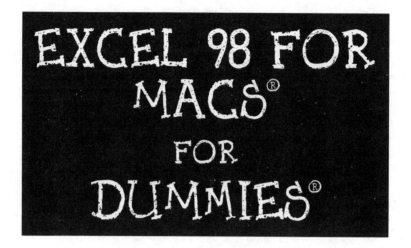

EXCEL 98 FOR MACS® FOR DUMMIES®

by Greg Harvey and Shane Gearing

IDG Books Worldwide, Inc.
An International Data Group Company

Foster City, CA ♦ Chicago, IL ♦ Indianapolis, IN ♦ New York, NY

Excel 98 For Macs® For Dummies®

Published by
IDG Books Worldwide, Inc.
An International Data Group Company
919 E. Hillsdale Blvd.
Suite 400
Foster City, CA 94404
www.idgbooks.com (IDG Books Worldwide Web site)
www.dummies.com (Dummies Press Web site)

Library of Congress Catalog Card No.: 98-85673

ISBN: 0-7645-0227-1

Printed in the United States of America

10 9 8 7 6 5 4 3 2 1

1O/SY/QV/ZY/IN

Distributed in the United States by IDG Books Worldwide, Inc.

Distributed by Macmillan Canada for Canada; by Transworld Publishers Limited in the United Kingdom; by IDG Norge Books for Norway; by IDG Sweden Books for Sweden; by Woodslane Pty. Ltd. for Australia; by Woodslane Enterprises Ltd. for New Zealand; by Longman Singapore Publishers Ltd. for Singapore, Malaysia, Thailand, and Indonesia; by Simron Pty. Ltd. for South Africa; by Toppan Company Ltd. for Japan; by Distribuidora Cuspide for Argentina; by Livraria Cultura for Brazil; by Ediciencia S.A. for Ecuador; by Addison-Wesley Publishing Company for Korea; by Ediciones ZETA S.C.R. Ltda. for Peru; by WS Computer Publishing Corporation, Inc., for the Philippines; by Unalis Corporation for Taiwan; by Contemporanea de Ediciones for Venezuela; by Computer Book & Magazine Store for Puerto Rico; by Express Computer Distributors for the Caribbean and West Indies. Authorized Sales Agent: Anthony Rudkin Associates for the Middle East and North Africa.

For general information on IDG Books Worldwide's books in the U.S., please call our Consumer Customer Service department at 800-762-2974. For reseller information, including discounts and premium sales, please call our Reseller Customer Service department at 800-434-3422.

For information on where to purchase IDG Books Worldwide's books outside the U.S., please contact our International Sales department at 650-655-3200 or fax 650-655-3295.

For information on foreign language translations, please contact our Foreign & Subsidiary Rights department at 650-655-3021 or fax 650-655-3281.

For sales inquiries and special prices for bulk quantities, please contact our Sales department at 650-655-3200 or write to the address above.

For information on using IDG Books Worldwide's books in the classroom or for ordering examination copies, please contact our Educational Sales department at 800-434-2086 or fax 817-251-8174.

For press review copies, author interviews, or other publicity information, please contact our Public Relations department at 650-655-3000 or fax 650-655-3299.

For authorization to photocopy items for corporate, personal, or educational use, please contact Copyright Clearance Center, 222 Rosewood Drive, Danvers, MA 01923, or fax 978-750-4470.

 is a trademark under exclusive license to IDG Books Worldwide, Inc., from International Data Group, Inc.

IDG
BOOKS
WORLDWIDE

About the Authors

Greg Harvey and **Shane Gearing** have been partners in business since 1984. Greg is author of more than a gazillion computer books (unfortunately, most of them for programs running on the Windows PCs). Shane, however, specializes in research and Macintosh applications for mind over media and has been waiting (for quite a while) for this opportunity to revise the original *Excel 5 For Macs For Dummies* book. To that end, Shane uttered the mantra, "Greg, don't count Apple out just yet!", several times since 1995.

In mid-1993, Greg and Shane started a multimedia publishing venture called mind over media. As multimedia developers, they hope to enliven their future computer books by making them into true interactive learning experiences that will vastly enrich and improve the training of users of all skill levels. You can send them e-mail at gharvey@mindovermedia.com and sgearing@mindovermedia.com. And you can visit their Web site at www.mindovermedia.com.

ABOUT IDG BOOKS WORLDWIDE

Welcome to the world of IDG Books Worldwide.

IDG Books Worldwide, Inc., is a subsidiary of International Data Group, the world's largest publisher of computer-related information and the leading global provider of information services on information technology. IDG was founded more than 25 years ago and now employs more than 8,500 people worldwide. IDG publishes more than 275 computer publications in over 75 countries (see listing below). More than 90 million people read one or more IDG publications each month.

Launched in 1990, IDG Books Worldwide is today the #1 publisher of best-selling computer books in the United States. We are proud to have received eight awards from the Computer Press Association in recognition of editorial excellence and three from *Computer Currents*' First Annual Readers' Choice Awards. Our best-selling *...For Dummies*® series has more than 50 million copies in print with translations in 38 languages. IDG Books Worldwide, through a joint venture with IDG's Hi-Tech Beijing, became the first U.S. publisher to publish a computer book in the People's Republic of China. In record time, IDG Books Worldwide has become the first choice for millions of readers around the world who want to learn how to better manage their businesses.

Our mission is simple: Every one of our books is designed to bring extra value and skill-building instructions to the reader. Our books are written by experts who understand and care about our readers. The knowledge base of our editorial staff comes from years of experience in publishing, education, and journalism — experience we use to produce books for the '90s. In short, we care about books, so we attract the best people. We devote special attention to details such as audience, interior design, use of icons, and illustrations. And because we use an efficient process of authoring, editing, and desktop publishing our books electronically, we can spend more time ensuring superior content and spend less time on the technicalities of making books.

You can count on our commitment to deliver high-quality books at competitive prices on topics you want to read about. At IDG Books Worldwide, we continue in the IDG tradition of delivering quality for more than 25 years. You'll find no better book on a subject than one from IDG Books Worldwide.

John Kilcullen
CEO
IDG Books Worldwide, Inc.

Steven Berkowitz
President and Publisher
IDG Books Worldwide, Inc.

*Eighth Annual
Computer Press
Awards ≥1992*

*Ninth Annual
Computer Press
Awards ≥1993*

*Tenth Annual
Computer Press
Awards ≥1994*

*Eleventh Annual
Computer Press
Awards ≥1995*

IDG Books Worldwide, Inc., is a subsidiary of International Data Group, the world's largest publisher of computer-related information and the leading global provider of information services on information technology. International Data Group publishes over 275 computer publications in over 75 countries. More than 90 million people read one or more International Data Group publications each month. International Data Group's publications include: **ARGENTINA:** Buyer's Guide, Computerworld Argentina, PC World Argentina; **AUSTRALIA:** Australian Macworld, Australian PC World, Australian Reseller News, Computerworld, IT Casebook, Network World, Publish, Webmaster; **AUSTRIA:** Computerwelt Österreich, Networks Austria, PC Tip Austria; **BANGLADESH:** PC World Bangladesh; **BELARUS:** PC World Belarus; **BELGIUM:** Data News; **BRAZIL:** Annuario de Informática, Computerworld, Connections, Macworld, PC Player, PC World, Publish, Reseller News, Supergamepower; **BULGARIA:** Computerworld Bulgaria, Network World Bulgaria, PC & MacWorld Bulgaria; **CANADA:** CIO Canada, Client/Server World, ComputerWorld Canada, InfoWorld Canada, NetworkWorld Canada, WebWorld; **CHILE:** Computerworld Chile, PC World Chile; **COLOMBIA:** Computerworld Colombia, PC World Colombia; **COSTA RICA:** PC World Centro America; **THE CZECH AND SLOVAK REPUBLICS:** Computerworld Czechoslovakia, Macworld Czech Republic, PC World Czechoslovakia; **DENMARK:** Communications World Danmark, Computerworld Danmark, Macworld Danmark, PC World Danmark, Techworld Denmark; **DOMINICAN REPUBLIC:** PC World Republica Dominicana; **ECUADOR:** PC World Ecuador; **EGYPT:** Computerworld Middle East, PC World Middle East; **EL SALVADOR:** PC World Centro America; **FINLAND:** MikroPC, Tietoverkko, Tietoviikko; **FRANCE:** Distributique, Hebdo, Info PC, Le Monde Informatique, Macworld, Reseaux & Telecoms, WebMaster France; **GERMANY:** Computer Partner, Computerwoche, Computerwoche Extra, Computerwoche FOCUS, Global Online, Macwelt, PC Welt; **GREECE:** Amiga Computing, GamePro Greece, Multimedia World; **GUATEMALA:** PC World Centro America; **HONDURAS:** PC World Centro America; **HONG KONG:** Computerworld Hong Kong, PC World Hong Kong, Publish in Asia; **HUNGARY:** ABCD CD-ROM, Computerworld Szamitastechnika, Internetto online Magazine, PC World Hungary, PC-X Magazin Hungary; **ICELAND:** Tolvuheimur PC World Island; **INDIA:** Information Communications World, Information Systems Computerworld, PC World India, Publish in Asia; **INDONESIA:** InfoKomputer PC World, Komputek Computerworld, Publish in Asia; **IRELAND:** ComputerScope, PC Live!; **ISRAEL:** Macworld Israel, People & Computers/Computerworld; **ITALY:** Computerworld Italia, Macworld Italia, Networking Italia, PC World Italia; **JAPAN:** DTP World, Macworld Japan, Nikkei Personal Computing, OS/2 World Japan, SunWorld Japan, Windows NT World, Windows World Japan; **KENYA:** PC World East African; **KOREA:** Hi-Tech Information, Macworld Korea, PC World Korea; **MACEDONIA:** PC World Macedonia; **MALAYSIA:** Computerworld Malaysia, PC World Malaysia, Publish in Asia; **MALTA:** PC World Malta; **MEXICO:** Computerworld Mexico, PC World Mexico; **MYANMAR:** PC World Myanmar; **NETHERLANDS:** Computer! Totaal, LAN Internetworking Magazine, LAN World Buyers Guide, Macworld Netherlands, Net, WebWereld; **NEW ZEALAND:** Absolute Beginners Guide and Plain & Simple Series, Computer Buyer, Computer Industry Directory, Computerworld New Zealand, MTB, Network World, PC World New Zealand; **NICARAGUA:** PC World Centro America; **NORWAY:** Computerworld Norge, CW Rapport, Datamagasinet, Financial Rapport, Kursguide Norge, Macworld Norge, Multimediaworld Norge, PC World Ekspress Norge, PC World Nettverk, PC World Norge, PC World ProduktGuide Norge; **PAKISTAN:** Computerworld Pakistan; **PANAMA:** PC World Panama; **PEOPLE'S REPUBLIC OF CHINA:** China Computer Users, China Computerworld, China InfoWorld, China Telecom World Weekly, Computer & Communication, Electronic Design China, Electronics Today, Electronics Weekly, Game Software, PC World China, Popular Computer Week, Software Weekly, Software World, Telecom World; **PERU:** Computerworld Peru, PC World Profesional Peru, PC World SoHo Peru; **PHILIPPINES:** Click!, Computerworld Philippines, PC World Philippines, Publish in Asia; **POLAND:** Computerworld Poland, Computerworld Special Report Poland, Cyber, Macworld Poland, Networld Poland, PC World Komputer; **PORTUGAL:** Cerebro/PC World, Computerworld/Correio Informático, Dealer World Portugal, Mac*In/PC*In Portugal, Multimedia World; **PUERTO RICO:** PC World Puerto Rico; **ROMANIA:** Computerworld Romania, PC World Romania, Telecom Romania; **RUSSIA:** Computerworld Russia, Mir PK, Publish, Seti; **SINGAPORE:** Computerworld Singapore, PC World Singapore, Publish in Asia; **SLOVENIA:** Monitor; **SOUTH AFRICA:** Computing SA, Network World SA, Software World SA; **SPAIN:** Communicaciones World España, Computerworld España, Dealer World España, Macworld España, PC World España; **SRI LANKA:** Infolink PC World; **SWEDEN:** CAP&Design, Computer Sweden, Corporate Computing Sweden, Internetworld Sweden, it.branschen, Macworld Sweden, MaxiData Sweden, MikroDatorn, Natverk & Kommunikation, PC World Sweden, PCaktiv, Windows World Sweden; **SWITZERLAND:** Computerworld Schweiz, Macworld Schweiz, PCtip; **TAIWAN:** Computerworld Taiwan, Macworld Taiwan, NEW ViSiON/Publish, PC World Taiwan, Windows World Taiwan; **THAILAND:** Publish in Asia, Thai Computerworld; **TURKEY:** Computerworld Turkiye, Macworld Turkiye, Network World Turkiye, PC World Turkiye; **UKRAINE:** Computerworld Kiev, Multimedia World Ukraine, PC World Ukraine; **UNITED KINGDOM:** Acorn User UK, Amiga Action UK, Amiga Computing UK, Apple Talk UK, Computing, Macworld, Parents and Computers UK, PC Advisor, PC Home, PSX Pro, The Web; **UNITED STATES:** Cable in the Classroom, CIO Magazine, Computerworld, DOS World, Federal Computer Week, GamePro Magazine, InfoWorld, I-Way, Macworld, Network World, PC Games, PC World, Publish, Video Event, THE WEB Magazine, and WebMaster; online webzines: JavaWorld, NetscapeWorld, and SunWorld Online; **URUGUAY:** InfoWorld Uruguay; **VENEZUELA:** Computerworld Venezuela, PC World Venezuela; and **VIETNAM:** PC World Vietnam.

5/7/98

Dedication

To all our long-suffering Mac enthusiasts and friends: This one's for you!

Acknowledgments

We want to take this opportunity to thank all the people at IDG Books whose dedication and talent combined to get this edition for Excel 98 out and into your hands in such great shape:

Tim Gallan, the project editor, for his helpful suggestions, humor, and all-around professionalism; Brian Kramer for his copy editing prowess; Tim Warner for his technical expertise; and Karen York, Linda Boyer, Michael Sullivan, and Rebecca Senninger on the Production team.

Publisher's Acknowledgments

We're proud of this book; please register your comments through our IDG Books Worldwide Online Registration Form located at http://my2cents.dummies.com.

Some of the people who helped bring this book to market include the following:

Acquisitions, Editorial, and Media Development

Senior Project Editor: Tim Gallan

Acquisitions Editor: Michael Kelly, Acquisitions Manager

Copy Editor: Brian Kramer

Technical Editor: Tim Warner

Editorial Manager: Leah P. Cameron

Editorial Assistant: Donna Love

Production

Project Coordinator: Karen York

Layout and Graphics: Lou Boudreau, Linda M. Boyer, Angela F. Hunckler, Brent Savage, Michael A. Sullivan

Proofreaders: Christine Berman, Kelli Botta, Vickie Broyles, Nancy Price, Rebecca Senninger, Janet M. Withers

Indexer: Anne Leach

General and Administrative

IDG Books Worldwide, Inc.: John Kilcullen, CEO; Steven Berkowitz, President and Publisher

IDG Books Technology Publishing: Brenda McLaughlin, Senior Vice President and Group Publisher

Dummies Technology Press and Dummies Editorial: Diane Graves Steele, Vice President and Associate Publisher; Mary Bednarek, Director of Acquisitions and Product Development; Kristin A. Cocks, Editorial Director

Dummies Trade Press: Kathleen A. Welton, Vice President and Publisher; Kevin Thornton, Acquisitions Manager

IDG Books Production for Dummies Press: Michael R. Britton, Vice President of Production; Beth Jenkins Roberts, Production Director; Cindy L. Phipps, Manager of Project Coordination, Production Proofreading, and Indexing; Kathie S. Schutte, Supervisor of Page Layout; Shelley Lea, Supervisor of Graphics and Design; Debbie J. Gates, Production Systems Specialist; Robert Springer, Supervisor of Proofreading; Debbie Stailey, Special Projects Coordinator; Tony Augsburger, Supervisor of Reprints and Bluelines; Leslie Popplewell, Media Archive Coordinator

Dummies Packaging and Book Design: Robin Seaman, Creative Director; Jocelyn Kelaita, Product Packaging Coordinator; Kavish + Kavish, Cover Design

♦

The publisher would like to give special thanks to Patrick J. McGovern, without whom this book would not have been possible.

♦

Contents at a Glance

Cartoons at a Glance

By Rich Tennant

page 93

page 7

page 189

page 301

page 235

page 325

Fax: 978-546-7747 • *E-mail:* the5wave@tiac.net

Table of Contents

Introduction

$\bullet\ \bullet$

*W*elcome to *Excel 98 For Macs For Dummies,* the definitive work on Excel 98 for those of you who have no intention of ever becoming a spreadsheet guru. In this book, you find all the information that you need to keep your head above water as you accomplish the everyday tasks that people do with Excel. The intention of this book is to keep things simple and not bore you with a lot of technical details that you neither need nor care anything about. As much as possible, this book attempts to cut to the chase by telling you in plain terms just what it is that you need to do to accomplish a task using Excel.

Excel 98 For Macs For Dummies covers all the fundamental techniques that you need to know in order to create, edit, format, and print your own worksheets. In addition to showing you around the worksheet, this book also exposes you to the basics of charting and creating databases. Keep in mind, though, that this book just touches on the easiest ways to get a few things done with these features — I make no attempt to cover charting and databases in a definitive way. In the main, this book concentrates on spreadsheets because spreadsheets are what most people need to create with Excel.

About This Book

This book is not meant to be read from cover to cover. Although its chapters are loosely organized in a logical order (progressing as you might when studying Excel in a classroom situation), each topic covered in a chapter is really meant to stand on its own.

Each discussion of a topic briefly addresses the question of what a particular feature is good for before launching into how to use it. In Excel, as with most other sophisticated programs, there is usually more than one way to do a task. For the sake of your sanity, I have purposely limited the choices by usually giving you only the most efficient ways to do a particular task. Later on, if you're so tempted, you can experiment with alternative ways of doing a task. For now, just concentrate on performing the task as described.

As much as possible, I've tried to make it unnecessary for you to remember anything covered in another section of the book. From time to time, however, you come across a cross-reference to another section or chapter in the book. For the most part, such cross-references are meant to help you get more complete information on a subject, should you have the time and interest. If you have neither, no problem; just ignore the cross-references as if they never existed.

How to Use This Book

This book is like a reference where you start out by looking up the topic you need information about (either in the table of contents or the index) and then refer directly to the section of interest. Most topics are explained conversationally (as though you were sitting in the back of a classroom where you can safely nap). Sometimes, however, my regiment-commander mentality takes over, and I list the steps you need to take to accomplish a particular task in a particular section.

What You Can Safely Ignore

When you come across a section that contains the steps you take to get something done, you can safely ignore all text accompanying the steps (the text that isn't in bold) if you have neither the time nor the inclination to wade through more material.

Whenever possible, I have also tried to separate background or footnote-type information from the essential facts by exiling this kind of junk to a sidebar. These sections are often flagged with icons that let you know what type of information you will encounter there. You can easily disregard text marked this way. (Icons used in this book are shown a little later.)

Foolish Assumptions

I'm going to make only one assumption about you (let's see how close I get): You have access to a Macintosh (at least some of the time) that has System 8 and Excel 98 installed on it (and, if you installed the rest of Office 98 on your Mac as well, I'll bet there isn't much room on your hard disk for anything more!). However, having said that, I make no assumption that you've ever launched Excel 98, let alone done anything with it.

This book is written expressly for users of Microsoft Excel 98 running under version System 8 of the Macintosh operating system. If you have a previous version of Excel for Macintosh (like Excel 5) running under the previous version of the operating system, like System 7.6 or earlier, please put this book down and instead pick up a copy of *Excel 5 For Macs For Dummies*, published by IDG Books Worldwide, Inc. If you have a version of Excel for Windows, you also need to put this book down, walk over to the Windows section of the store, and pick up a copy of *Excel 97 For Windows For Dummies*.

If you happen to be using Excel 5 for Macintosh (either because you just haven't seen the need for upgrading yet or you're just too cheap to purchase the upgrade), you can use this book to learn Excel 5 for Macintosh, provided that you promise to pay strict attention to the Excel 98 icon shown in the left margin. Anytime you see this baby, it means that I'm talking about a feature or set of features that are brand-new in Excel 98 (which means that they weren't yet invented in your version of Excel). I don't want any flame mail from you saying how the book's all wrong about some feature that doesn't appear in your copy of Excel. If that happens, I'll have to write you back and tell you that you weren't paying attention to the Excel 98 icon. Shame on you.

How This Book Is Organized

This book is organized in six parts (which gives you a chance to see at least six of those great Rich Tennant cartoons!). Each part contains two or more chapters (to keep the editors happy) that more or less go together (to keep you happy). Each chapter is further divided into loosely related sections that cover the basics of the topic at hand. You should not, however, get too hung up about following along with the structure of the book; ultimately, it doesn't matter at all if you learn how to edit the worksheet before you learn how to format it, or you learn printing before you learn editing. The important thing is that you find the information — and understand it when you find it — when you need to perform a particular task.

Just in case you're interested, a brief synopsis of what you find in each part follows.

Part I: Getting In on the Ground Floor

As the name implies, Part I covers such fundamentals as how to start the program, identify the parts of the screen, enter information in the worksheet, save a document, and so on. If you're starting with absolutely no background in using spreadsheets, you definitely want to glance at the information in Chapter 1 to discover what this program is good for before you move on to how to create new worksheets in Chapter 2.

Part II: Editing without Tears

Part II gives you the skinny on how to edit spreadsheets to make them look good as well as how to make major editing changes to them without courting disaster. Refer to Chapter 3 when you need information on formatting the data to improve the way it appears in the worksheet. Refer to Chapter 4 when you need information on rearranging, deleting, or inserting new information in the worksheet. And refer to Chapter 5 when you need information on how to print out your finished product.

Part III: Getting Organized and Staying That Way

Part III gives you all kinds of information on how to stay on top of the data that you've entered in your spreadsheets. Chapter 6 is full of good ideas on how to keep track of and organize the data in a single worksheet. Chapter 7 gives you the ins and outs of working with data in different worksheets in the same workbook and gives you information on transferring data between the sheets of different workbooks.

Part IV: Life beyond the Spreadsheet

Part IV explores some of the other aspects of Excel besides the spreadsheet. In Chapter 8, you find out just how ridiculously easy it is to create a chart using the data in a worksheet. In Chapter 9, you discover just how useful Excel's database capabilities can be when you have to track and organize a large amount of information. In Chapter 10, you find out about adding hyperlinks to jump to new places in a worksheet, to new documents, and even to Web pages, as well as how to convert worksheet data into HTML tables so that they can be published on your company's Web site.

Part V: Doing a Custom Job

Part V gives you ideas about how to customize the way you work with Excel. In Chapter 11, you find out how to record and play back macros to automate tasks. In Chapter 12, you see how to customize the built-in toolbars and create new toolbars of your own.

Part VI: The Part of Tens

As is the tradition in these ...For Dummies books, the last part contains lists of the top ten most useful and useless facts, tips, and suggestions. Don't worry, you won't have to read ten more chapters when you flip to this part.

Conventions Used in This Book

The following information gives you the lowdown on how things look in this book — publishers call these the book's *conventions*. (No campaigning, flag-waving, name-calling, or finger-pointing is involved, however.)

Excel 98 is a sophisticated program with lots of fancy boxes, plenty of bars, and more menus than you can count. In Chapter 1, I explain all about these features and how to use them. Be sure to review Chapter 1 if you have any questions about how to get around the program.

Although you use the mouse and keyboard shortcut keys to move your way in, out, and around the Excel worksheet, you do have to take some time to enter the data so that you can eventually mouse around with it. Therefore, this book occasionally encourages you to type something specific into a specific cell in the worksheet. Of course, you can always choose not to follow the instructions. When I tell you to enter a specific function, the part you should type generally appears in **bold** type. For example, **=SUM(A2:B2)** means that you should type exactly what you see: an equal sign, the word **SUM**, a left parenthesis, the text **A2:B2** (complete with a colon between the letter-number combos), and a right parenthesis. You then, of course, have to press Enter to make the entry stick.

When Excel isn't talking to you by popping up message boxes, it displays highly informative messages in the status bar at the bottom of the screen. This book renders many messages that you see on-screen like this:

```
=SUM(A2:B2)
```

Occasionally I may ask you to press a *key combination* in order to perform a certain task. Key combinations are written like this: ⌘+S. That plus sign in between means that you should hold down both the ⌘ key (the one with the Apple symbol and pretzel on it) and the S key at the same time before releasing them. This (sometimes cruel) type of finger aerobics may take some practice for you novices, but don't worry; you'll soon be a key-combo pro!

When you need to wade through one or more menus to get to the selection you want, I sometimes (though not often, mind you) use *command arrows* to lead you from the initial menu to the submenu and so on to the command you ultimately want. For example, if you need to first open the File menu to get to the Open command, I may write that instruction like this: File⇨Open.

Icons Used in This Book

The following icons are strategically placed in the margins to point out stuff you may or may not want to read.

This icon alerts you to nerdy discussions that you may well want to skip (or read when no one else is around).

This icon alerts you to shortcuts or other valuable hints related to the topic at hand.

This icon alerts you to information to keep in mind if you want to meet with a modicum of success.

This icon alerts you to information to keep in mind if you want to avert complete disaster.

This icon alerts you to brand-new features never before seen until the release of Excel 98.

Where to Go from Here

If you've never worked with a computer spreadsheet, I suggest that, right after getting your chuckles with the cartoons, you go first to Chapter 1 and find out what you're dealing with. If you're already familiar with the ins and outs of electronic spreadsheets but don't know anything about creating worksheets with Excel, jump into Chapter 2, where you find out how to get started entering data and formulas. Then, as specific needs arise (like "How do I copy a formula?" or "How do I print just a particular section of my worksheet?"), you can go to the table of contents or the index to find the appropriate section and go right to that section for answers.

Part I
Getting In on the
Ground Floor

The 5th Wave   By Rich Tennant

"Before I go on to explain more advanced procedures like the 'Zap-Rowdy-Students-who-Don't-Pay-Attention' function, we'll begin with some basics."

In this part . . .

One look at the Excel 98 screen (with all its boxes, buttons, and tabs), and you realize that there's a whole lot of stuff going on here. Well, not to worry: Chapter 1's only reason for being is to break down the parts of the Excel 98 screen and make some sense out of the rash of icons, buttons, and boxes that you're going to be facing day after day after day.

Of course, it's not enough to just sit back and have someone like me explain what's what on the screen. To get any good out of Excel, you've got to start learning how to use all these bells and whistles (or buttons and boxes, in this case). That's where Chapter 2 comes in, giving you the lowdown on how to use some of the screen's more prominent buttons and boxes to get your spreadsheet data entered. From this humble beginning, it's a quick trip to total screen mastery.

Chapter 1
What Is All This Stuff?

*J*ust because electronic spreadsheets like Excel 98 have become almost as commonplace on today's personal computers as word processors and games doesn't mean that they're either well understood or well used. In fact, I've encountered scads of users, even those who are reasonably well versed in the art of writing and editing in Microsoft Word, who have little or no idea of what they could or should do with Excel.

If you're one of the folks who has Office 98 on your computer but doesn't know a spreadsheet from a bedsheet, this means that Excel 98 is just sitting there taking up a lot of space. Well, it's high time to change all that.

What the Hell Would I Do with Excel?

Excel is a great organizer for all types of data, be they numeric, textual, or otherwise. Because the program has loads of built-in calculating capabilities, most people turn to Excel when they need to set up financial spreadsheets. These spreadsheets tend to be filled to the gills with formulas for computing stuff like total sales, net profits and losses, growth percentages, and that sort of thing.

Also popular are Excel's charting capabilities that enable you to create all types of charts and graphs from the numbers you crunch in your financial worksheets. Excel makes it really easy to turn columns and rows of boring, black-and-white numbers into colorful and snappy charts and graphs. You can then use these charts to add some pizazz to written reports (like those created with Word 98) or to punch up overheads used in formal business presentations (like those created with PowerPoint 98) or even to publish them in Web pages (using the Internet Assistant Wizard — see Chapter 10 for details).

Now, even if your job doesn't involve creating worksheets with a lot of fancy-Dan financial calculations or la-di-da charts, you probably have plenty of things for which you could and should be using Excel. For instance, you may have to keep lists of information or maybe even put together tables of information for your job. Excel is a great list keeper (even though we tend to refer to such lists as *databases* in Excel) and one heck of a table maker. Therefore, you can use Excel anytime you need to keep track of the products you sell, clients you service, employees you oversee, or you name it.

Little boxes, little boxes . . .

There's a really good reason why Excel is such a whiz at doing financial calculations by formula and keeping lists and tables of information organized. Look at any blank Excel worksheet (the one in Figure 1-1 will do fine) and just what do you see? Boxes, lots of little boxes, that's what! These little boxes (and there are millions of them in each worksheet you encounter) are called *cells* in spreadsheet jargon. And each piece of information (like a name, address, monthly sales figure, even your Aunt Sally's birthdate) goes into its own box (cell) in the worksheet you're building.

TECHNICAL STUFF

Why spreadsheet programs produce nothing but worksheets

Spreadsheet programs like Excel 98 refer to their electronic sheets as *worksheets* rather than *spreadsheets*. And, although it is perfectly acceptable (even preferable) to call one of its electronic sheets a worksheet, you never, never refer to Excel as a worksheet program — it is always called a spreadsheet program. So you can think of Excel as a spreadsheet program that produces worksheets, but *not* as a worksheet program that produces spreadsheets. (On the other hand, I often refer to worksheets as spreadsheets in this book — and so can you.)

If you're used to word processing, this idea of entering different types of information in little, bitty cells can be somewhat strange to get used to. If you're thinking in word-processing terms, you need to think of the process of building an Excel worksheet as being more like setting up a table of information in a Word document than writing a letter or report.

Send it to my cell address

As you can see in Figure 1-1, the Excel worksheet contains a frame used to label the columns and rows. Columns are given letters of the alphabet, while the rows are numbered. The columns and rows must be labeled because the Excel worksheet is humongous (Figure 1-1 shows only a tiny part of the total worksheet). The column and row labels act like street signs in a city — they can help you identify your current location, even if they don't prevent you from becoming lost.

Figure 1-1:
Little boxes, little boxes, and they all look just the same!

Cells: The building blocks of all worksheets

The cells in an Excel worksheet are formed by the intersection of the column and row grid. Technically, such an arrangement is known as an *array*. An array keeps track of different pieces of information stored in it by referring to its row position and its column position (something you'll see more clearly when the subject of the R1C1 cell referencing system is discussed in the sidebar called "Cell A1 a.k.a. Cell R1C1," later in this chapter). To display your worksheet data in its grid and tabular format, Excel just reads off the row and column position associated with the data you entered there.

As shown in Figure 1-2, Excel constantly shows you your current position in the worksheet in three different ways:

- ✔ Above the worksheet display at the beginning of what's called the *formula bar,* Excel lists the current cell location by its column and row reference as D5 when the cell at the intersection of column D and row 5 is current (the so-called *A1 cell reference system*).

- ✔ In the worksheet itself, the *cell pointer* (see the callout in Figure 1-2), shown by a heavy border, appears in the cell that's currently selected.

- ✔ On the frame of the worksheet, the letter of the column and the number of the row containing the cell pointer appear in bold, and these parts of the frame have shadows making them appear more sculpted.

You wonder why Excel makes such a big deal about telling you which cell is current in the worksheet? That's a good question, and the answer is important:

In the worksheet, you can only enter or edit information in the cell that's current.

The repercussions of this seemingly innocuous little statement are enormous. It means that if you're paying more attention to what you need to enter in your spreadsheet than to which cell is current, you can end up replacing something you've already entered. It also means that you'll never be able to edit a particular cell entry if you haven't first selected the cell to make it current.

Current Cell Reference   Cell Pointer

Figure 1-2:
Excel
shows you
where you
are in the
worksheet
with the cell
pointer,
current cell
reference,
and bold
type for the
column
letter and
row number
in the
worksheet
frame.

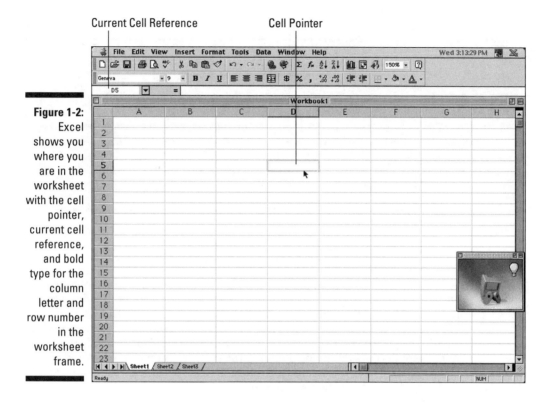

So just how many cells are we talking about here?

It's no exaggeration to say that each worksheet contains millions of cells, any of which can be filled with information. Each worksheet has 256 columns (of which, only the first 11 or 12 [A through K or L] are normally visible in a new worksheet) and 65,536 rows (of which, only the first 35 or 36 are normally visible in a new worksheet) depending upon the size of your monitor. If you multiply 256 by 65,536, you come up with a total of 16,777,216 empty cells in each worksheet you use. (That's more than 16 million of those suckers!)

And, as if that weren't enough, each new workbook that you start comes equipped with three of these worksheets, each with its own 16,777,216 blank cells. This gives you a grand total of 50,331,648 cells at your disposal in any one Excel file you happen to have open. And, should that prove to be too few (yeah, right!), you can add more worksheets (each with its 16,777,216 cells) to the workbook.

Cell A1 a.k.a. Cell R1C1

The A1 cell reference system is a holdover from the VisiCalc days (VisiCalc being the granddaddy of spreadsheet programs for personal computers). In addition to the A1 system, Excel 98 supports a much older, technically more correct system of cell references called the *R1C1 cell reference system*. In this system, both the columns and rows in the worksheet are numbered, and the row number precedes the column number. For example, in this system, cell A1 is called R1C1 (row 1, column 1); cell A2 is R2C1 (row 2, column 1); and cell B1 is R1C2 (row 1, column 2).

Assigning 26 letters to 256 columns

When it comes to labeling the 256 columns in a worksheet, our alphabet — with its measly 26 letters — is not up to the task. To make up the difference, Excel doubles up the cell letters in the column reference so that column AA immediately follows column Z. This is followed by column AB, AC, and so on to AZ. After column AZ, you find column BA, and then BB, BC, and so on. According to this system for doubling the column letters, the 256th (and last) column of the worksheet is column IV. This, in turn, gives the very last cell of any worksheet the cell reference IV65536.

What you should know about Excel at this point

Thus far, you know (or should know) the following things about Excel:

- Each Excel file is referred to as a *workbook*.

- Each new workbook you open contains three blank worksheets.

- Each worksheet in a workbook is divided into more than 16 million cells (16,777,216 actually) made by the intersection of the 256 columns and 65,536 rows.

- Each worksheet is surrounded on the left and the top with a frame that labels the columns with letters of the alphabet and rows with numbers. Columns beyond column Z have a double-letter designation such as AA, AB, and so on.

- All spreadsheet information is stored in the individual cells of the worksheet. You can, however, only enter information into the cell that is current.

More worksheet size trivia

If you were to produce the entire worksheet grid on paper, you would need a sheet that was approximately 21 feet wide by 1,365 feet long to do it! On a 14-inch computer screen, you can normally see no more than 10 or 11 complete columns and 21 or 22 complete rows of the entire worksheet. With columns being about 1 inch wide and rows about ¼ inch high, 10 columns represent a scant 3.9 percent of the total width of the worksheet, while 22 rows fill only about 0.03 percent of its total length. This should give you some idea of how little of the total worksheet is visible on the screen as well as just how much area is available.

✔ Excel indicates which of the more than 16 million cells in the worksheet is the current one by displaying its cell reference on the formula bar and displaying the cell pointer in the worksheet itself. (Refer to Figure 1-2.)

✔ The system for referencing cells in a worksheet — the so-called A1 cell reference system — combines the column letter (or letters) with the row number.

What you still need to know about Excel

Armed with the preceding information alone, however, you could easily get the mistaken idea that a spreadsheet program like Excel is little more than a quirky word processor with a gridlock that forces you to enter your information in tiny, individual cells instead of offering you the spaciousness of full pages.

Well, I'm here to say that Bill Gates didn't become a mega billionaire by selling a quirky word processor (all you Microsoft Word users out there, please hold your tongues!). The big difference between the cell of a worksheet and the pages of a word processor is that each cell offers computing power along with text-editing and formatting capabilities. This computing power takes the form of formulas that you create in various cells of the worksheet.

Quite unlike a paper spreadsheet, which contains only values computed somewhere else, an electronic worksheet can store both the formulas and the computed values returned by these formulas. Even better, your formulas can use values stored in other cells of the worksheet, and, as explained later, Excel automatically updates the computed answer returned by such a formula anytime you change these values in the worksheet.

Excel's computational capabilities, combined with its editing and formatting capabilities, make the program perfect for generating any kind of document that uses textual and numeric entries and requires you to perform calculations on the values. Because you can make your formulas *dynamic* — so that their calculations are automatically updated when you change referenced values stored in other cells of the worksheet — you will find it much easier to keep the calculated values in a worksheet document both current and correct.

Getting the Darn Thing Started

Please note that Office 98 and Excel 98 are only available on Mac Power PC or PPC computers running System 7.5 or System 8 or later. If you're at all familiar with using System 8 of the Macintosh operating system, it will come as no shock to find out that you have about a zillion ways to get Excel up and running (actually, there are only about five, and I'm only going to talk about four of them). All methods, however, require you to turn on your Mac and get the operating system up and running before you can use any of them to get Excel 98 going.

Starting Excel from the Office Manager pop-up menu on the menu bar

Starting Excel from the Office 98 pop-up menu on the menu bar is the easiest way to get the program up and running. The only problem with this method is that you can't use it unless you have the Office 98 Manager control panel installed.

With the Office 98 pop-up menu installed, you only have to click the Office Manager icon (see Figure 1-3) and then select Microsoft Excel on the Office Manager menu to start the program.

Starting Excel from the Office 98 folder

Even if you don't have the luxury of starting Excel 98 from the Office 98 pop-up menu on the menu bar (because you didn't install the Office 98 Manager), you can still start Excel 98 from the Microsoft Office 98 folder.

Figure 1-3:
To start
Excel 98,
click the
Office
Manager
icon, then
select
Microsoft
Excel on the
pop-up
menu.

To start Excel 98, follow these simple steps:

1. **Locate the icon for the hard drive on which you installed Office 98 and then double-click the icon to open it.**

2. **Locate the Microsoft Office 98 folder icon on the hard drive window and then double-click the folder icon to open it.**

3. **Locate the Microsoft Excel icon in the Microsoft Office 98 folder; then double-click this icon to launch the program (see Figure 1-4).**

As soon as you complete Step 3, the program loads, indicated by the display of the Microsoft Excel 98 opening (splash) screen. When Excel finishes loading, you are presented with a screen like the one shown in Figure 1-1, containing a new workbook where you can begin working.

You can also launch Excel 98 by opening any of the spreadsheet documents that you create with it. To launch Excel and open a particular Excel workbook file, open the folder containing the file, and double-click the document's icon (indicated by the XL icon on the right side of the page icon).

Figure 1-4:
To start
Excel 98
from the
Microsoft
Office 98
folder,
double-
click the
Microsoft
Excel icon.

Starting Excel from its alias

Not content with just two ways for starting Excel 98 (three if you count double-clicking an Excel document)? Well, how about another — this one by creating an Excel 98 alias (a desktop icon that is linked to the Microsoft Excel program icon in the Office folder) that you can double-click to launch the program?

To create an alias for Excel 98, you follow these steps:

1. **Locate the icon for the hard drive on which you installed Office 98; then double-click the icon to open it.**

2. **Locate the Microsoft Office 98 folder icon on the hard drive window and then double-click the folder icon to open it.**

3. **Locate the Microsoft Excel icon in the Microsoft Office 98 folder, click this icon to select it, and press ⌘+M to create an alias for it (indicated by the text** *Microsoft Excel alias* **in italic type).**

4. **Drag the Microsoft Excel alias icon out of the Microsoft Office 98 folder and place it on the desktop as suits your fancy.**

After adding the Microsoft Excel alias to the desktop of your Mac, you can launch Excel from the desktop by double-clicking its icon.

Starting Excel from the Launcher by adding its alias as a button

System 7.5 on the Macintosh introduced the Launcher window to the Mac desktop as a place where you can launch your favorite programs simply by clicking their buttons. If you're one of those users who has set up the

Launcher to load automatically each time you start your Mac, you will definitely want to add an Excel 98 alias (described in the section, "Starting Excel by clicking its alias," immediately preceding this one) to the Launcher as a button that you can click anytime you want to open Excel.

Here are the steps for adding the Microsoft Excel alias to the Launcher:

1. **If the Launcher isn't open on the desktop of your Macintosh, click the Apple icon at the far left of the menu bar; then click the Launcher alias on the Apple pop-up menu.**

2. **If it's not already pressed, click the Applications button at the top of the Launcher window to display the buttons for the programs you've added to the Launcher.**

3. **Drag the icon for Microsoft Excel alias (see "Starting Excel by clicking its alias" in the preceding section for details) from the desktop to the Launcher window (see Figure 1-5).**

After you complete Step 3, the Mac OS adds a Microsoft Excel button to the Launcher. After adding this Microsoft Excel button to the Launcher window, you only have to click this button anytime you feel the need to fire up Excel 98.

Figure 1-5:
To add an Excel button to the Launcher, drag its alias to the Launcher window.

Mousing Around

Although most of Excel's capabilities are accessible from the keyboard, in most cases the mouse is the most efficient way to select a command or perform a particular procedure. For that reason alone, if you need to use Excel regularly in getting your work done, mastering the program's various mouse techniques is well worth your time.

Minding your mouse manners

Programs such as Excel use three basic mouse techniques to select and manipulate various objects in the program and workbook windows:

- **Clicking an object:** positioning the pointer on something and then pressing and immediately releasing the mouse button.

- **Double-clicking an object:** positioning the pointer on something and then pressing and immediately releasing the mouse button rapidly twice in a row.

- **Dragging an object:** positioning the pointer on something and then pressing and holding down the mouse button as you move the mouse in the direction you want to drag the object. When you position the object in the desired location on the screen, you then release the mouse button to place it (a technique referred to, appropriately enough, as drag-and-drop).

When clicking an object to select it, you must make sure that the point of the arrowhead is touching the object you want to select before you click. To avoid moving the pointer slightly before you click, grasp the sides of the mouse between your thumb (on one side) and your ring and little fingers (on the other side) and then click the button with your index finger. If you run out of room on your desktop for moving the mouse, just pick up the mouse and reposition it on the desk (this does not move the pointer). A vast array of shortcuts are also available when clicking and pressing one or more modifier keys like ⌘, Control, Option, and Shift keys.

Getting your mouse pointer in shape

The shape of the mouse pointer is anything but static in the Excel program. As you move the mouse pointer to different parts of the Excel screen, the pointer changes shape to indicate a change in function. Table 1-1 shows you the various faces of the mouse pointer as well as the use of each shape.

Mouse Pointer Shape	What It Means
⊕	This thick, white cross pointer appears as you move the pointer around the cells of the current worksheet. You use this pointer to select the cells you need to work with, which is then outlined by the cell pointer.
▷	The arrowhead pointer appears when you position the pointer on the toolbar, menu bar, or on one of the edges of the block of cells that you've selected. You use the arrowhead pointer to choose Excel commands or to move or copy a cell selection with the drag-and-drop technique.
I	The I-beam pointer appears when you click the entry in the formula bar, double-click a cell, or press ⌘+U to edit a cell entry. You use this pointer to locate your place when editing a cell entry either in the cell itself or on the formula bar.
+	The fill handle (the thin, black cross) appears only when you position the pointer on the lower-right corner of the cell that contains the cell pointer. You use this pointer to create a series of sequential entries in a block or to copy an entry or formula in a block of cells.
⟷	The double-headed arrow pointer appears when you move over the side of some object that can be sized diagonally.
⊣⊢	The split double-headed arrow pointer appears when you position the pointer over the horizontal or vertical split box or the tab split bar. You use this pointer to split the workbook window into different panes or to increase or decrease the size of the horizontal scroll bar.
⊕	The crossed double-headed arrow pointer appears when you click the pointer on an embedded object to move or resize it.

Table 1-1   Minding the Shape of the Mouse Pointer in Excel

Don't confuse the mouse pointer with the cell pointer. The mouse pointer changes shape as you move it around the screen. The *cell pointer* always maintains its shape as an outline around the current cell or cell selection (whereupon it expands to include all the selected cells). The mouse pointer responds to any movement of your mouse on the desk and always moves independently of the cell pointer. You can use the mouse pointer to reposition the cell pointer, however. You do this by positioning the thick, white cross pointer in the cell that you want to hold the cell pointer and then clicking the mouse button.

So What Do All These Buttons Do?

Figure 1-6 identifies the different parts of the Excel program window that appear when you first start the program (assuming that you haven't selected an existing workbook to open at the same time as the program). As you can see, the Excel window, upon opening, is chock-full of all kinds of useful, though potentially confusing, stuff!

Turning on to the menu bar

The first bar in the Excel window is called the *menu bar*. Following the Apple icon, you find the menus for whatever application is running. In Figure 1-6, the Excel 98 menus appear on the menu bar. At the far right of the menu bar, you see the Excel icon (XL), indicating that it is Excel which is currently running and that the menus (File through Help) that appear on the menu bar belong to it.

You can click the Excel icon in the far right of the menu bar to open a menu where you can access the Finder or other programs that you have open.

You use the Excel 98 menus that appear on the menu bar to select the Excel commands you need in creating your spreadsheets and charts (jump ahead to the section "Ordering Directly from the Menus" for more information on how to select their commands).

Working with the Workbook title bar

The Workbook title bar is located at the top of the active Excel window containing the title, Workbook1. In the left-hand corner of the title bar you find the Close box. When you click the Close box (or press the shortcut keys ⌘+W), you close the current Excel workbook without exiting the Excel program.

Formula Bar

Menu Bar with Excel 98 Menu

Vertical Scroll Bar

Standard Toolbar   Title Bar   Collapse Box

Formatting Toolbar   Zoom Box

Close Box

Figure 1-6:
The Excel
program
window
contains a
veritable
smorgasbord
of buttons
and
toolbars.

Horizontal Scroll Bar with Sheet Tabs   Status Bar

Workbook Window with New Workbook

The Zoom box on the right side of the title bar enables you to maximize the current workbook so that its window becomes full-size and occupies all the space between the formula and status bars. Clicking the Zoom box again restores the original workbook window size. If you click the Collapse box, the Excel workbook window shrinks down to just the Workbook title bar (with the workbook still in memory and all its information still open). If you click the Collapse box again, the workbook is restored to its original size.

Tiptoe through the tooltips

To display the name of a tool on any toolbar shown on the screen, simply position the mouse pointer on the tool. Excel then displays the name of the tool in a little box below the tool.

Scrutinizing the Standard toolbar

The Standard toolbar occupies the second bar of the Excel program window. Each button (more commonly called a *tool*) in this bar performs a particular function when you click it with the mouse. For example, you can use the first tool to open a new workbook, the second one to open an existing workbook file, the third one to save the current workbook, and the fourth one to print the workbook. Table 1-2 shows you the name and function of each tool on the Standard toolbar. Rest assured, you will come to know each one intimately as your experience with Excel grows.

Table 1-2	The Cool Tools on the Standard Toolbar	
Tool in Question	*Tool Name*	*What the Tool Does When You Click It*
	New	Opens a new workbook with three blank worksheets
	Open	Opens an existing Excel workbook
	Save	Saves changes in the active workbook
	Print	Prints the active worksheet
	Print Preview	Previews how the worksheet will appear when printed
	Spelling	Checks the spelling of text in your worksheet
	Cut	Cuts the current selection to the Clipboard
	Copy	Copies the current selection to the Clipboard
	Paste	Pastes the contents of the Clipboard in the current worksheet
	Format Painter	Applies all the formatting used in the current cell to any cell selection you choose

Tool in Question	Tool Name	What the Tool Does When You Click It
	Undo	Undoes your last action
	Redo	Repeats your last action
	Insert Hyperlink	Lets you insert a hypertext link to another file, Internet address (URL), or specific location in another document (see Chapter 10 for information on using hyperlinks)
	Web Toolbar	Displays and hides the Web toolbar with the tools for navigating the hyperlinks in your worksheet or surfing the World Wide Web (see Chapter 10 for information on using this toolbar)
	AutoSum	Adds a list of values with the SUM function
	Paste Function	Lets you use one of Excel's many built-in functions (see Chapter 2 for details)
	Sort Ascending	Sorts data in a cell selection in alphabetical and/or numerical order, depending upon the type of data in the cell
	Sort Descending	Sorts data in a cell selection in reverse alphabetical and/or numerical order, depending upon the type of data in the cells
	ChartWizard	Steps you through the creation of a new chart in the active worksheet (see Chapter 8 for details)
	PivotTable Wizard	An advanced function for analyzing data in an interactive format.
	Drawing	Displays and hides the Drawing toolbar, which lets you draw various shapes and arrows (see Chapter 8 for details)
100%	Zoom	Changes the screen magnification to zoom in or out on your worksheet data
	Office Assistant	Activates the Office Assistant and lets you get tips on using Excel or ask him a question (see "Conferring with your Office Assistant" later in this chapter for details)

Finding your way around the Formatting toolbar

Beneath the Standard toolbar, you see the Formatting toolbar, so called because its buttons are mainly used to format cells in your worksheet. Table 1-3 shows you the name of each tool on this toolbar, along with a brief description of its function.

Table 1-3	**The Cool Tools on the Formatting Toolbar**	
Tool	*Tool Name*	*What the Tool Does When You Click It*
Geneva	Font	Applies a new font to the entries in the cell selection
9	Font Size	Applies a new font size to the entries in the cell selection
B	Bold	Applies bold to the cell selection
I	Italic	Applies italics to the cell selection
U	Underline	Underlines the *entries* in the cell selection (not the cells); if the entries are already underlined, clicking this tool removes the underlining
≡	Align Left	Left-aligns the entries in the cell selection
≡	Center	Centers the entries in the cell selection
≡	Align Right	Right-aligns the entries in the cell selection
⊞	Merge and Center	Centers the entry in the active cell across selected columns by merging their cells into one
$	Currency Style	Applies a Currency number format to the cell selection to display all values with a dollar sign, with commas between thousands, and two decimal places

Tool	Tool Name	What the Tool Does When You Click It
%	Percent Style	Applies a Percentage number format to the cell selection; the values are multiplied by 100 and displayed with a percent sign and no decimal places
,	Comma Style	Applies a Comma number format to the cell selection to display commas separating thousands and adds two decimal places
+.0 .00	Increase Decimal	Adds one decimal place to the number format in the cell selection each time you click the tool; reverses direction and reduces the number of decimal places when you hold the Shift key as you click this tool
.00 +.0	Decrease Decimal	Reduces one decimal place from the number format in the cell selection each time you click the tool; reverses direction and adds one decimal place when you hold the Shift key as you click this tool
⇐	Decrease Indent	Outdents the entry in the current cell to the left by one character width of the standard font
⇒	Increase Indent	Indents the entry in the current cell to the right by one character width of the standard font
⊞ ▾	Borders	Selects a border for the cell selection from the pop-up palette of border styles
⬠ ▾	Fill Color	Selects a new color for the background of the cells in the cell selection from the pop-up color palette
A ▾	Font Color	Selects a new color for the text in the cells in the cell selection from the pop-up color palette

The Standard and Formatting toolbars contain the most commonly used tools and are the ones that are automatically displayed in the Excel window when you first start the program. Excel does, however, include several other toolbars that you can display as your work requires their special tools. As you soon discover, Excel's toolbars are a real boon to productivity because they make the program's standard routines so much more accessible than the Excel menus.

Fumbling around the formula bar

The formula bar displays the cell address and the contents of the current cell. This bar is divided into three sections: The first, leftmost section (called the Name Box) contains the current cell address with a drop-down button to its right; the second, middle section is shaded and displays only a single button with an equal sign on it (called the Edit Formula button); and the third, rightmost section is the white area that takes up all the rest of the bar. If the current cell is empty, the third section of the formula bar is blank. As soon as you begin typing an entry or building a worksheet formula, the second and third sections of the formula bar come alive.

As soon as you press a key, the Cancel and Enter buttons appear in the second section (see Figure 1-7) between the drop-down button in the Name Box and the Edit Formula buttons (refer to Chapter 2 for information on using these buttons).

After this string of buttons, you see the characters that you've typed in the third section of the bar, mirroring the characters that appear in the worksheet cell itself. After you complete the entry in the cell — either by clicking the Enter button on the formula bar or by pressing Return or an arrow key — Excel displays the entire entry or formula in the formula bar, and the string of buttons disappears from the center section of the formula bar. The contents of that cell thereafter appear in the formula bar whenever that cell contains the cell pointer.

Cancel Button

Enter Button

New Box   Edit Formula Button

Figure 1-7:
Cancel and
Edit buttons
appear on
the formula
bar to the
left of
the Edit
Formula
button as
soon as
you begin
typing.

Winding your way through the workbook window

A blank Excel workbook appears in a workbook window right below the formula bar when you first start the program (assuming that you don't start it by double-clicking an Excel workbook icon). As you can see in Figure 1-8, when you first start Excel 98, the workbook window is somewhat less than full-size and quite a bit larger than a collapsed workbook title bar. The title bar at the top of the workbook window displays the workbook's filename (at first, before you've had a chance to save a new document, the title bar carries a temporary filename like Workbook1, and then Workbook2 when you open your next new workbook, and so on).

On the bottom of the workbook window, you see sheet-tab scrolling buttons, the sheet tabs for activating the various worksheets in your workbook (remember that you have three new sheets to start), followed by the horizontal scroll bar that you can use to bring new columns of the current worksheet into view. On the right side of the workbook window, you see a vertical scroll bar that you can use to bring new rows of the current worksheet into view (keeping in mind that you're only viewing a small percentage of the total columns and rows in each worksheet). At the intersection of the horizontal and vertical scroll bars, in the lower-right corner, you find the *sizer,* which you can use to manually modify the size and shape of the less-than-maximized workbook window.

Figure 1-8:
Each
workbook
window in
Excel
contains its
own title
bar and
sizing
buttons as
shown
here.

As soon as you start Excel, you can immediately begin creating a new
spreadsheet in Sheet1 of Workbook1.

When a workbook sheet is not a worksheet

Worksheets are not the only type of sheet that you can have in an Excel
workbook. In addition to worksheets, your workbook can contain *chart
sheets,* which contain charts (see Chapter 8) created from data in one of the
worksheets, and/or *macro sheets* (see Chapter 11), which in turn contain the
code for macros that automate various tasks that you perform on your
worksheets or charts.

Manually manipulating the workbook window

As I mention in the preceding section, when you're working with a less-than-maximized workbook window (like the one shown in Figure 1-8), you can manually size and move the window with the sizer (the box that appears in the lower-right corner at the intersection of the horizontal and vertical scroll bars).

To manipulate the size of a workbook window, position the mouse pointer on the sizer box and then drag the mouse as needed to adjust the size of the side or sides of the window.

- ✔ If you drag the sizer straight up, the workbook window becomes shorter. If you drag the sizer straight down, the window becomes longer.

- ✔ If you drag the sizer straight to the left, the workbook window becomes narrower; if you drag it straight to the right, the window becomes wider.

- ✔ If you drag the sizer diagonally toward the upper-left corner of the window, the workbook becomes both shorter and narrower; if you drag the sizer diagonally away from the upper-left corner of the window, the workbook becomes longer and wider.

When the outline of the workbook window reaches the desired size, you then release the mouse button, and Excel redraws the workbook window to your new size.

After using the sizer box to change the size and shape of a workbook window, you must use the sizer again to manually restore the window to its original shape and dimensions. After clicking the zoom box to maximize a window, the next time you click the zoom box, Excel restores the window to whatever shape and size you last created with the sizer box.

Besides resizing workbook windows, you can also move them around within the area between the formula bar and status bar in the Excel program window. To move a workbook window

1. **Simply pick it up by the scruff of its neck — which, in this case, corresponds to the window's title bar or the outer edge of the window.**

2. **After you've got it by the title bar or outer edge, drag the window to the desired position and release the mouse button.**

Slipping through the sheets

At the very bottom of the Excel workbook window that contains the horizontal scroll bar, you see the sheet-tab scrolling buttons followed by the sheet tabs for the three worksheets in the workbook. Excel shows which worksheet is active by displaying its sheet tab on top in white as part of the displayed worksheet (rather than belonging to unseen worksheets below). To activate a new worksheet (thus bringing it to the top and displaying its information in the workbook window), you click its sheet tab.

If you add more sheet tabs to your workbook (see Chapter 7 for details on how to add more worksheets to your workbook) and the sheet tab for the worksheet you want to work with is not displayed, you can use the sheet-tab scrolling buttons to bring the worksheet into view. Click the buttons with the triangles pointing left and right to scroll one worksheet at a time in either direction (left to scroll left and right to scroll right). Click the buttons with the triangles pointing left and right to the vertical lines to scroll the sheets so that the tabs for the very first or very last worksheets are displayed at the bottom.

Scoping out the status bar

The bar at the very bottom of the Excel program window is called the status bar because it displays information that keeps you informed of the current state of Excel. The left part of the status bar displays messages indicating the current activity you're undertaking or the current command you've selected from the Excel menu bar. When you first start Excel, the message Ready is displayed in this area (as shown in Figure 1-9), telling you that the program is ready to accept your next entry or command.

The right side of the status bar contains various boxes that display different indicators telling you when you've placed Excel in a particular state that somehow affects how you work with the program. For example, normally, when you first start Excel, the Num Lock indicator shows NUM in this part of the status bar.

You AutoCalculate my totals

The widest box (the second one from the left) in the status bar contains the AutoCalculate indicator. You can use the AutoCalculate indicator to get a running total of any group of values in your worksheet. (See the beginning of Chapter 3 if you need information on how to select groups of cells that you select in a worksheet.) For example, Figure 1-9 shows you a typical spreadsheet after selecting part of a column of cells, many of which contain values. The total of all the values in the cells that are currently selected in this worksheet automatically appears in the AutoCalculate indicator on the status bar.

	File Edit View Insert Format Tools Data Window Help			Mon 5:10:10 PM

Arial ▼ 10 ▼ **B** *I* U ≡ ≡ ≡ ⊞ $ % , .00 .00 ⊞ ▾ ⬧ ▾ **A** ▾

B3 ▼ = 80138.58

Mother Goose - 1998 Sales

	A	B	C	D	E	F	G
1	Mother Goose Enterprises - 1998 Sales						
2		Jan	Feb	Mar	Qtr 1 Total		
3	Jack Sprat Diet Centers	80138.58	59389.56	19960.06	159488.2		
4	Jack and Jill Trauma Centers	123456.2	89345.7	25436.84	238238.74		
5	Mother Hubbard Dog Goodies	12657.05	60593.56	42300.28	115550.89		
6	Rub-a-Dub-Dub Hot Tubs and Spas	17619.79	40635	42814.99	101069.78		
7	Georgie Porgie Pudding Pies	57133.56	62926.31	12408.73	132468.6		
8	Hickory, Dickory, Dock Clock Repair	168291	124718.1	41916.13	334925.23		
9	Little Bo Peep Pet Detectives	30834.63	71111.25	74926.24	176872.12		
10	Total	490130.81	508719.48	259763.27	1258613.6		
11							

⊩ ◀ ▶ ▶⊩ \Sheet1 / Sheet2 / Sheet3 /

Ready   Sum=159488.2   NUM

Auto Calculate Indicator

Figure 1-9:
The
AutoCalculate
indicator
automatically
displays the
sum of the
values
in the
selected
(highlighted)
cells in the
worksheet.

Not only does the AutoCalculate indicator on the status bar give you the sum of the values in the cells you currently have selected, but it can also give you the count or the average of these values. To get the count of all the cells that contain values (cells containing text entries are not counted), you Control+click the AutoCalculate indicator and select COUNT on this indicator's shortcut menu. To get the average of the values in the current cell selection, you Control+click the AutoCalculate indicator and select AVERAGE on this indicator's shortcut menu. To return the AutoCalculate indicator to its normal totaling function, you Control+click it and choose SUM on the indicator's shortcut menu.

The Num Lock indicator and the numeric keypad

The NUM in the Num Lock indicator tells you that you can use the numbers on the numeric keypad to enter values in the worksheet. When you press Shift and the Num Lock key, NUM disappears from the Num Lock indicator. This is your signal that the cursor-movement functions that are also assigned to this keypad are now in effect. This means, for example, that pressing 6 moves the cell pointer one cell to the right instead of entering this value in the formula bar!

Of course, you need never disable Num Lock if your keyboard is already equipped with dedicated cursor and arrow keys, as are all the keyboards that offer you a separate numeric keypad.

You Gotta Get Me Out of This Cell!

Excel provides several methods for getting around each of the huge worksheets in your workbook. One of the easiest ways is to click the tab for the sheet you want to work with and then use the scroll bars in the workbook window to bring new parts of this worksheet into view. In addition, the program provides a wide range of keystrokes that you can use not only to move a new part of the worksheet into view but also to make a new cell active by placing the cell pointer in it.

The secrets of scrolling

 To understand how scrolling works in Excel, imagine the worksheet as a humongous papyrus scroll attached to rollers on the left and right. To bring into view a new section of a papyrus worksheet that is hidden on the right, you crank the left roller until the section with the cells you want to see appears. Likewise, to scroll into view a new section of the worksheet that is hidden on the left, you crank the right roller until the section of cells appears.

Calling up new columns with the horizontal scroll bar

You can use the *horizontal scroll bar* to scroll back and forth through the columns of a worksheet. To scroll new columns into view from the right, you click the right-arrow scroll button on the horizontal scroll bar. To scroll new columns into view from the left (anytime except when column A is the first column displayed), you click the left-arrow scroll button.

To scroll very quickly through columns in one direction or the other, you click the appropriate arrow scroll button in the scroll bar and *continue to hold down* the mouse button until the columns you want to see are displayed on the screen.

 You can use the scroll box in the horizontal scroll bar to make big jumps to the left and right in the columns of the worksheet. Simply drag the scroll box in the appropriate direction along the bar. As you drag, the letter of the column that would appear as the leftmost column in the worksheet (should you then release the mouse button) is displayed above the horizontal scroll bar (this feature of showing how far you've scrolled is known as *scroll tips*). You can use the column letter display in the horizontal scroll tips to gauge when to release the mouse button to stop the horizontal scrolling.

Raising up new rows with the vertical scroll bar

You can use the *vertical scroll bar* to scroll up and down through the rows of a worksheet. To scroll to new rows below those currently in view, you click the down-arrow scroll button on the vertical scroll bar. To scroll back up to rows above that are no longer in view (anytime except when row 1 is the first one displayed), you click the up-arrow scroll button.

To scroll very quickly through rows in one direction or the other, you click and hold down the appropriate arrow scroll button in the vertical scroll bar just as you do in the horizontal scroll bar.

You can use the vertical scroll box to make big jumps up and down the rows of the worksheet by dragging the vertical scroll box in the appropriate direction along the bar. As you drag, the scroll tips shows you the number of the row that would appear at the very top of the worksheet area (should you release the mouse button at that very moment). You can use this row number display in the vertical scroll tips to tell when you should release the mouse button to stop the vertical scrolling.

Scrolling from screen to screen

You can also use the horizontal and vertical scroll bars to scroll through the columns and rows of your worksheet a screenful at a time. To do this, you click the light gray area of the scroll bar *not* occupied by the scroll box or the arrow scroll buttons. For example, to scroll to the right by a screenful of columns when the scroll box is snug against the left-arrow scroll button, you simply click the light gray area of the scroll bar behind the scroll box, between it and the right-arrow scroll button. Then, to scroll back to the left by a screenful of columns, you click the light gray area in front of the scroll box, between it and the left-arrow scroll button.

Likewise, to scroll up and down the rows of the worksheet a screenful at a time, you click the light gray area either above or below the vertical scroll, between it and the appropriate arrow scroll button.

The keys to moving the cell pointer

The only disadvantage to using the scroll bars to move around is that the scrolls only bring new parts of the worksheet into view — they don't actually change the position of the cell pointer. This means that if you want to start making entries in the cells in a new area of the worksheet, you still have to remember to select the cell (by clicking it) or the group of cells (by dragging through them) where you want the data to appear before you begin entering the data.

Excel offers a wide variety of keystrokes for moving the cell pointer to a new cell. When you use one of these keystrokes, the program automatically scrolls a new part of the worksheet in view, if this is required in moving the cell pointer. Table 1-4 summarizes these keystrokes and how far each one moves the cell pointer from its starting position.

Table 1-4	Keystrokes for Moving the Cell Pointer
Keystroke in Question	*Where the Cell Pointer Moves*
→ or Tab	Cell to the immediate right
← or Shift+Tab	Cell to the immediate left
↑	Cell up one row
↓	Cell down one row
Home	Cell in Column A of the current row
⌘ or Control+Home	First cell (A1) of the worksheet
⌘ or Control+End or End, Home	Cell in the worksheet at the intersection of the last column that has any data in it and the last row that has any data in it (that is, the last cell of the so-called *active area* of the worksheet)
Page Up	Cell one screenful up in the same column
Page Down	Cell one screenful down in the same column
⌘ or Control+→ or End, →	First occupied cell to the right in the same row that is either preceded or followed by a blank cell
⌘ or Control+← or End, ←	First occupied cell to the left in the same row that is either preceded or followed by a blank cell
⌘ or Control+↑ or End, ↑	First occupied cell above in the same column that is either preceded or followed by a blank cell
⌘ or Control+↓ or End, ↓	First occupied cell below in the same column that is either preceded or followed by a blank cell
⌘ +Page Down	Last occupied cell in the next worksheet of that workbook
⌘ +Page Up	Last occupied cell in the previous worksheet of that workbook

Block moves

The keystrokes that combine the ⌘ or Control or End key with an arrow key listed in Table 1-4 are among the most helpful for moving quickly from one edge to the other in large tables of cell entries or in moving from table to table in a section of the worksheet that contains many blocks of cells.

- ✔ If the cell pointer is positioned on a blank cell somewhere to the left of a table of cell entries that you want to view, pressing ⌘ or Control+→ moves the cell pointer to the first cell entry at the leftmost edge of the table (in the same row, of course).

- ✔ When you then press ⌘ or Control+→ a second time, the cell pointer moves to the last cell entry at the rightmost edge (assuming that there are no blank cells in that row of the table).

- ✔ If you switch direction and press ⌘ or Control+↓, Excel moves right to the last cell entry at the bottom edge of the table (again assuming that there are no blank cells below in that column of the table).

- ✔ If, when the cell pointer is at the bottom of the table, you press ⌘ or Control+↓ again, Excel moves the pointer to the first entry at the top of the next table located below (assuming that there are no other cell entries above this table in the same column).

- ✔ If you press ⌘ or Control or End and arrow key combinations and there are no more occupied cells in the direction of the arrow key you selected, Excel advances the cell pointer right to the cell at the very edge of the worksheet in that direction.

- ✔ If the cell pointer is located in cell C15 and there are no more occupied cells in row 15, when you press ⌘ or Control+→, Excel moves the cell pointer to cell IV at the rightmost edge of the worksheet.

- ✔ If you are in cell C15 and there are no more entries below in Column C and you press ⌘ or Control+↓, Excel moves the pointer to cell C65536 at the very bottom edge of the worksheet.

When you use End and an arrow-key alternative, you must press and then release the End key *before* you press the arrow key (indicated by the comma in keystrokes such as End, →). Pressing and releasing the End key causes the END indicator to appear on the status bar. This is your sign that Excel is ready for you to press one of the four arrow keys.

Because you can keep the ⌘ or Control key depressed as you press the different arrow keys you need to use, the ⌘ or Control-plus-arrow-key method provides a more fluid method for navigating blocks of cells than the End-then-arrow-key method.

When you gotta go to that cell now!

Excel's Go To feature provides an easy method for moving directly to a distant cell in the worksheet. To use this feature, you display the Go To dialog box by selecting the Edit⇨Go To command on the Excel menu bar or by pressing ⌘+G or the function key F5. In the Reference text box of the Go To dialog box, type the address of the cell you want to go to and select OK or press Return. When typing in the cell address in the Reference text box, you can type the column letter or letters in upper- or lowercase letters.

When you use the Go To feature to move the cell pointer, Excel remembers the references of the last four cells that you visited. These cell references then appear in the Go To list box. Notice that the address of the cell you last came from is also listed in the Reference box. This makes it possible to move quickly from your present location to your previous location in a worksheet by pressing F5 and Return (provided that you used the Go To feature to move to your present position).

Lotsa luck with Scroll Lock

You can use the Scroll Lock key to "freeze" the position of the cell pointer in the worksheet so that you can scroll new areas of the worksheet in view with keystrokes such as Page Up and Page Down without changing the cell pointer's original position (in essence, making these keystrokes work in the same manner as the scroll bars).

After engaging Scroll Lock, by pressing Shift+Scroll Lock (F14 on many keyboards), when you scroll the worksheet with the keyboard, Excel does not select a new cell as it brings a new section of the worksheet into view. To "unfreeze" the cell pointer when scrolling the worksheet via the keyboard, just press the Shift+Scroll Lock key again.

Ordering Directly from the Menus

For those occasions when the Standard and Formatting toolbars don't provide you with a ready-made tool for getting a particular task done, you have to turn to the program's system of menu commands. Excel exhibits a little bit of menu overkill in that, in addition to the regular menus found on the menu bar of nearly all applications, the program also offers a secondary system of *shortcut menus*.

Shortcut menus are so called because they offer just those menu commands that are normally used to manipulate the particular screen object that the menu is attached to (such as a toolbar, workbook window, or worksheet cell). As a result, shortcut menus often bring together commands that you otherwise find on several individual menus on the Excel menu bar.

Encountering the Excel menus

As when moving the cell pointer in the worksheet, Excel offers you a choice between using the mouse or the keyboard to select commands from the menu bar. To open an Excel menu with the mouse, you simply click a menu to open it and then click the command name on the open menu. To open a menu with the keyboard, press function key F10 to access the menu bar, and then press the → key until you highlight the menu you want to open. Then, to open the menu, you press the ↓ key.

Prior to System 8, Mac users had to click and hold down the mouse button while navigating menus. In System 8 and later, you only have to click the menu, and it stays open.

After you open your menu, you can select any of its commands by clicking the command with the mouse, or by pressing the ↓ key until you highlight the command and then pressing the Return key.

As an alternative to using the arrow keys with F10, you can activate *hot keys* on the menu and command names (indicated by underlining) that you access by pressing F10 followed by the underlined letter in the menu and command names (just like Windows users do!?!). To activate the hot keys, choose Tools⇨Preferences and then click the On or Automatic radio button in the Command underline section of the General tab.

As you learn the Excel commands, you can combine opening a menu and selecting one of its menu commands. With the mouse, you have to click the menu and then drag the pointer down the open menu until you highlight the desired command, whereupon you release the mouse button. Some commands on the Excel menus have shortcut keystrokes assigned to them (shown after the command on the drop-down menu). You can use the shortcut keystrokes to select the desired command instead of having to access the drop-down menus. For example, to save changes to your workbook, you press the shortcut keys ⌘+S instead of having to select the Save command from the File menu.

Many commands on the Excel menus lead to the display of a dialog box, which contains further commands and options (see "Digging Those Dialog Boxes" later in this chapter). You can tell which commands on a menu lead to dialog boxes because the command name is followed by three periods (known as an *ellipsis*). For example, you know that selecting the Save As command on the File menu opens a dialog box because the command is listed as Save As... on the File menu.

Also, note that not all menu commands are always available to you. You can tell when a command is not currently available because the command name is in light gray (or *dimmed*) on the menu. A command on a menu remains dimmed until the conditions under which it operates exist in your document. For example, the Paste command on the Edit menu remains dimmed as long as the Clipboard is empty. But as soon as you move or copy some information into the Clipboard with the Cut or Copy commands on the Edit menu, the Paste option is no longer dimmed and appears in normal bold type when you open the Edit menu — indicating, of course, that this command is now available for your use.

Sizing up the shortcut menus

Shortcut menus are attached to particular objects on the Excel screen — like a workbook window, toolbar, or worksheet cell. Because different shortcut menus are attached to different kinds of Excel objects, you need to click the object in order to end up with the shortcut menu that is associated with it. When clicking the object, however, you must be holding down the Control (and not the ⌘ key) to have Excel open the object's shortcut menu rather than simply select the object itself.

After you open a shortcut menu, you can select one of its commands by clicking it (or by pressing the ↓ or ↑ key until you highlight the desired command and then pressing the Return key to select it).

The one shortcut menu that you can open with the keyboard is the shortcut menu attached to cells in a worksheet. To open this special type of shortcut menu, you select a cell or cells and then press Shift+F10. Note that this keystroke works for any type of Excel sheet except a chart, which doesn't have this type of shortcut menu attached to it.

Digging Those Dialog Boxes

Many an Excel command is attached to a dialog box that presents you with a variety of options that you can apply to the command. Figures 1-10 and 1-11 show you the Save As and Preferences dialog boxes. Between these two dialog boxes, you can find almost all the different types of buttons, tabs, and boxes used by Excel and described in Table 1-5.

Figure 1-10:
The Save As
dialog box
contains a
text box, list
box, and
pop-up list
box, along
with a
bunch of
command
buttons.

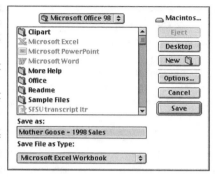

Figure 1-11:
The
Preferences
dialog box
contains a
variety of
tabs, check
boxes, radio
buttons, and
command
buttons.

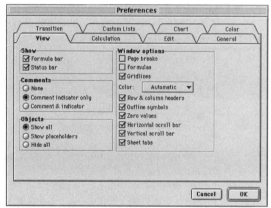

Table 1-5	The Parts of a Dialog Box
Button or Box in Question	*What It's Good For*
Tab	Provides a means of displaying a certain set of options in a complex dialog box like the Preferences dialog box (shown in Figure 1-11), bringing together a whole mess of different types of program settings that you can change.
Text box	Provides a place for typing a new entry. Many text boxes contain default entries that you can alter or replace entirely.

(continued)

Table 1-5 *(continued)*

Button or Box in Question	*What It's Good For*
List box	Provides a list of options from which you can choose. If the list box contains more options than can be displayed in its box, the list box contains a scroll bar that you can use to bring new options into view. Some list boxes are attached to a text box, allowing you to make a new entry in the text box either by typing it or by selecting it in the related list box.
Pop-up list box	Provides a condensed version of a standard list box that, instead of displaying several options in its list, shows only the current option (which originally is also the default option). To open the list box and display the other options, you click the pop-up button that accompanies the box. After the list is displayed, you can select a new option from it as you would in any standard list box.
Check box	Presents a dialog box option that you can turn on or off. When the check box is selected, you know that its option is selected. When a check box is blank, you know that its option is not selected.
Radio button	Presents items that have mutually exclusive options. The option button consists of a circle followed by the named option. Radio buttons are always arranged in groups, and only one of the buttons in the group can be selected at one time. Excel lets you know which option is currently selected by placing a dot in the middle of its circle (when an option button is selected, it looks like a knob on an old-fashioned radio, thus the name radio button).
Spinner buttons	Spinner buttons appear as a pair of small boxes one on top of the other. The spinner button on the top has an upward-pointing arrowhead on it, whereas the spinner button on the bottom has a downward-pointing arrowhead on it. You use the spinner buttons to scroll up and down through a series of preset options as you select the one you want.
Command button	Initiates an action. The command button is rectangular in shape, and the name of the command is displayed within the button. If a name in a command button is followed by an ellipsis (. . .), Excel displays another dialog box containing even more options when you select the button.

Note: Although you can move a dialog box out of the way of some data in your worksheet, you cannot change the box's size or shape — these dimensions are permanently fixed by the program.

Many dialog boxes contain default options or entries that are automatically selected unless you make new choices before you close the dialog box.

 ✔ To close a dialog box and put your selections into effect, you choose the OK button (or the Close button in the upper-left corner if the dialog box lacks an OK button).

 ✔ If the OK button is surrounded by a border, which is very often the case, you can also press Return or Enter to put your selections into effect.

 ✔ To close a dialog box without putting your selections into effect, you can either select Cancel in the dialog box or press Esc.

Most dialog boxes group related options together as an item (often, this is done by placing a box around the options). When making selections in a dialog box with the mouse, you simply click the selection you want to use or, in the case of text entries, click the pointer in the entry to set the insertion point and then modify the entry.

You can also select an item in the current list box option by typing the first few characters of its name — as soon as you begin typing, Excel jumps to the first option in the list box whose name begins with the characters you enter.

In addition to the more elaborate dialog boxes shown in Figures 1-10 and 1-11, you also encounter a simpler type of dialog box used to display messages and warnings (these dialog boxes are appropriately known as *alert boxes*). Many dialog boxes of this type contain just an OK button that you must click to close the dialog box after reading the message.

Ogling the Online Help

You can get online help with Excel 98 anytime you need it while using the program. The only problem with the traditional online Help system is that it is only truly helpful when you're familiar with the Excel jargon. If you don't know what Excel calls a particular feature, you may have trouble locating it in the Help topics (just like trying to look up in a dictionary a word that you have no idea how to spell). To help alleviate this problem, Excel has added a new Office Assistant that lets you type in a question about how to do something in Excel in your own words. The Office Assistant then attempts to translate your question, phrased in perfectly good English, into its horrible Excel-technobabble so that it can then display the Help topics that give you the information you need.

Conferring with your Office Assistant

The Office Assistant personalizes the online Help system, while at the same time giving you the opportunity to ask questions in plain English about using Excel. When you first call upon the Office Assistant, he appears in the form of a rather animated Macintosh with feet, named Max. To call upon Max and ask him a question about using Excel, you open the Office Assistant window by following these steps:

1. **Click the Office Assistant button on the Standard toolbar (the very last one) or choose Help⇨Microsoft Excel Help on the Excel menu bar.**

   Max appears in his own window with a question-and-answer balloon extending from the window, which asks you what you would like to do (just like the one shown in Figure 1-12).

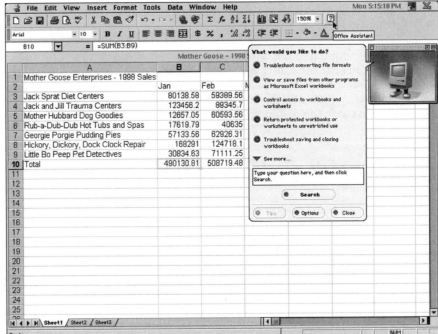

Figure 1-12: Meet Max, your personal Office Assistant, who is ready to answer your every question about Excel.

2. **Type in plain English your question about using Excel; then click the Search button or press Return.**

   As you type, Max pretends to be writing your question down in his notebook. After you select Search, Max searches for related Help topics and then displays the results as bulleted points in a new question and answer balloon that extends from the Office Assistant window.

3. **Click the Help topic that interests you the most in the list to open a new window containing the Help topic.**

   When there are more related Help topics than will all fit into Max's question and answer balloon, a triangular button appears at the end of the bulleted list. To see more Help topics, click this triangle. When you locate the Help topic you want to read, click its bullet in the question and answer balloon.

4. **When you finish reading or printing the Help topic, close the Help window by clicking the window's Close box.**

If you want to consult another one of the topics that Max displayed in response to your question, you simply need to click somewhere on the open Office Assistant window to reopen the question-and-answer balloon (Max remembers your question until you replace it with a new one) and then click the Search button or press Return to ask your question again. Max then redisplays the same Help topics displayed in the question-and-answer balloon in response to your original question. To print a Help topic, choose File⇨Print Topic or press ⌘+P.

If the Office Assistant can't even figure out where to look for Help topics because you asked a completely zany question, at least as it relates to using Excel, such as, "When will I win the lottery?", Excel beeps and then displays an alert box stating

```
Sorry, but I don't know what you mean. Please rephrase your
question.
```

which is the Office Assistant's way of saying, "I don't have a clue as to what you're talking about!"

If the Office Assistant doesn't find any related topics, maybe because you asked a really ambiguous question, at least according to its limited, technical vocabulary, Excel beeps and then displays an alert box stating

```
There are several Help topics that may be related to your
request. If you don't see a topic that looks helpful,
please rephrase your question.
```

Most of the time, however, the Office Assistant fetches a bunch of Help topics (whether they're helpful or not), no matter how irrelevant or stupid your question. For example, I asked the Tip Wizard, Max,

```
Why is Excel so hard to use?
```

and its reply was to go and get a whole bunch of disparate Help topics, including tips on entering text, using Excel data in a mailing list, speeding searches with the Find feature, using Excel 98 files with previous versions of Excel or other programs, along with a bunch of unrelated topics like copying Excel data to Word or PowerPoint or how Excel calculates PivotTable data. When you think about it, I guess this screen is a pretty good answer to the question, "Why is Excel so hard to use?"

Sometimes, you may think that the Help topics returned by the Office Assistant have nothing to do with your question, only later to discover that the weird topics listed in the question-and-answer balloon were exactly what you needed to know. A lot of this is just the result of not yet being familiar with the bulk of Excel's technobabble.

After consulting the Office Assistant, you can close the question-and-answer balloon while leaving the Office Assistant window open. To close the balloon, just press the Esc key or the Close command button. To move the Office Assistant window out of the way as you work, drag the window by its title bar (which just happens to be completely empty).

If you later decide that you need to close the Office Assistant window altogether, you need to click its Close box.

Choosing a new persona for the Office Assistant

Max is just one of the many different "personalities" that you can assign to the Office Assistant. In addition, you can choose between:

- A bouncing ball with a smiley face (of all things) called The Dot.
- A three-dimensional Albert Einstein knockoff named (what else?) The Genius.
- A vacuum cleaner-like robot (that only R2-D2 could love) called Hoverbot.
- A two-legged robot with two big eyes called F1.
- A smiling paper clip called Clippit.
- A animated butler called Bosgrove.
- A spinning Microsoft Office Logo showing the four interlocking colors called Office Logo.

✔ An animated planet Earth that turns into a flower and then back into a planet called Mother Nature.

✔ A cartoon dog in a red cape called Power Pup.

✔ A cartoon retriever called Rocky.

✔ An cartoon cat named Earl.

✔ An origami cat named Scribble.

✔ A two-dimensional representation of the Bard of Avon himself called, simply, Will (the persona my editors all seem to be really wild about).

Some of these various Office Assistants are installed on the Office CD in the Value Pack Installer, which is recommended for those users with adequate hard disk space (that is, lots of room!).

Each Office Assistant personality available in what's referred to as the Gallery comes with its own animation and sounds (some make more noise than others). To select a new persona for your Office Assistant, follow these steps:

1. **If you haven't already done so, click the Office Assistant button on the Standard toolbar or choose Help⇨Microsoft Excel Help on the menu bar to open the Office Assistant window.**

2. **Click the Office Assistant to open the Office Assistant dialog box.**

3. **Click the Options button at the bottom of the Office Assistant dialog box.**

4. **Click the Gallery tab and then click the >Next or Back> buttons until you display the Office Assistant persona that you want to use.**

5. **Click the OK button to close the Office Assistant dialog box and replace Max with the new persona in the Office Assistant window.**

Note that if you find yourself getting bored with the same old staid antics from the Office Assistant, you can get him (or her, if you're using Mother Nature) to dance (or at least become a little more animated) by choosing the Animate! command on the Office Assistant's shortcut menu (opened by Control+clicking the window).

Taking tips from the Office Assistant

As you go about building and editing your worksheets in Excel, the Office Assistant, like some spy in the background, is silently analyzing everything you do. As you select commands and push buttons, the Office Assistant is busy trying to amass a list of tips and tricks related to the tasks that you just did. You can always tell when the Office Assistant has come up with some new tips because a light bulb icon appears in the Office Assistant window along with the Office Assistant persona.

To see the tip that the Office Assistant has dug up for you, just click the light bulb in the Office Assistant window or click the Office Assistant window and click the Tips button in the question-and-answer balloon to open a tip balloon. To see earlier tips in the tip balloon, click the Back button. To return to later tips, click the Next button. When you finish looking at the tips and want to put the tip balloon away, just click the Close button.

Carving out context-sensitive Balloon help

You can get context-sensitive help by choosing Help⇨Show Balloons on the menu bar. With Balloon help turned on, help balloons spring up all over the place as you pass the mouse pointer over various objects in Excel and parts of the Excel screen, including Excel menus, tools on the various toolbars, not to mention the worksheet title bar, worksheet frame, and so on and so forth.

After you tire of balloons popping up all over the place (and you *will* get tired of them), you can turn off the Balloon help by choosing Help⇨Hide Balloons (which replaces the Show Balloons command).

If you turn on Balloon help in Excel 98 and then switch to another Microsoft program like Word 98, Balloon help is turned on in that program as well. You can then turn off Balloon help in the new program by choosing Help⇨Hide Balloons on that program's menu bar. When you then return to Excel, you will find Balloon help has been deflated there as well.

Tackling the Help topics

Beyond using the Office Assistant to get straight answers to your Excel questions or the Balloon help to identify parts of the Excel screen, you can, if all else fails, resort to using the MS Excel Help window to get even more online information on Excel. To open this window, you choose Help⇨ Contents and Index on the menu bar. The MS Excel Help window contains four buttons: Contents, Index, Back, and History. Select the Contents button to get information performing essential techniques like creating, printing, or saving a worksheet. Select the Index button to find information on a particular item or term such as *current cell, data entry,* or *fonts.* Select the Back button to back up the very last topic you visited. Select the History button to quickly revisit a particular Help topic.

To select a topic on the Contents button, click the book icon with the topic of interest to display all the subtopics. Then to display help on a particular subtopic, click its page icon (containing a question mark).

To locate a Help topic in the index, click the Index button, then, in the first text box, type the first letter or letters of the name of the item or term (for example, **hy** for hyperlink) that you want to look up. Doing this scrolls up the list of Help topics to those that begin with the letter(s) you typed. To see all the subtopics pertaining to a particular topic displayed in the list box, click its description and then click the Show Topics button. The Help system then displays a list of all related subtopics in the list box below. To display the Help information for a particular subtopic in the lower list box, click it and then click the Go To button to display its Help information in a new window. (Click the Back button to return to the Index.)

When reading a Help topic in the MS Excel Help window, you may notice that certain terms appear in green underlined with dots, and certain icons appear in gray-shaded boxes on the screen. On some help screens, you may see small buttons (with >> on them) preceding certain help procedures.

- ✔ Click any term that appears in green underlined with dots or graphic that appears in a gray shaded box to display a balloon explaining the term or graphic (like Balloon help). Click somewhere outside of the balloon on the help screen to hide its text.

- ✔ Click the >> button that precedes a particular step or procedure to display a new help screen with more information on that procedure. Click the Back button when you are ready to return to the previous help screen.

If you come upon a Help topic that you want to print out, you can select the Print Topic command on the File⇨Print Topic on the menu bar or you can simply press ⌘+P.

You can also copy information from an Excel Help topic to your word processor or even to an Excel document. To copy Help information, choose the Edit⇨Copy command on the menu bar or simply press ⌘+C.

After you copy the Help topic in this manner, you can copy the Help information into a word-processing document or worksheet by starting the program and opening the document (if necessary) and then choosing the Edit⇨Paste command on the program's menu bar or by pressing ⌘+V.

After you finish with reviewing and printing the Help information in the MS Excel Help window, you can return to Excel by clicking File⇨Quit on the menu bar (⌘+Q) or by clicking the MS Excel Help window's Close button.

When It's Quitting Time

When you're ready to call it a day and quit Excel, you have a couple of choices for shutting down the program:

✔ Choose File⇨Quit command on the menu bar.

✔ Press ⌘+Q.

If you try to exit Excel after working on a workbook and you haven't saved your latest changes, the program beeps at you and displays an alert box asking you whether you want to save your changes. To save your changes before exiting, choose the Save command button (for detailed information on saving documents, see Chapter 2). If you've just been playing around in the worksheet and don't want to save your changes, you can abandon the document by choosing the Don't Save button.

Chapter 2

Creating a Spreadsheet from Scratch

*A*fter you know how to get into Excel 98, it's time to find out how to get yourself into trouble by actually using it! In this chapter, you're gonna find out how to put all kinds of information into all those little, blank worksheet cells described in Chapter 1. Here, you find out about the Excel AutoCorrect and AutoComplete features and how they can help cut down on errors and speed up your work. You also get some basic pointers on other smart ways to minimize the drudgery of data entry, such as filling out a series of entries with the AutoFill feature and entering the same thing in a bunch of cells all at the same time.

And after discovering how to fill up a worksheet with all this raw data, you find out what has to be the most important lesson of all: how to save all the information on disk so that you don't ever have to enter the stuff again!

So What Ya Gonna Put in That New Workbook of Yours?

When you start Excel without specifying a document to open, as happens when you start the program by selecting Microsoft Excel on the Office 98 menu on the menu bar (refer to Chapter 1), you get a blank workbook in a new workbook window. This workbook, temporarily named Workbook1, contains three blank worksheets (named Sheet1, Sheet2, and Sheet3). To begin to work on a new spreadsheet, you simply start entering information in the first sheet of the Workbook1 workbook window.

The ins and outs of data entry

Here are a few simple guidelines (a kind of data-entry etiquette, if you will) that you should keep in mind when you start creating a spreadsheet in Sheet1 of your new workbook:

- ✔ Whenever you can, organize your information in tables of data that use adjacent (neighboring) columns and rows. Start the tables in the upper-left corner of the worksheet and work your way down the sheet, rather than across the sheet, whenever possible. When it's practical, separate each table by no more than a single column or row.

- ✔ When you set up tables, don't skip columns and rows just to "space out" the information. In Chapter 3, you see how to place as much white space as you want between information in adjacent columns and rows by widening columns, heightening rows, and changing the alignment.

- ✔ Reserve a single column at the left edge of the table for the table's row headings.

- ✔ Reserve a single row at the top of the table for the table's column headings.

- ✔ If your table requires a title, put the title in the row above the column headings. Put the title in the same column as the row headings. You see how to center a title across the columns of the entire table in Chapter 3.

You may wonder why, after making such a big stinking deal about how big each of the worksheets in a workbook is back in Chapter 1, I'm now on your case about not using that space to spread out the data you enter into it. After all, given all the real estate that comes with each and every Excel worksheet, you'd think conserving space would be one of the last things you'd have to worry about.

And you'd be 100 percent correct . . . except for one little, itty-bitty thing: Space conservation in your worksheet equals memory conservation. You see, as a table of data grows and expands into columns and rows in new areas of the worksheet, Excel decides that it had better reserve a certain amount of computer memory and hold it open just in case you go crazy and fill that area full of cell entries. This means that if you skip columns and rows that you really don't need to skip (just to cut down on all that clut-tered data), you end up wasting computer memory that you can otherwise use to store more information in your worksheet.

You must remember this . . .

So now you know: It's the amount of computer memory available to Excel that determines the ultimate size of the spreadsheet you can build, not the total number of cells in the worksheets of your workbook. When you run out of memory, you've effectively run out of space — no matter how many columns and rows are still left to fill. To maximize the information you can get into a worksheet, always adopt the "covered wagon" approach to worksheet design by keeping your data close together.

To check out how much computer memory is available to Excel at any given time, choose the About Microsoft Excel command on the Apple menu to open the About Microsoft Excel dialog box. The About Microsoft Excel dialog box displays the Available Memory in *kilobytes* (thousands of bytes). When you finish viewing this information, click the OK button in the About Microsoft Excel dialog box or press Return to close it.

Doing the Data-Entry Thing

Let's start by reciting (in unison) the basic rule of worksheet data entry. All together now:

> To enter data in a worksheet, position the cell pointer in the cell where you want the data, and then begin typing the entry.

Note that before you can position the cell pointer in the cell where you want the entry, Excel must be in Ready mode (as evidenced by the Ready indicator on the status bar). When you start typing the entry, however, Excel goes through a mode change from Ready to Enter mode (and "Enter" replaces "Ready" on the status bar).

If you're not in Ready mode, try pressing Esc or ⌘+. (period).

As soon as you begin typing in Enter mode, the characters you type appear both in a cell in the worksheet area and on the formula bar near the top of the screen. Starting to type something that's ultimately destined to go into the current cell also triggers a change to the formula bar because two new boxes, Cancel and Enter, appear in between the Name Box (containing the address of the current cell) and the Edit Formula button.

As you continue to type, Excel displays your progress both on the formula bar and in the active cell in the worksheet (see Figure 2-1). However, the insertion point (the flashing vertical bar that acts as your cursor) is displayed only at the end of the characters displayed in the cell.

After you finish typing your cell entry, you still have to get the information into the cell so that it stays put. In doing this, you also change the program from Enter mode back to Ready mode so that you can move the cell pointer to another cell and, perhaps, enter or edit the data there.

Figure 2-1:
The stuff
you type
appears
both in the
current cell
and on the
formula bar.

To complete your cell entry and, at the same time, get Excel out of Enter mode and back into Ready mode, you can click the Enter box on the formula bar, press Return, or press one of the arrow keys like ↓, ↑, →, or ← to move to another cell.

Now, even though each of these alternatives gets your text into the cell, each does something a little different afterwards, so please take note:

- ✔ If you click the Enter box on the formula bar, the text goes into the cell, and the cell pointer just stays in the cell containing the brand new entry.

- ✔ If you press Return, the text goes into the cell, and the cell pointer moves down to the cell below in the next row.

- ✔ If you press one of the arrow keys, the text goes into the cell, and the cell pointer moves the next cell in the direction of the arrow. If you press ↓, the cell pointer moves below in the next row just as when you finish off a cell entry with the Return key. However, if you press →, the cell pointer moves right to the cell in the next column; if you press ←, the cell pointer moves left to the cell in the previous column; and if you press ↑, the cell pointer moves up to the cell in the next row above.

If you have an extended keyboard, you can also press the Enter key on the 10-key numeric keypad to complete a cell entry. When you press the Enter key, the cell pointer stays put in the cell with the new entry (just like when you click the Enter box on the Formula bar) rather than moving to the next cell down (as happens when you press the Return key).

No matter which of the methods you choose when putting an entry in its place, as soon as you complete your entry in the current cell, Excel deactivates the formula bar by removing the Cancel and Enter boxes. Thereafter, the data you entered continues to appear in the cell in the worksheet (with certain exceptions that I discuss later in this chapter), and every time you put the cell pointer into that cell, the data reappears on the formula bar as well.

If, while still typing an entry or after finishing typing but prior to completing the entry, you realize that you're just about to stick it in the wrong cell, you can clear and deactivate the formula bar by clicking the Cancel box (the one with the X in it) or by pressing Esc. If, however, you don't realize that you had the wrong cell current until after you enter your data there, you have to either move the entry to the correct cell (something you find out how to do in Chapter 4) or delete the entry (see Chapter 4) and then reenter the data in the correct cell.

Getting the Return key to put the cell pointer where you want it

Excel automatically advances the cell pointer to the next cell down in the column every time you press Return to complete the cell entry. If you want to customize Excel so that pressing Return doesn't move the cell pointer as the program enters your data, or to have it move the cell pointer to the next cell up, left, or right, choose Tools⇨Preferences on the menu bar and select the Edit tab in the dialog box.

To prevent the cell pointer from moving at all, choose the Move Selection after Return option to remove the check mark from its check box. To have the cell pointer move in another direction, choose the Direction pop-up list box right below the Move Selection after Return check box and then select the new direction you want to use (Right, Up, or Left). When you're finished changing this setting, click the OK button or press Return.

It Takes All Types (Of Data, That Is)

Unbeknownst to you as you go about happily entering data in your spreadsheet, Excel is constantly analyzing the stuff you type and classifying it into one of three possible data types: a piece of *text,* a *value,* or a *formula.*

If Excel finds that the entry is a formula, the program automatically calculates the formula and displays the computed result in the worksheet cell. (You continue to see the formula itself, however, on the formula bar.) If Excel is satisfied that the entry does not qualify as a formula (I give you the qualifications for an honest-to-goodness formula a little later in this chapter), the program then determines whether the entry should be classified as text or as a value.

Excel makes the distinction between text and values so that it knows how to align the entry in the worksheet. It aligns text entries with the left edge of the cell and values with the right edge. Also, because most formulas work properly only when they are fed values, by differentiating text from values, the program knows which will and will not work in the formulas you build. Suffice to say, you can foul up your formulas good if they refer to any cells containing text where Excel expects values to be.

The telltale signs of text

A text entry is simply an entry that Excel can't pigeonhole as either a formula or value. This makes text the catchall category of Excel data types. As a practical rule, most text entries (also known as *labels*) are a combination of letters and punctuation or letters and numbers. Text is used mostly for titles, headings, and notes in the worksheet.

You can tell right away whether Excel has accepted a cell entry as text because text entries are automatically aligned at the left edge of their cells. If the text entry is wider than the cell can display, the data spills over into the neighboring cell or cells on the right, *as long as those cells remain blank* (see Figure 2-2).

This means that if, sometime later, you enter information in a cell that contains spillover text from a cell to its left, Excel cuts off the spillover of the long text entry (see Figure 2-3). Not to worry: Excel doesn't actually lop these characters off the cell entry — it simply shaves the display to make room for the new entry. To redisplay the suddenly "missing" portion of the long text entry, you have to widen the column that contains the cell that contains the text. (To find out how to do this, skip ahead to Chapter 3.)

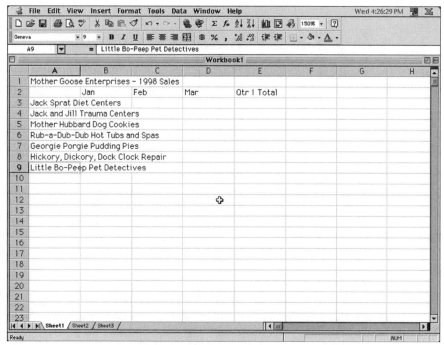

Figure 2-2:
Long text entries spill over into neighboring blank cells.

	A	B	C	D	E	F	G	H
1	Mother Goose Enterprises - 1998 Sales							
2		Jan	Feb	Mar	Qtr 1 Total			
3	Jack Sprat Di	80138.58						
4	Jack and Jill	123456.2						
5	Mother Hubbe	12657.05						
6	Rub-a-Dub-D	17619.79						
7	Georgie Porç	57133.56						
8	Hickory, Dick	168291						
9	Little Bo-Peep Pet Detectives							

Figure 2-3: Cell entries in the cells to the right cut off the spillover text.

How Excel evaluates its values

Values are the building blocks of most of the formulas that you create in Excel. As such, they come in two flavors: numbers that represent quantities (such as 14 stores or $140,000 dollars) and numbers that represent dates (such as July 30, 1995) or times (such as 2:00 p.m.).

You can tell whether Excel has accepted your entry as a value because values are automatically aligned at the right edge of their cells. If the value you enter is wider than the column containing the cell can display, Excel automatically converts the value to (of all things) *scientific notation* (for example, 6E+08 indicates that the 6 is followed by eight zeros for a grand total of 600 million!). To restore a value that's been converted into that weird scientific notation stuff back to a regular number, simply widen the column for that cell. (Chapter 3 shows you how.)

Making sure that Excel's got your number

In building a new worksheet, you'll probably spend a lot of your time entering numbers, representing all types of quantities from money you made (or lost) to the percentage of the office budget that went for coffee and donuts. (You mean you don't get donuts?)

To Excel, text is nothing but a big zero

You can use the AutoCalculate indicator to prove to yourself that Excel gives all text entries the value of 0 (zero). Simply enter a number like 10 in one cell and then some stupid piece of text, like "Using Excel is like eating a box of chocolates," in the cell directly below.

Then drag up so that both cells (the one with 10 and the one with the text) are highlighted. Then take a gander at the AutoCalculate indicator on the status bar, and you see that it reads SUM=10, proving that the text adds nothing to the total value of these two cells.

To enter a numeric value that represents a positive quantity, like the amount of money you made last year, just select a cell, type the numbers — for example, **459600** — and complete the entry in the cell by clicking the Enter box, pressing the Enter key, and so on. To enter a numeric value that represents a negative quantity, like the amount of money the office spent on coffee and donuts last year, begin the entry with the minus sign or hyphen (–) before typing the numbers — for example, type **–175** (that's not too much to spend on coffee and donuts when you just made $459,600) — and then complete the entry.

If you're trained in accounting, you can enclose the negative number (that's *expense* to you) in parentheses as in (175). Just note that, if you go to all the trouble to use parentheses for your negatives (expenses), Excel goes ahead and automatically converts the number so that it begins with a minus sign; meaning that if you type **(175)** in the Coffee and Donut expense cell, Excel spits back **–175.** (Relax, you can find out how to get your beloved parentheses back for the expenses in your spreadsheet in Chapter 3).

With numeric values that represent dollar amounts, like the amount of money you made last year, you can include dollar signs ($) and commas (,) just as they appear in the printed or handwritten numbers you are working from. Just be aware that when you enter a number with commas, Excel assigns a number format to the value that matches your use of commas. (For more information on number formats and how Excel uses them, see Chapter 3.) Likewise, when you preface a financial figure with a dollar sign, Excel assigns an appropriate dollar-number format to the value (one that automatically inserts commas between the thousands).

When entering numeric values with decimal places, use the period as the decimal point. When you enter decimal values, the program automatically adds a zero before the decimal point (Excel inserts **0.34** in a cell when you type **.34**) and drops trailing zeros entered after the decimal point (Excel inserts **12.5** in a cell when you type **12.50**).

If you don't know the decimal equivalent for a value that contains a fraction, you can just go ahead and enter the value with its fraction. For example, if you don't know that 2.1875 is the decimal equivalent for $2^3/_{16}$, just type **2 3/16** (making sure to add a space between the 2 and 3) in the cell. After completing the entry, when you put the cell pointer in that cell, you see $2^3/_{16}$ in the cell of the worksheet, but 2.1875 appears on the formula bar. As you see in Chapter 3, it's then a simple trick to format the display of $2^3/_{16}$ in the cell so that it matches the 2.1875 on the formula bar.

Note that, if you need to enter simple fractions such as $^3/_4$ or $^5/_8$, you must enter them as a mixed number preceded by zero; for example, type **0 3/4** or **0 5/8** (and be sure to include a space between the zero and the fraction). Otherwise, Excel gets mixed up and thinks that you're entering the dates March 4th (3/4) and May 8 (5/8).

When entering in a cell a numeric value that represents a percentage (so much out of a hundred), you have a choice:

- ✔ You can divide the number by 100 and enter the decimal equivalent (by moving the decimal point two places to the left like your teacher taught you; for example, type **.12** for 12 percent).
- ✔ You can enter the number with the percent sign (for example, type **12%**).

Either way, Excel stores the decimal value in the cell (0.12 in this example). If you use the percent sign, Excel assigns a percentage-number format to the value in the worksheet so that it appears as 12%.

How to get your decimal places fixed (when you don't even know if they're broken)

If you find that you need to enter a whole slew of numbers that use the same number of decimal places, you can turn on Excel's Fixed Decimal setting and have the program enter the decimals for you. This feature really comes in handy when you have to enter hundreds of financial figures that all use two decimal places (for example, for the number of cents).

To *fix* the number of decimal places in a numeric entry, follow these steps:

1. **Choose Tools⇨Preferences on the menu bar.**

    The Preferences dialog box appears.

2. **Choose the Edit tab in the dialog box.**

3. **Choose Fixed Decimal in the Settings section to select its check box.**

    By default, Excel fixes the decimal place two places to the left of the last number you type. To change the default Places setting, go to Step 4; otherwise move to Step 5.

4. Type a new number in the Places text box or use the spinner buttons (the ones with the up and down arrows) to change the value.

For example, you can change the Places setting to 3 to enter numbers with the following decimal placement: 00.000.

5. Click OK or press Return.

Excel displays the FIX status indicator on the status bar to let you know that the Fixed Decimal feature is active.

After fixing the decimal place in numeric values, Excel automatically adds the decimal point to any numeric value you enter — all you do is type the digits and complete the entry in the cell. For example, to enter the numeric value 100.99 in a cell after fixing the decimal point to 2 places, type the digits **10099**. When you complete the cell entry, Excel automatically inserts a decimal point two places from the right in the number you typed, leaving 100.99 in the cell.

When you're ready to return to normal data entry for numerical values (where you enter any decimal points yourself), open the Preferences dialog box, choose the Edit tab again, deselect the Fixed Decimal check box, and click OK or press Return. Excel removes the FIX indicator from the status bar.

Tapping on the old ten-key

If your Mac is equipped with a numeric keypad, you can make the Fixed Decimal feature work even better by selecting the block of the cells where you want to enter the numbers (see "Entries all around the block," later in this chapter) and then doing all the data entry for this cell selection with the keypad.

Don't get in a fix over your decimal places!

While the Fixed Decimal setting is turned on, Excel adds a decimal point to all the numeric values you enter. However, if you want to enter a number without a decimal point, or one with a decimal point in a position different from the one called for by this feature, you have to remember to type the decimal point (period) yourself. For example, to enter the number 1099 instead of 10.99 when the decimal point is fixed at 2 places, type **1099.** in the cell.

And, for heaven's sake, please don't forget to turn off the Fixed Decimal feature before you start work on another worksheet or exit Excel. Otherwise, when you intend to enter a value like 20, you'll end up with 0.2 instead, and you won't have a clue what's going on!

Using this approach, all you have to do to enter the range of values in each cell is type the number's digits and press Enter on the numeric keypad — Excel inserts the decimal point in the proper place as it moves the cell pointer right to the cell in the next column. When you reach the cell in the last column of the cell selection, pressing the Enter key moves the cell pointer to the cell in the first column of the row below. When you reach the very last cell in the selection, pressing Enter jumps the cell pointer back up to the very first cell in the selection.

If, instead of entering data across each column as you move down the rows of the cell selection, you prefer entering data down each column as you move across the rows, complete each entry by pressing the Return key on the regular keyboard instead of the Enter key on the numeric pad.

Figures 2-4 and 2-5 illustrate how you can make the ten-key method work for you. In Figure 2-4, the Fixed Decimal feature has been turned on (using the default of two decimal places), and the block of cells from B3 through D9 has been selected. You also see that six entries have already been made in cells B3 through D4 and a seventh, 12657.05, is about to be completed in cell B5. To make this entry when the Fixed Decimal feature is turned on, you simply type **1265705** from the numeric keypad.

Figure 2-5 shows you what happens when you press Enter on the numeric keypad. As you can see, not only does Excel automatically add the decimal point to the value in cell B5, but it also moves the cell pointer over to cell C5 where you can continue entering the values in this row.

	A	B	C	D	E	F	G	H
1	Mother Goose Enterprises - 1998 Sales							
2		Jan	Feb	Mar	Qtr 1 Total			
3	Jack Sprat Di	80138.58	59389.56	19960.06				
4	Jack and Jill	123456.2	89345.7	25436.84				
5	Mother Hubb	1265705	es					
6	Rub-a-Dub-Dub Hot Tubs and Spas							
7	Georgie Porgie Pudding Pies							
8	Hickory, Dickory, Dock Clock Repair							
9	Little Bo-Peep Pet Detectives							
10								
11								
12								
13								
14								
15								

Figure 2-4: To enter the value 12657.05 in cell B5, you simply type **1265705** and press Enter.

Figure 2-5:
When you
press Enter
to complete
the 12657.05
entry in cell
B5, the
program
automatically
moves the
cell pointer
to cell C5.

Entering dates with no debate

At first look, it may strike you as a bit odd that you enter dates and times as values in the cells of a worksheet rather than as text. The reason for this is simple, really: Dates and times entered as values can be used in formula calculations, whereas dates and times entered as text cannot. For example, if you enter two dates as values, you can then set up a formula that subtracts the more recent date from the older date and returns the number of days between them. This kind of thing just couldn't happen if you were to enter the two dates as text entries.

Excel determines whether the date or time you type is entered as a value or as text by the format you follow. If you follow one of Excel's built-in date and time formats, the program recognizes the date or time as a value. If you don't follow one of the built-in formats, the program enters the date or time as a text entry — it's as simple as that.

Excel recognizes the following time formats:

- 3:21 PM
- 3:21:04 PM
- 15:21
- 15:21:04

The dating game

Dates are stored as serial numbers that indicate how many days have elapsed from a particular starting date; times are stored as decimal fractions indicating the elapsed part of the 24-hour period. Excel supports two date systems: the 1900 date system used by Excel for Windows, where January 1, 1900 is the starting date (serial number 1) and the 1904 system used by Excel for the Macintosh, where January 2, 1904 is the starting date.

If you ever get a hold of a workbook created with Excel for Windows that contains dates that seem all screwed up when you open the file, you can rectify this problem by choosing Preferences from the Tools menu, selecting the Calculation tab in the Preferences dialog box, and then selecting the 1904 date system check box under Workbook options before you click OK.

Excel knows the following date formats. (Note that month abbreviations always use the first three letters of the name of the month, as in Jan, Feb. . . .)

- November 24, 1998 or November 24, 98
- 11/24/98 or 11-24-98
- 25-Nov-98
- 25-Nov
- Nov-98

Fabricating those fabulous formulas!

As entries go in Excel, formulas are the real workhorses of the worksheet. If you set up a formula properly, it computes the right answer when you first enter it into a cell. From then on, it keeps itself up-to-date, recalculating the results whenever you change any of the values that the formula uses.

You let Excel know that you're about to enter a formula, rather than some text or a value, in the current cell by starting the formula with the equal sign (=). Most simple formulas follow the equal sign with a built-in function such as SUM or AVERAGE. (See "Inserting a function into a formula with the Paste Function and the Formula Palette" later in this chapter, for more information on using functions in formulas.) Other simple formulas use a series of values or cell references that contain values separated by one or more of the following mathematical operators:

- ✔ + (plus sign) for addition
- ✔ – (minus sign or hyphen) for subtraction
- ✔ * (asterisk) for multiplication
- ✔ / (slash) for division
- ✔ ^ (caret) for raising a number to a power

For example, to create a formula in cell C2 that multiplies a value entered in cell A2 by a value in cell B2, type the following formula in cell C2:

```
=A2*B2
```

To enter this formula in cell C2, follow these steps:

1. **Select cell C2.**
2. **Type the entire formula =A2*B2 in the cell.**
3. **Press Return.**

Or

1. **Select Cell C2.**
2. **Type = (equal sign).**
3. **Select cell A2 in the worksheet by using the mouse or the keyboard.**

   This action places the cell reference A2 in the formula in the cell (as shown in Figure 2-6).

4. **Type *.**

   The asterisk is used for multiplication rather than the x you used in school.

5. **Select cell B2 in the worksheet by using the mouse or the keyboard.**

   This action places the cell reference B2 in the formula (as shown in Figure 2-7).

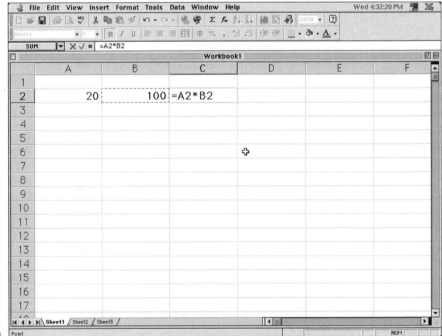

Figure 2-6:
To start the formula, type = and then select cell A2.

Figure 2-7:
To complete the second part of the formula, type * and select cell B2.

6. Click the Enter box to complete the formula entry, while at the same time keeping the cell pointer in cell C2.

Excel displays the calculated answer in cell C2 and the formula =A2*B2 in the formula bar (as shown in Figure 2-8).

When you finish entering the formula =A2*B2 in cell C2 of the worksheet, Excel displays the calculated result depending on the values currently entered in cells A2 and B2. The major strength of the electronic spreadsheet is the capability of formulas to automatically change their calculated results to match changes in the cells referenced by the formulas.

Now comes the fun part: After creating a formula like the preceding one that refers to the values in certain cells (rather than containing those values itself), you can change the values in those cells, and Excel automatically recalculates the formula, using these new values and displaying the updated answer in the worksheet! Using the example shown in Figure 2-8, say that you change the value in cell B2 from 100 to 50. The moment you complete this change in cell B2, Excel recalculates the formula and displays the new answer, 1000, in cell C2.

Figure 2-8:
When you click the Enter box, Excel displays the answer in cell C2 while the formula appears in the formula bar above.

If you want it, just point it out

The method of selecting the cells you use in a formula, rather than typing their cell references, is known as *pointing*. Pointing is not only quicker than typing cell references, it also reduces the risk that you might type the wrong cell reference. When you type a cell reference, you can easily type the wrong column letter or row number and not realize your mistake just by looking at the calculated result returned in the cell.

If you select the cell you want to use in a formula, either by clicking it or moving the cell pointer to it, there is less chance that you'll enter the wrong cell reference.

Altering the natural order of operations

Many formulas you create perform more than one mathematical operation. Excel performs each operation, moving from left to right, according to a strict pecking order (the natural order of arithmetic operations). In this order, multiplication and division pull more weight than addition and subtraction and are, therefore, performed first, even if these operations don't come first in the formula (when reading from left to right).

Consider the series of operations in the following formula:

```
=A2+B2*C2
```

If cell A2 contains the number 5, B2 contains the number 10, and C2 contains the number 2, Excel evaluates the following formula:

```
=5+10*2
```

In this formula, Excel multiplies 10 times 2 to equal 20 and then adds this result to 5 to produce the result 25.

If you want Excel to perform the addition between the values in cells A2 and B2 before the program multiplies the result by the value in cell C2, enclose the addition operation in parentheses as follows:

```
=(A2+B2)*C2
```

The parentheses around the addition tell Excel that you want this operation performed before the multiplication. If cell A2 contains the number 5, B2 contains the number 10, and C2 contains the number 2, Excel adds 5 and 10 to equal 15 and then multiplies this result by 2 to produce the result 30.

In fancier formulas, you may need to add more than one set of parentheses, one within another (like the wooden Russian dolls that nest within each other) to indicate the order in which you want the calculations to take place. When nesting parentheses, Excel first performs the calculation contained in the most inside pair of parentheses and then uses that result in further calculations as the program works its way outward. For example, consider the following formula:

```
=(A4+(B4-C4))*D4
```

Excel first subtracts the value in cell C4 from the value in cell B4, then adds the difference to the value in cell A4, and finally multiplies that sum by the value in D4.

Without the additions of the two sets of nested parentheses, left to its own devices, Excel would first multiply the value in cell C4 by that in D4, add the value in A4 to that in B4, and then perform the subtraction.

When nesting parentheses in a formula, always try to pair them properly so that you have a right parenthesis for every left parenthesis in the formula. If you do not include a right parenthesis for every left one, however, Excel 98's new AutoCorrect feature displays an alert dialog box that suggests how it thinks you should fix up the formula so that parentheses are balanced. To have Excel make the suggested correction, you only have to click the Yes button in the alert dialog box.

Formula flub-ups

Under certain circumstances, even the best formulas can appear to have freaked out after you get them in your worksheet. You can tell right away that a formula's gone haywire because instead of the nice calculated value you expected to see in the cell, you get a strange, incomprehensible message in all uppercase letters beginning with the number sign (#) and ending with an exclamation point (!) or, in one case, a question mark (?). This weirdness is known, in the parlance of spreadsheets, as an *error value*. Its purpose is to let you know that some element — either in the formula itself or in a cell referred to by the formula — is preventing Excel from returning the anticipated calculated value.

The worst thing about error values is that they can contaminate other formulas in the worksheet. If a formula returns an error value to a cell and a second formula in another cell refers to the value calculated by the first formula, the second formula returns the same error value and so on down the line.

After an error value shows up in a cell, you have to discover what caused the error and edit the formula in the worksheet. Table 2-1 lists some error values that you may run into in a worksheet and explains the most common causes.

Table 2-1	Error Values That You Can Encounter from Faulty Formulas
What Shows Up in the Cell	*What's Going On Here?*
#DIV/0!	Appears when the formula calls for division by a cell that either contains the value 0 or, as is more often the case, is empty. Division by zero is a no-no according to our math.
#NAME?	Appears when the formula refers to a *range name* (see Chapter 6 for info on naming ranges) that doesn't exist in the worksheet. This error value appears when you type the wrong range name or fail to enclose in quotation marks some text used in the formula, causing Excel to think that the text refers to a range name.
#NULL!	Appears most often when you insert a space (where you should have used a comma) to separate cell references used as arguments for functions.
#NUM!	Appears when Excel encounters a problem with a number in the formula, such as the wrong type of argument in an Excel function or a calculation that produces a number too large or too small to be represented in the worksheet.
#REF!	Appears when Excel encounters an invalid cell reference, such as when you delete a cell referred to in a formula or paste cells over the cells referred to in a formula.
#VALUE!	Appears when you use the wrong type of argument or operator in a function, or when you call for a mathematical operation that refers to cells that contain text entries.

Fixing Up Those Data Entry Flub-Ups

We all wish we were perfect, but alas, because so few of us are, we are best off preparing for those inevitable times when we mess up. When entering vast quantities of data, it's really easy for those nasty little typos to creep into your work. In your pursuit of the perfect spreadsheet, there are things you can do: First, get Excel to automatically correct certain typos right as they happen with its AutoCorrect feature; second, manually correct any of the disgusting little errors that get through, either while you're still in the process of making the entry in the cell or after the entry has gone in.

You really AutoCorrect that for me

The AutoCorrect feature is a godsend for those of us who tend to make the same stupid typos over and over again. With AutoCorrect, you can alert Excel 98 to your own particular typing gaffes and tell the program how it should automatically fix them for you.

When you first install Excel, the AutoCorrect feature already knows to automatically correct two initial capital letters in an entry (by lowercasing the second capital letter), capitalize the name of the days of the week, and to replace a set number of text entries and typos with particular substitute text.

You can add to the list of text replacements at any time when using Excel. These text replacements can be of two types: typos that you routinely make along with the correct spellings, and abbreviations or acronyms that you type all the time along with their full forms. To add to the replacements

1. **Choose Tools⇨AutoCorrect on the menu bar to open the AutoCorrect dialog box.**

2. **Type the typo or abbreviation in the Replace text box.**

3. **Type the correction or full form in the With text box.**

4. **Click the Add button or press Return to add the new typo or abbreviation to the AutoCorrect list.**

5. **Click the OK button to close the AutoCorrect dialog box.**

Figure 2-9 shows the AutoCorrect dialog box after I entered "mge" in the Replace text box and "Mother Goose Enterprises" in the With text box. After clicking the Add button to add this abbreviation to the AutoCorrect list and closing the AutoCorrect dialog box, I no longer have to take the time to spell out Mother Goose Enterprises in any of the spreadsheets that I create because AutoCorrect is there, ready to convert my "mge" to "Mother Goose Enterprises" as soon as I type it.

Figure 2-9:
Entering my
favorite
acronym
and the
automatic
correction
that Excel is
to replace
it with.

Cell editing etiquette

Despite the help of AutoCorrect, some mistakes are bound to get you. How you correct them really depends upon whether you notice before or after you complete the cell entry.

- ✔ If you catch the mistake before you complete an entry, you can delete it by pressing Delete until you remove all the incorrect characters from the cell. Then you can retype the rest of the entry or the formula before you complete the entry in the cell.

- ✔ If you don't discover the mistake until after you complete the cell entry, you have a choice of replacing the whole thing or editing just the mistakes.

- ✔ When dealing with short entries, you'll probably want to go the replacement route. To replace a cell entry, you have only to position the cell pointer in that cell, type your replacement entry, and then complete the replacement entry by clicking the Enter box or pressing Return or one of the arrow keys.

- ✔ When the error in an entry is relatively easy to fix and the entry is on the long side, you'll probably want to edit the cell entry rather than replace it. To edit the entry in the cell, simply double-click the cell or select the cell and then press ⌘+U.

✔ Doing either one reactivates the formula bar by once again displaying the Enter and Cancel boxes while at the same time placing the insertion point in the cell entry in the worksheet. (If you double-click, the insertion point is positioned wherever you click; if you press ⌘+U, the insertion point is positioned after the last character in the entry.)

✔ Notice also that the mode indicator changes to Edit. While in this mode, you can use the mouse or the arrow keys to position the insertion point at the place in the cell entry that needs fixing.

Table 2-2 lists the keystrokes you can use to reposition the insertion point in the cell entry and delete unwanted characters. If you want to insert new characters at the insertion point, simply start typing. If you want to delete existing characters at the insertion point, press the Del key. When you finish making corrections, you must reenter the edited entry before Excel updates the contents of the cell.

While Excel is in Edit mode, you must reenter the edited cell contents by either clicking the Enter box or pressing Return. You can use the arrow keys as a way to complete an entry only when the program is in Enter mode. When the program is in Edit mode, the arrow keys move the insertion point only through the entry that you're editing, not to a new cell.

Table 2-2	Keystrokes for Fixing Those Cell Entry Flub-Ups
Keystroke	*What the Keystroke Does*
Delete	Deletes the character to the left of the insertion point
Del (next to the End key)	Deletes the character to the right of the insertion point
→	Positions the insertion point one character to the right
←	Positions the insertion point one character to the left
↑	Positions the insertion point, when it is at the end of the cell entry, at its last position to the left
End or ↓	Moves the insertion point after the last character in the cell entry
Home	Moves the insertion point in front of the first character of the cell entry
Control+→	Positions the insertion point in front of the next word in the cell entry
Control+←	Positions the insertion point in front of the preceding word in the cell entry

A Tale of Two Edits: Cell versus formula bar editing

Excel gives you a choice between editing a cell's contents either in the cell (as discussed earlier) or on the formula bar. Whereas, most of the time, editing right in the cell is just fine, when dealing with really, really long entries (like humongous formulas that seem to go on forever or text entries that take up paragraphs and paragraphs), you may prefer to do your editing on the formula bar. This is because Excel expands the formula bar to as many rows as are necessary to display the entire cell contents; in the worksheet display, the cell contents may be running right off the screen.

To edit the contents in the formula bar rather than in the cell itself, you click somewhere (probably the first place that needs changing) in the cell contents on the formula bar to position the insertion point and put Excel into Edit mode.

Taking the Drudgery out of Data Entry

Before leaving the topic of data entry, I feel duty bound to cover some of the shortcuts that really help to cut down on the drudgery of this task. These data-entry tips include using the AutoComplete and AutoFill features as well as doing data entry in a preselected block of cells and entering the same things in a bunch of cells all at the same time.

I'm just not complete without you

The AutoComplete feature in Excel 98 is not something you can do anything about; it's just something to be aware of as you enter your data. In an attempt to cut down on your typing load, our friendly software engineers at Microsoft came up with the AutoComplete feature.

AutoComplete is kinda like a moronic mind reader who anticipates what you might want to enter next based upon what you just entered earlier. This feature comes into play only when you're entering a column of text entries. (It does not come into play when entering values or formulas or when entering a row of text entries.) When entering a column of text entries, AutoComplete looks at the kinds of entries you make in that column and automatically duplicates them in subsequent rows whenever you start a new entry that begins with the same letter as an existing entry.

For example, say I type **Jack Sprat Diet Centers** (one of the companies owned and operated by Mother Goose Enterprises) in cell A3 and then move the cell pointer down to cell A4 in the row below and press J (lowercase or uppercase, it doesn't matter), AutoComplete immediately inserts "ack Sprat Diet Centers" in this cell after the J, as shown in Figure 2-10.

Now this is great if I happen to need Jack Sprat Diet Centers as the row heading in both cells A3 and A4. Anticipating that I may be typing a different entry that just happens to start with the same letter as the one above, AutoComplete automatically selects everything after the first letter in the duplicated entry it inserted (from "ack" on, in this example). This enables me to replace the duplicate supplied by AutoComplete just by continuing to type (which is what I did after shooting Figure 2-10 because I needed to enter Jack and Jill Trauma Centers — another of Mother's companies — in cell A4).

If you override a duplicate supplied by AutoComplete in a column by typing one of your own (as in my example with changing Jack Sprat Diet Centers to Jack and Jill Trauma Centers in cell A4), you effectively shut down its ability to supply any more duplicates for that particular letter. So, for instance, in my example, after changing Jack Sprat Diet Centers to Jack and Jill Trauma Centers in cell A4, AutoComplete doesn't do anything if I then type **J** in cell A5. In other words, you're on your own if you don't continue to accept AutoComplete's typing suggestions.

Fill 'er up with AutoFill

Many of the worksheets you create with Excel require the entry of a series of sequential dates or numbers. For example, a worksheet may require you to title the columns with the 12 months, from January through December, or to number the rows from 1 to 100.

Figure 2-10: AutoComplete duplicates a previous entry if you start a new entry in the same column that begins with the same letter.

Excel's AutoFill feature makes short work of this kind of repetitive task. All you have to enter is the starting values for the series. In most cases, AutoFill is smart enough to figure out how to extend the series for you when you drag the fill handle to the right (to take the series across columns to the right) or down (to extend the series to the rows below).

Remember that the AutoFill handle looks like this + and appears only when you position the mouse pointer on the lower-right corner of the cell (or the last cell, when you select a block of cells). Keep in mind that if you drag a cell selection with the white-cross mouse pointer rather than the AutoFill handle, Excel simply extends the cell selection to those cells you drag through (see Chapter 3). If you drag a cell selection with the arrowhead pointer, Excel moves the cell selection (see Chapter 4).

When creating a series with the fill handle, you can drag only in one direction at a time. For example, you can extend the series or fill the range to the left or right of the cell range that contains the initial values, or you can extend the series or fill the range above or below the cell range that contains the initial values. You can't, however, extend the series or fill the range in two directions at the same time (such as down and to the right by dragging the fill handle diagonally).

As you drag the mouse, the program keeps you informed of whatever entry would be entered into the last cell selected in the range by displaying that entry next to the mouse pointer (as a kind of AutoFill tip, if you will). When you release the mouse button after extending the range with the fill handle, Excel either creates a series in all the cells you selected or fills the entire range with the initial value.

Figures 2-11 and 2-12 illustrate how to use AutoFill to enter a row of months, starting with January in cell B2 and ending with June in cell G2. To do this, you simply type **January** in cell B2 and then position the mouse pointer on the fill handle in the lower-right corner of this cell before you drag through to cell G2 on the right (as shown in Figure 2-11). When you release the mouse button, Excel fills in the names of the rest of the months (February through June) in the selected cells (as shown in Figure 2-12). Note that Excel keeps the cells with the series of months selected, giving you another chance to modify the series. (If you went too far, you can drag the fill handle to the left to cut back on the list of months; if you didn't go far enough, you can drag it to the right to extend the list of months farther.)

Table 2-3 shows some of the different initial values that AutoFill can use and the types of series that Excel can create from them.

Figure 2-11:
To create a
series of
months,
type
January in
the first cell
and then
use the fill
handle to
select the
range of
cells where
the months
will be
entered.

Figure 2-12:
As soon you
release the
mouse
button,
Excel fills
the cell
selection
with the
rest of the
months.

Working with a spaced series

AutoFill uses the initial value you select (date, time, day, year, and so on) to "design" the series. All the sample series shown in Table 2-3 change by a factor of one (one day, one month, or one number). You can tell AutoFill to create a series that changes by some other value: Enter two sample values in neighboring cells that describe the amount of change you want between each value in the series. Make these two values the initial selection that you extend with the fill handle.

For example, to start a series with Saturday and enter every other day across a row, type **Saturday** in the first cell and **Monday** in the cell next door. After selecting both cells, drag the fill handle across the cells to the right as far you need to extend the series. When you release the mouse button, Excel follows the example set in the first two cells by entering every other day (Wednesday to the right of Monday, Friday to the right of Wednesday, and so on).

Table 2-3   Samples of Series You Can Create with AutoFill

Value Entered in First Cell	Extended Series Created by AutoFill in the Next Three Cells
June	July, August, September
Jun	Jul, Aug, Sep
Tuesday	Wednesday, Thursday, Friday
Tue	Wed, Thu, Fri
4/1/98	4/2/98, 4/3/98, 4/4/98
Jan-98	Feb-98, Mar-98, Apr-98
15-Feb	16-Feb, 17-Feb, 18-Feb
10:00 PM	11:00 PM, 12:00 AM, 1:00 AM
8:01	9:01, 10:01, 11:01
Quarter 1	Quarter 2, Quarter 3, Quarter 4
Qtr2	Qtr3, Qtr4, Qtr1
Q3	Q4, Q1, Q2
Product 1	Product 2, Product 3, Product 4
1st Product	2nd Product, 3rd Product, 4th Product

Copying with AutoFill

You can use AutoFill to copy a text entry throughout a cell range (rather than fill in a series of related entries). To copy a text entry to a cell range, you must hold down the Option key as you click and drag the fill handle. When you hold down the Option key as you click the fill handle, a plus sign appears to the right of the fill handle — your sign that AutoFill will *copy* the entry in the active cell instead of creating a series using it. (You can also tell because the entry that appears as the AutoFill tip next to the mouse pointer as you drag contains the same text as the original cell.)

Although holding down Option as you drag the fill handle copies a text entry, just the opposite is true when it comes to values! If you enter a number like 17 in a cell and then drag the fill handle across the row, Excel just copies the number 17 in all the cells you select. If, however, you hold down Option as you drag the fill handle, Excel then fills out the series (17, 18, 19, and so on).

Creating custom lists for AutoFill

In addition to varying the increment in a series created with AutoFill, you can also create your own custom series. For example, in the bosom of Mother Goose Enterprises, you will find the following companies:

- ✔ Jack Sprat Diet Centers
- ✔ Jack and Jill Trauma Centers
- ✔ Mother Hubbard Dog Goodies
- ✔ Rub-a-Dub-Dub Hot Tubs and Spas
- ✔ Georgie Porgie Pudding Pies
- ✔ Hickory, Dickory, Dock Clock Repair
- ✔ Little Bo Peep Pet Detectives

Rather than have to type this list of companies in the cells of each new worksheet (or even copy them from an existing worksheet), you can create a custom series that produces the whole list of companies simply by entering Jack Sprat Diet Centers in the first cell and then dragging the fill handle to the blank cells where the rest of the companies should appear.

To create this kind of custom series, follow these steps:

1. **Choose Tools⇨Preferences on the menu bar to open the Preferences dialog box.**

2. **Select the Custom Lists tab to display the Custom lists and List entries boxes.**

   If you've already gone to the time and trouble of typing the custom list in a range of cells, go to Step 3a. If you haven't yet typed the series in an open worksheet, go to Step 3b instead.

3a. **Click in the Import list from cells text box and then click the Mini-mize button on its right to reduce the Preferences dialog box to just the Import list from cells text box so that you can see your list in the worksheet and select the range of cells (see Chapter 3 for details).**

After selecting the cells (and clicking the Restore button to restore the Preferences dialog box), click the Import button to copy this list into the List entries list box and skip to Step 5 (as shown in Figure 2-13).

3b. **Choose the List entries box and then type each entry (in the desired order), being sure to press Return after typing each one.**

When all the entries in the custom list appear in the List entries box in the order you're going to want them, proceed to Step 4.

4. **Choose the Add button to add the list of entries to the Custom lists box.**

Finish creating all the custom lists you need, using the preceding steps. When you're done, move on to Step 5.

5. **Choose OK or press Return to close the Preferences dialog box and return to the current worksheet in the active workbook.**

After adding a custom list to Excel, from then on you need only enter the first entry in a cell and then use the fill handle to extend it to the cells below or to the right.

If you don't even want to bother with typing the first entry, use the AutoCorrect feature — refer to "You really AutoCorrect that for me" earlier in this chapter — to create an entry that will fill in as soon as you type your favorite acronym for it (such as "jsdc" for "Jack Sprat Diet Centers").

Figure 2-13: Creating a custom company list from existing worksheet entries.

Entries all around the block

When you want to enter a table of information in a new worksheet, you can simplify the job of entering the data if you select all the empty cells in which you want to make entries before you begin entering any information. Just position the cell pointer in the first cell of what is to become the data table and then select all the cells in the subsequent columns and rows. (For information on the ways to select a range of cells, see Chapter 3.) After you select the block of cells, you can begin entering the first entry.

When you select a block of cells (also known as a *range*) before you start entering information, Excel restricts data entry to that range as follows:

- ✔ The program automatically advances the cell pointer to the next cell in the range when you click the Enter box or press Return to complete each cell entry.

- ✔ In a cell range that contains several different rows and columns, Excel advances the cell pointer down each row of the column as you make your entries. When the cell pointer reaches the cell in the last row of the column, the cell pointer advances to the first selected row in the next column to the right. If the cell range uses only one row, Excel advances the cell pointer from left to right across the row.

- ✔ When you finish entering information in the last cell in the selected range, Excel positions the cell pointer in the first cell of the now-completed data table. To deselect the cell range, click the mouse pointer on one of the cells in the worksheet (inside or outside the selected range — it doesn't matter) or press one of the arrow keys.

Be sure that you don't press one of the arrow keys to complete a cell entry within a preselected cell range instead of clicking the Enter box or pressing Return. Pressing an arrow key deselects the range of cells when Excel moves the cell pointer. To move the cell pointer around a cell range without deselecting the range, try these methods:

- ✔ Press Return to advance to the next cell down each row and then across each column in the range. Press Shift+Return to move up to the previous cell.

- ✔ Press Tab to advance to the next cell in the column on the right and then down each row of the range. (You can also do this by pressing the Enter key on the numeric keypad.) Press Shift+Tab to move left to the previous cell.

- ✔ Press Control+. (period) to move from one corner of the range to another.

Data entry express

You can save a lot of time and energy when you want the same entry (text, value, or formula) to appear in many cells of the worksheet; you can enter the information in all the cells in one operation. You first select the cell ranges to hold the information. (Excel lets you select more than one cell range for this kind of thing — see Chapter 3 for details.) Then you construct the entry on the formula bar and press ⌘+Return or Control+Return to put the entry into all the selected ranges.

The key to making this operation a success is to hold the ⌘ or Control key as you press Return so that Excel inserts the entry on the formula bar into all the selected cells. If you forget to hold ⌘ or Control and you just press Return, Excel only places the entry in the first cell of the selected cell range.

How to Make Your Formulas Function Even Better

Earlier in this chapter, I showed you how to create formulas that perform a series of simple mathematical operations such as addition, subtraction, multiplication, and division. Instead of creating more complex formulas from scratch out of an intricate combination of these operations, you can find an Excel function to get the job done.

A *function* is a predefined formula that performs a particular type of computation. All you have to do to use a function is supply the values that the function uses when performing its calculations. (In the parlance of the Spreadsheet Guru, such values are known as the *arguments of the function*.) As with simple formulas, you can enter the arguments for most functions either as a numerical value (for example, **22** or **–4.56**) or, as is more common, as a cell reference (for example, **B10**) or as a cell range (for example, **C3:F3**).

Just as with a formula that you build yourself, each function you use must start with an equal sign (=) so that Excel knows to enter the function as a formula rather than as text. Following the equal sign, you enter the name of the function (in uppercase or lowercase — it doesn't matter, as long as you don't misspell the name). Following the name of the function, you enter the arguments required to perform the calculations. All function arguments are enclosed in a pair of parentheses.

If you type the function directly in a cell, remember not to insert spaces between the equal sign, function name, and the arguments enclosed in parentheses. Some functions use more than one value when performing their designated calculations. When this is the case, you separate each function with a comma (not a space).

After you type the equal sign, function name, and the left parenthesis that marks the beginning of the arguments for the function, you can point to any cell or cell range you want to use as the first argument instead of typing the cell references. When the function uses more than one argument, you can point to the cells or cell ranges you want to use for the second argument right after you type the , (comma) to complete the first argument.

After you finish entering the last argument, type a right parenthesis to mark the end of the argument list and then click the Enter box or press Return or an arrow key to insert the function in the cell and have Excel calculate the answer.

Inserting a function into a formula with Paste Function and the Formula Palette

Although you can enter a function by typing it directly in a cell, Excel provides a Paste Function button on the Standard toolbar that displays the Paste Function dialog box from which you select the function to use. After you select your function, Excel opens the Formula Palette right below the formula bar. This Formula Palette enables you to specify the function arguments. The real boon comes when you're fooling with an unfamiliar function or one that's kind of complex (some of these puppies can be really hairy) and you open the Formula Palette when the Office Assistant is open. (Refer to "Conferring with your Office Assistant" in Chapter 1.) Under those conditions, the Office Assistant is ready to give you loads of help in completing the argument text boxes that the Formula Palette presents to you by keeping track of all the arguments you need to use and checks that you don't mess up on your parentheses or commas separating the argument list.

To open the Paste Function dialog box, you select the cell that needs the formula and then click the Paste Function button (the one marked *fx*) on the Standard toolbar. When you click the Paste Function button, the Paste Function dialog box appears, similar to the one shown in Figure 2-14.

Figure 2-14:
Select the
function
you want to
use in the
Paste
Function
dialog box.

The Paste Function dialog box contains two list boxes: Function category and Function name. When you open this dialog box, Excel automatically selects Most Recently Used as the category in the Function category list box and displays the functions you usually use in the Function name list box.

If your function isn't among the most recently used, you must then select the appropriate category of your function in the Function category list box (if you don't know the category, choose All). After that, of course, you still need to choose the particular function in the Function name list box.

When you select a function in the Function name list box, Excel displays the required arguments for the function at the bottom of this dialog box and inserts the function name (along with the obligatory parentheses) in the current cell. For example, suppose that you select the SUM function (the "crown jewel" of the Most Recently Used function category) in the Function name list box. As soon as you do, the program puts an equal sign into the cell (and on the formula bar) and shows the arguments as

```
SUM(number1,number2,...)
```

at the bottom of the first Paste Function dialog box.

To continue and fill in the number arguments for the SUM function, you then click the OK button or press Return. As soon as you do, Excel inserts

```
SUM( )
```

in the current cell and on the formula bar (following the equal sign), and the Formula Palette with the SUM arguments appears below the formula bar (as shown in Figure 2-15). This is where you add the arguments for the SUM function.

As the Formula Palette in Figure 2-15 points out, you can select up to 30 numbers to be summed. What it doesn't tell you, however (there's always some trick, huh?), is that these numbers don't have to be in single cells. In fact, most of the time you will be selecting a whole slew of numbers in nearby cells (in a multiple cell selection — that range thing) that you want to total.

To select your first number argument in the dialog box, you click the cell (or drag through the block of cells) in the worksheet while the insertion point is in the Number1 text box. Excel then displays the cell address (or range address) in the Number1 text box while, at the same time, showing the value in the cell (or values, if you've selected a bunch of cells) in the box to the right. Excel displays the total so far near the bottom of the Formula Palette after the words Formula result=.

Figure 2-15:
You specify the arguments to use in the selected function in the Formula Palette.

Keep in mind, when selecting cells, that you can minimize this arguments dialog box down to just the contents of the Number1 text box and a maximize button by clicking the minimize button on the right of the Number1 text box. After minimizing the arguments dialog box so that you can select the cells to be used as the first argument, you can expand it again by clicking the maximize button (the only button displayed on the far right). Instead of minimizing the dialog box, you can also temporarily move it out of the way by clicking any part and then dragging the dialog box to its new destination on the screen.

If you're adding more than one cell (or bunch of cells) in a worksheet, you press the Tab key or click the Number2 text box to move the insertion point there (Excel responds by extending the argument list with a Number3 text box). Here is where you specify the second cell (or cell range) that is to be added to the one now showing in the Number1 text box. After you click the cell or drag through the second cell range, the program displays the cell address(es), with the numbers in the cell(s) to the right and the running total near the bottom of the Formula Palette after the words Formula result= (as shown in Figure 2-16). Note that you can minimize the entire arguments dialog box down to just the contents of the argument text box you're dealing with (Number2, Number3, and so on) and a maximize button by clicking its particular minimize button if the dialog box obscures the cells that you need to select.

Figure 2-16:
To specify additional arguments for a function in the Formula Palette, press Tab to expand the argument list.

When you finish pointing out the cells or bunches of cells to be summed, you then click the OK button to close the Formula Palette and put the SUM function in the current cell.

Editing a function with the Edit Formula button

Excel 98's new Edit Formula button lets you edit formulas (especially those with functions) right from the formula bar. To use it, you select the cell with the formula to be edited before you click the Edit Formula button (the one sporting the equal sign that appears immediately in front of the current cell entry on the formula bar).

As soon as you click the Edit Formula button, Excel responds in these two ways:

✔ The contents of the Name Box at the beginning of the formula bar displays the function at the top of the list of Most Recently Used functions instead of the address of the current cell. When you click the pop-up button to the right of the Name Box, Excel displays a pop-up list containing all functions on the Most Recently Used function list.

✔ The Formula Palette showing the result of the formula in the current cell appears in the upper-left corner of the workbook window. If this formula uses a function, the Formula Palette shows the current arguments of the function (similar to the ones shown earlier in Figure 2-15 and 2-16).

You can then edit the formula as required. If you want to replace a function that's used in the formula, select (by highlighting) the function's name on the formula bar, then click the pop-up button on the Name Box, and select the new function in the list that's to replace the one you've highlighted. (To have access to more functions than those in the Most Recently Used category, click More Functions at the bottom of the list box and Excel displays the Paste Function dialog box like the one shown earlier in Figure 2-14.)

To edit just the arguments of a function, select the cell references in the appropriate argument's text box (marked Number1, Number2, Number3, and so on) and then make whatever changes are required to the cell addresses or select a new range of cells. Keep in mind that Excel automatically adds any cell or cell range that you highlight in the worksheet to the current argument. If you want to replace the current argument, you need to highlight it and then get rid of its cell addresses by pressing the Delete key before you highlight the new cell or cell range to be used as the argument. (Remember that you can always minimize this dialog box or move it to a new location if it obscures the cells you need to select.)

When you finish editing the formula, click the OK button or press Return in the Formula Palette to put it away, update the formula, and return the Name Box on the formula bar to normal (so that the Name Box once again displays the address of the current cell instead of the name of the function at the top of the Most Recently Used list).

I'd be totally lost without AutoSum

Before leaving this fascinating discussion on entering functions, I want you to get to the AutoSum tool on the Standard toolbar (the one with the Σ). This little tool is worth its weight in gold, as it not only enters the SUM function but also selects the most likely range of cells in the current column or row that you want totaled and automatically enters them as the function's argument. And nine times out of ten, Excel selects (by highlighting) the correct cell range to be totaled. For that tenth case, you can manually correct the range by simply dragging the cell pointer through the block of cells that need to be summed.

Figure 2-17 shows how to use the AutoSum tool to total the sales of Jack Sprat Diet Centers in Row 3. To total the sales in this row, position the cell pointer in cell E3, where the first-quarter total is to appear, and click the AutoSum tool. Excel inserts the SUM function (equal sign and all) onto the formula bar; places a *marquee* (the moving dotted line) around the cells B3, C3, and D3; and uses the cell range B3:D3 as the argument of the SUM function.

Figure 2-17: Using the AutoSum button to total the sales of Jack Sprat Diet Centers in Row 3.

Figure 2-18 shows the worksheet after you insert the function in cell E3. The calculated total appears in cell E3 while the following SUM formula appears in the formula bar:

```
=SUM(B3:D3)
```

After entering the function to total the sales of Jack Sprat Diet Centers, you can copy this formula to total sales for the rest of the companies by dragging the fill handle down Column E until the cell range E3:E9 is highlighted.

Figure 2-19 illustrates how you can use the AutoSum tool to total the January sales for all the Mother Goose Enterprises in Column B. Position the cell pointer in cell B10 where you want the total to appear. When you click the AutoSum tool, Excel places the marquee around cells B3 through B9 and correctly enters the cell range B3:B9 as the argument of the SUM function.

Figure 2-20 shows the worksheet after inserting the function in cell B10 and using the AutoFill feature to copy the formula to cells C10, D10, and E10 to the right. (To use AutoFill, drag the fill handle through the cells to the right until you reach cell E10 before you release the mouse button.)

Figure 2-18:
The worksheet with the first-quarter total for Jack Sprat Diet Centers.

	A	B	C	D	E	F	G	H
1	Mother Goose Enterprises – 1998 Sales							
2		Jan	Feb	Mar	Qtr 1 Total			
3	Jack Sprat Di	80138.58	59389.56	19960.06	159488.2			
4	Jack and Jill	123456.2	89345.7	25436.84				
5	Mother Hubba	12657.05	60593.56	42300.28				
6	Rub-a-Dub-D	17619.79	40635	42814.99				
7	Georgie Porg	57133.56	62926.31	12408.73				
8	Hickory, Dick	168291	124718.1	41916.13				
9	Little Bo Pee	30834.63	71111.25	74926.24				
10	Total							
11								
12								
13								
14								
15								

Figure 2-19:
Using the
AutoSum
button to
add the
January
sales in
Column B.

Figure 2-20:
The
worksheet
after
copying the
SUM
formulas.

Making Sure the Data's Safe and Sound

All the work you do in any of the worksheets in your workbook is at risk
until you save the workbook as a disk file. Should you lose power or should
your computer crash for any reason before you save the workbook, you're
out of luck. You have to re-create each and every keystroke — a painful task,
made all the worse because it's so unnecessary. To avoid this unpleasant-
ness altogether, adopt this rule of thumb: Save your work anytime you've
entered more information than you could possibly bear to lose.

To encourage frequent saving on your part, Excel even provides you with a Save button on the Standard toolbar (the one with the picture of the disk, third from the left). You don't even have to take the time and trouble to choose the Save command from the File menu (or even press ⌘+S); you can simply click this tool whenever you want to save new work on disk.

The first time you click the Save tool, Excel displays the Save As dialog box (similar to the one shown in Figure 2-21). You can use this dialog box to replace the temporary document name (Workbook1, Workbook2, and the like) with a more descriptive filename and to select a new drive and folder before you save the workbook as a disk file. It's just this easy:

Figure 2-21:
The Save As
dialog box.

✔ To rename the workbook, type the filename in the Save as text box. When you first open the Save As dialog box, the suggested Workbook1-type filename is selected; you can just start typing the new filename to replace it.

✔ To change the drive on which the workbook is stored, click the Desktop button and then double-click the appropriate drive name, such as Macintosh Hard disk in the Desktop list box.

✔ To change the folder in which the workbook is saved, select the drive if necessary (as described previously) and then double-click the desired folder. If you want to save the workbook in a folder that's inside one of the folders shown in the list box, just double-click that folder. When all is said and done, the name of the folder where the workbook file will be saved should appear on the pop-up button at the top of the Save As dialog box. If you want to save the file in a brand-new folder, click the New button (refer to Figure 2-21) and enter the folder name in the Name of new folder text box before clicking OK or pressing Return.

When you finish making changes in the Save As dialog box, click the Save button or press Return to have Excel 98 save your work. When Excel saves your workbook file, the program saves all the information in every worksheet in your workbook (including the last position of the cell pointer) in the designated folder and disk. You don't have to fool with the Save As dialog box again unless you want to rename the workbook or save a copy of it in a different directory. If you want to do either of these things, you must choose the Save As command from the File menu rather than click the Save tool or press ⌘+S.

Part II
Editing without Tears

In this part . . .

The business world wouldn't be half bad if it just weren't for the fact that right around the time you master your job, somebody goes and changes it on you. When your life must always be flexible, changing gears and "going with the flow" can really grate on a person! The sad truth is that a big part of the work that you do with Excel 98 is changing the stuff you slaved so hard to enter into the spreadsheet in the first place.

Part II breaks this editing stuff down into three phases: formatting the raw data, rearranging the formatting data and/or in some cases deleting it, and, finally, spitting the final formatted and edited data out in printed form. Take it from me, after you know your way around editing your spreadsheets (as presented in this part of the book), you're more than halfway home with Excel 98.

Chapter 3

Making It All Look Pretty

*I*n spreadsheet programs like Excel, you don't normally worry about how the stuff looks until after you've entered all the data in the worksheets of your workbook and saved it all safe and sound (see Chapters 1 and 2). Only then do you begin to pretty up the information so that it's clearer and easy to read.

After you decide on the types of formatting you want to apply to a portion of the worksheet, you select all the cells you want to beautify and then click the appropriate tool or choose the menu command to apply those formats to the cells. This means that before you find out about all the fabulous formatting features you can use to dress up cells, you first need to know how to pick out the group of cells that you want to apply the formatting to — a process formally known as *selecting the cells* or alternately, *making a cell selection*.

Be aware, also, that entering data into a cell and formatting that data are two completely different things in Excel. Because they're separate, you can change the entry in a formatted cell, and the new entry will assume the cell's formatting. This enables you to format blank cells in a worksheet, knowing that when you get around to making entries in those cells, those entries will automatically assume the formatting assigned to those cells.

Choosing a Select Group of Cells

Given the monotonously rectangular nature of the worksheet and its components, you shouldn't be surprised to find that all the cell selections you make in the worksheet have the same kind of cubist feel to them. After all, worksheets are just blocks of cells of varying numbers of columns and rows.

A *cell selection* (also known as a *cell range*) is whatever collection of neighboring cells you pick out for formatting or editing. The smallest possible cell selection in a worksheet is just one cell (the so-called *active cell;* the cell with the cell pointer is really just a single cell selection). The largest possible cell selection in a worksheet is all the cells in that worksheet (the whole enchilada, so to speak). Most of the cell selections you need for formatting a worksheet will probably be somewhere in between, consisting of cells in several adjacent columns and rows.

Excel shows a cell selection in the worksheet by highlighting the block. (Figure 3-1 shows several cell selections of different sizes and shapes.)

In Excel, you can select more than one cell range at a time (a phenomenon somewhat ingloriously called a *discontiguous* or *nonadjacent selection*). In fact, although I bill Figure 3-1 as having several cell selections, it is really just one big, nonadjacent cell selection with cell D12 (the active one) as the cell that was selected last.

Point-and-click cell selections

The mouse is a natural for selecting a range of cells. Just position the mouse pointer (in its thick, white-cross form) on the first cell and drag in the direction that you want to extend the selection.

- ✔ To extend the cell selection to columns to the right, drag right, highlighting neighboring cells as you go.
- ✔ To extend the selection to rows to the bottom, drag down.
- ✔ To extend the selection down and to the right at the same time, drag diagonally toward the cell in the lower-right corner of the block you're highlighting.

Figure 3-1:
Several cell
selections
of various
shapes and
sizes.

Shifty cell selections

To speed up the old cell-selection procedure, you can use the old Shift+click method, which goes as follows:

1. **Click the first cell in the selection.**

   Doing so selects that cell.

2. **Position the mouse pointer in the last cell in the selection.**

   This would be kitty-corner from the first cell if you're selecting a rectangular block.

3. **Press the Shift key and hold it down as you click the mouse button again.**

   When you click the mouse button the second time, Excel selects all the cells in the columns and rows between the first cell and last cell.

The Shift key works with the mouse like an *extend* key to extend a selection from the first object you select through to, and including, the second object you select (see "Extending that cell selection," later in this chapter). The Shift key enables you to select the first and last cells as well as all the intervening cells in a worksheet or all the document names in a dialog list box.

If, when making a cell selection with the mouse, you notice that you have included the wrong cells before you release the mouse button, you can deselect the cells and resize the selection by moving the pointer in the opposite direction. If you've already released the mouse button, click the first cell in the highlighted range to select just that cell (and deselect all the others) and then start the whole selection process again.

Nonadjacent cell selections

To select a nonadjacent cell selection made up of more than one discontiguous block of cells, drag through the first cell range and then hold down the ⌘ (Command) key as you click the first cell of the second range and drag the pointer through the cells in this range. As long as you hold down ⌘ while you select the subsequent ranges, Excel doesn't deselect any of the previously selected cell ranges.

The ⌘ key works with the mouse like an _add_ key to include non-neighboring objects in Excel (see "Nonadjacent cell selections with the keyboard," later in this chapter). With ⌘, you can add to the selection of cells in a worksheet without having to deselect those already selected.

Going for the "big" cell selections

You can select the cells in entire columns or rows or even all the cells in the worksheet by applying the following clicking-and-dragging techniques to the worksheet frame:

✔ To select every single cell in a particular column, click its column letter on the frame at the top of the worksheet document window.

✔ To select every cell in a particular row, click its row number on the frame at the left edge of the document window.

✔ To select a range of entire columns or rows, drag through the column letters or row numbers on the frame surrounding the workbook.

✔ To select more than entire columns or rows that are not right next to each other (that old discontiguous stuff, again), press and hold down the ⌘ key while you click the column letters or row numbers of the columns and rows that you want to add to the selection.

✔ To select each and every cell in the worksheet, click the unmarked button in the upper-left corner of the workbook frame formed by the intersection of the row with the column letters and the column with the row numbers.

Selecting the cells in a table of data, courtesy of AutoSelect

Excel provides a really quick way (called AutoSelect) to select all the cells in a table of data entered as a solid block. (Don't try this when you need to select empty cells or on a table of data that has blanks in the first column or top row.) To use AutoSelect, simply follow these steps:

1. **Click the first cell of the table to select it.**

   That's the one in the table's upper-left corner.

2. **Hold down the Shift key as you double-click either the right or bottom edge of the selected cell with the arrowhead mouse pointer (see Figure 3-2).**

   If you double-click the bottom edge of the cell, the cell selection expands to that cell in the last row of the first column (as shown in Figure 3-3). If you double-click the right edge of the cell, the cell selection expands to the cell in the last column of the first row.

3a. **Double-click somewhere on the right edge of the cell selection (see Figure 3-3) if the cell selection now consists of the first column of the table.**

   Excel selects all the remaining rows of the table of data (as shown in Figure 3-4).

3b. **Double-click somewhere on the bottom edge of the current cell selection if the cell selection now consists of the first row of the table.**

   Excel selects all the rest of the rows in the table.

Figure 3-2:
Position the
mouse
pointer on
the bottom
edge of the
first cell to
select the
cells in the
first column
of the data
table with
AutoSelect.

Figure 3-3:
Double-clicking the bottom edge of the selected cells while holding down the Shift key selects the first column of the data table.

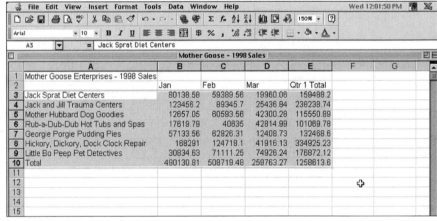

Figure 3-4:
Double-clicking the right edge of the current column selection while pressing Shift selects the rest of the columns in the data table.

Although the preceding steps make it sound like you have to select the first cell of the table when you use AutoSelect, you can actually select any of the cells in the four corners of the table. Then, when expanding the cell selection in the table with the Shift key depressed, you can choose whatever direction you like (left by clicking the left edge, right by clicking the right edge, up by clicking the top edge, or down by clicking the bottom edge) to select either the first or last row of the table or the first or last column. After expanding the cell selection to include either the first or last row or first or last column, you need to click whichever edge of the cell selection that will cause the selection to expand to include all the remaining table rows or columns.

Keyboard cell selections

If you're not really keen on always using the mouse, you can switch to the keyboard to select the cells you want. In keeping with the Shift+click method of selecting cells, the easiest way to select cells with the keyboard is to combine the Shift key with other keystrokes that move the cell pointer. (Chapter 1 lists these keystrokes.)

Start by positioning the cell pointer in the first cell of the selection and then holding the Shift key as you press the appropriate cell-pointer movement keys. When you hold the Shift key as you press direction keys such as the arrow keys (↑, ←, ↓, →), Page Up, or Page Down, Excel anchors the selection on the current cell and not only moves the cell pointer as usual but also highlights cells as it goes.

When making a cell selection this way, you can continue to alter the size and shape of the cell range with the cell-pointer movement keys as long as you don't release the Shift key. After you let up on the Shift key, pressing any of the cell-pointer movement keys immediately collapses the selection, reducing your selection to just the cell with the cell pointer.

Extending that cell selection

If holding the Shift key as you move the cell pointer is too tiring, you can place Excel in Extend mode by pressing (and promptly releasing) F8 before you press any cell-pointer movement key. Excel displays the EXT (for Extend mode) indicator on the status bar — your sign that the program will select all the cells that you move the cell pointer through (just as though you were holding down the Shift key).

After you highlight all the cells you want in the cell range, press F8 again to turn off Extend mode. The EXT indicator disappears from the status bar, and then you can once again move the cell pointer with the keyboard without highlighting everything in your path.

AutoSelect keyboard style

For the keyboard equivalent of AutoSelect with the mouse (refer to "Selecting the cells in a table of data, courtesy of AutoSelect" earlier in this chapter), you combine the use of the F8 (Extend key) or the Shift key with the ⌘+arrow keys or End+arrow keys to zip the cell pointer from one end of a block to the other, merrily selecting all the cells in its path as it goes.

To select an entire table of data with a keyboard version of AutoSelect, follow these steps:

1. **Position the cell pointer in the first cell.**

   That's the one in the upper-left corner of the table.

2. **Press F8 (or hold the Shift key) and then press ⌘+→ (or End, → if you prefer) to extend the cell selection to the cells in the columns on the right.**

3. **Then press ⌘+↓ (or End, ↓ if you prefer) to extend the selection to the cells in the rows below.**

Keep in mind that the directions in the above steps are arbitrary — you can just as well press ⌘+↓ (or End, ↓) before you press ⌘+→ (or End, →). Just be sure (if you're using the Shift key instead of F8) that you don't let up on the Shift key until after you finish performing these two directional maneuvers. Also, if you press F8 to get the program into Extend mode, don't forget to press this key again to get out of Extend mode after the table cells are all selected (or you'll end up selecting cells that you don't want included when you next move the cell pointer).

You can also combine the Control key with the Shift and arrow key to extend a selection.

Nonadjacent cell selections with the keyboard

Selecting more than one cell range is a little more complicated with the keyboard than it is with the mouse. When using the keyboard, you alternate between anchoring the cell pointer and moving the cell pointer to select the cell range, unanchoring the cell pointer and repositioning it at the beginning of the next range. To unanchor the cell pointer so that you can move it into position for selecting another range, press Shift+F8. Doing so puts you in Add mode, in which you can move to the first cell of the next range without selecting any more cells. Excel lets you know that the cell pointer is unanchored by displaying the ADD indicator on the status bar.

To select more than one cell range using the keyboard, you follow these general steps:

1. **Move the cell pointer to the first cell of the first cell range you want to select.**

2. **Press F8 to get into Extend mode.**

   Move the cell pointer to select all the cells in the first cell range. Alternatively, hold the Shift key as you move the cell pointer.

3. **Press Shift+F8 to switch to Add mode.**

   The ADD indicator appears in the status bar.

4. **Move the cell pointer to the first cell of the next nonadjacent range you want to select.**

5. **Press F8 again to get back into Extend mode and then move the cell pointer to select all the cells in this new range.**

6. **If you still have other nonadjacent ranges to select, repeat Steps 3, 4, and 5 until you select and add all the cell ranges you want to use.**

Cell selections à la Go To

If you want to select a really big cell range that would take a long time to select by pressing various cell-pointer movement keys, use the Go To feature to extend the range to a far distant cell. All you gotta do is follow this pair of steps:

1. **Start by positioning the cell pointer in the first cell of the range; then press F8 to anchor the cell pointer and get Excel into Extend mode.**

2. **Press F5 to open the Go To dialog box, type the address of the last cell in the range (the cell kitty-corner from the first cell), and then press Return.**

Because Excel is in Extend mode at the time you use the Go To feature to jump to another cell, the program not only moves the cell pointer to the designated cell address but also selects all the intervening cells as well. After selecting the range of cells with the Go To feature, don't forget to press F8 (the Extend key) again to prevent the program from messing up your selection by adding on more cells the next time you move the cell pointer.

Trimming Your Tables with AutoFormat

Here's a formatting technique that doesn't require you to do any prior cell selecting. (Kinda figures, doesn't it?) In fact, the AutoFormat feature is so automatic that, to use it, the cell pointer just has to be somewhere within the table of data prior to your choosing the Format⇨AutoFormat on the Excel menu bar.

As soon as you open the AutoFormat dialog box, Excel automatically selects all the cells in the table. (You get a rude message in an alert box if you choose the command when the cell pointer isn't within the confines of the table or in one of the cells directly bordering the table.)

You can make short work of formatting a table of data by choosing one of the 16 built-in table formats. Here's how:

1. **Choose Format⇨AutoFormat to open the AutoFormat dialog box.**

2. **Select a format in the Table format list box to see a preview of its formats in the Sample area.**

   This sample should give you an idea of what kind of formatting is included in a particular table format and how it makes the table look. (Unfortunately, Excel can't display a miniature of your table in the Sample area.)

3. **Continue selecting formats from the list box in this manner to preview other table formats until you find the one you want to use.**

4. **Click the OK button or press Return to close the AutoFormat dialog box and apply the selected format to the table in the worksheet.**

When you're familiar enough with the table formats to know which one you want to use, you can save time by double-clicking the desired format in the Table format list box to both close the AutoFormat dialog box and apply the formatting to the selected table.

If you ever goof up and select a table format that you just absolutely hate after you see it in the worksheet, choose the Edit⇨Undo AutoFormat on the menu bar (or press ⌘+Z) before you do anything else; Excel restores the table to its previous state. (For more on getting yourself out of a jam with the Undo feature, see Chapter 4.) If you decide later on that you don't want any of the automatic table formatting, you can get rid of all of it (even when it's too late to use Undo) by opening the AutoFormat dialog box and selecting None in the Table format list box (located at the very bottom of the list) before you click OK or press Return.

Each of the built-in table formats offered by AutoFormat is nothing more than a particular combination of various kinds of cell and data formatting that Excel applies to the cell selection in a single operation. (Boy, does this ever save time!) Each one enhances the headings and values in the table in a slightly different way.

Figure 3-5 shows the first quarter 1998 sales table for Mother Goose Enterprises (introduced in Chapter 2) just before the Simple table format is selected in the AutoFormat dialog box. Figure 3-6 shows the sales table with the Simple table format applied to it. Notice that not only did AutoFormat bold the worksheet title and headings in Rows 1 and 2 and draw borderlines to separate these headings from the rest of the table data, but it also centered the title *Mother Goose Enterprises — 1998 Sales* over Columns A through E and the headings in cells B2 through E2. Note, however, that the Simple table format does nothing to spruce up the dollar amounts in the table.

Figure 3-5:
Using
AutoFormat to
select and
format the
Mother Goose
Enterprises
first quarter
sales table.

Figure 3-6:
Mother's first
quarter sales
table in the
Simple table
format.

Figure 3-7 shows the table after reopening the AutoFormat dialog box and, this time, choosing the 3D Effects 2 table format for the same cell range. As you can see, after selecting this table format, Excel increased the width of Column A to contain the entire worksheet title, *Mother Goose Enterprises — 1998 Sales* in cell A1. This kind of column sizing is known as *best-fit* (somewhat misapplied in this case) and is accomplished with the AutoFit feature. To rectify this little boo-boo, you simply narrow Column A until it's just wide enough to display all the company names in Rows 3 through 9 of Column A and let the worksheet title in cell A1 once again overhang Columns B through E as it naturally wants to do. (For information on how to widen and narrow columns, both manually and with the AutoFit feature, see "Calibrating Columns," later in this chapter.)

The 3D Effects 2 AutoFormat is not the only table format that uses AutoFit to apply this type of *best-fit* to all the selected columns (and therefore can give you a really wide first column if your table has a long title in the first cell like the ones shown in Figure 3-5 through 3-7). You also get this best-fit-which-is-not situation — shown in Figure 3-7 — if you choose the Classic 2; Financial 1, 2, or 3; Accounting 1, 2, 3, 4; Colorful 3; List 1 or 2; or 3D Effects 1 table formats. All the others prefer to center long titles in the first cell across all the columns in the table (which can give you the problem illustrated in Figure 3-6!).

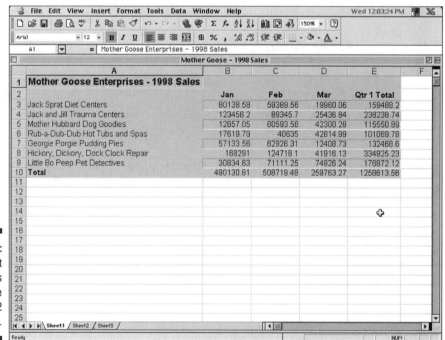

Figure 3-7: Mother's first quarter sales table, in the 3D Effects 2 table format.

Fancying Up Your Cells with the Formatting Toolbar

Some worksheets require a lighter touch than the AutoFormat feature offers. For example, you may have a table where the only emphasis you want to add is to make the column headings bold at the top of the table and to underline the row of totals at the bottom (done by drawing a borderline along the bottom of the cells).

With the tools on the Formatting toolbar, which appears right below the Standard toolbar, you can accomplish most data and cell formatting without ever venturing into the shortcut menus, let alone (heaven forbid) opening up the pull-down menus.

You can use the tools on the Formatting toolbar to assign new fonts and number formats to cells, to change the alignment of their contents, or to add borders, patterns, and colors to them. (Refer to Table 1-3 in Chapter 1 for a complete rundown on the use of each of these tools.)

Transient toolbars

Normally, the Standard and Formatting toolbars appear at the top of the Excel 98 program window (right below the menu bar) in a stationary position politely referred to as being in a *docked* position (*beached* is more like it). Although Excel automatically docks these toolbars at the top of the screen, you are free to move them (as well as any other toolbars that you open — see Chapter 13 for details on using and customizing other toolbars) around by dragging them by their move handles (kicking and screaming) into new positions.

When you drag the Standard or Formatting toolbar down by its move handle into the work area containing the open workbook, the toolbar then appears in a separate little window like the one containing the Formatting toolbar shown in Figure 3-8. Such toolbars-in-a-window are referred to as *floating toolbars* because they float like clouds above the open workbook below (how poetic!). And not only can you move these little dears, but you can resize them as well:

- ✔ You can move a floating toolbar into new positions over the worksheet document by dragging it by its tiny title bar.

- ✔ You can resize a floating toolbar by dragging the tab displayed in its lower-right corner.

Move Handle

Figure 3-8:
The
Formatting
toolbar
peacefully
floating
above the
worksheet.

✔ As you drag a side of the floating toolbar, the outline of the toolbar assumes a new shape to accommodate the tools in a prescribed tool arrangement. When the toolbar outline assumes the shape you want, release the mouse button, and Excel redraws the toolbar.

✔ To close a floating toolbar when you no longer want it in the document window, click the close box (the small box in the upper-left corner of the toolbar window).

✔ To minimize a floating toolbar down to just its title bar, double-click somewhere on the title bar or click the collapse box (the little box in the upper-right corner of the toolbar window). To restore the toolbar window to its previous size and shape, double-click somewhere on the title bar or click the collapse box again.

To restore a floating toolbar to its original docked position in the Excel window, just double-click somewhere on the toolbar outside of the title bar and outside of its buttons (which activates the button's function).

Toolbar docking maneuvers

Face it, sometimes a floating toolbar can be a real pain because you're constantly having to move it out of the way as you add to and edit your worksheet data. To get a toolbar out of the way so that it no longer obscures any of the worksheet cells, you can simply dock it.

Excel has four docking stations: the top of the screen above the formula bar, the very left edge of the screen, the very right edge of the screen, or the bottom of the screen right above the status bar. Figure 3-9 shows the Formatting toolbar after docking it at the bottom of the work area.

To dock a floating toolbar in one of these four areas, drag it by the title bar as far to the side of the window as possible and release the mouse button when the outline of the bar assumes a shape that accommodates a single column (when docking left or right) or a single row (when docking top or bottom). Toolbars you dock on the left or right of the document window reorient their tools so that they run vertically down the toolbar.

Figure 3-9: The Formatting toolbar safely docked at the bottom of the work area.

	A	B	C	D	E	F	G
1	Mother Goose Enterprises - 1998 Sales						
2		Jan	Feb	Mar	Qtr 1 Total		
3	Jack Sprat Diet Centers	80138.58	59389.56	19960.06	159488.2		
4	Jack and Jill Trauma Centers	123456.2	89345.7	25436.84	238238.74		
5	Mother Hubbard Dog Goodies	12657.05	60593.56	42300.28	115550.89		
6	Rub-a-Dub-Dub Hot Tubs and Spas	17619.79	40635	42814.99	101069.78		
7	Georgie Porgie Pudding Pies	57133.56	62926.31	12408.73	132468.6		
8	Hickory, Dickory, Dock Clock Repair	168291	124718.1	41916.13	334925.23		
9	Little Bo Peep Pet Detectives	30834.63	71111.25	74926.24	176872.12		
10	Total	490130.81	508719.48	259763.27	1258613.6		

Formatting Toolbar

When you dock the Standard or Formatting toolbar on the left or right side of the screen, the toolbars lose buttons like the Font and Zoom buttons that use pop-up text boxes, as the text in these boxes can't be aligned with the new vertical orientation. This same type of button loss occurs when docking the Chart and Web toolbars on the left or right side of the screen, as they also contain buttons that use pop-up text boxes.

Sometimes, after you dock a toolbar, the active document window loses one or the other of the scroll bars. To get the missing scroll bar back, click the document Maximize button to max out the current document. If you're working with an empty workbook (like Workbook1), you can properly size the document window and restore the scroll bars by closing the workbook with the File⇨Close command on the menu bar and then opening a new workbook in its place by clicking the New tool on the Standard toolbar (the very first tool). When Excel opens the new workbook (Workbook2), the document window fits nicely (with all the scroll bars intact) and reflects your current toolbar-docking arrangement.

Using the Format Cells Dialog Box

Excel's Format⇨Cells command on the menu bar (⌘+1 for short) makes it a snap to apply a whole rash of different kinds of formatting to a cell selection. The Format Cells dialog box that this command calls up contains six tabs: Number, Alignment, Font, Border, Patterns, and Protection. In this chapter, I show you how to use the Number, Alignment, Font, Border, and Patterns tabs in the Format Cells dialog box to assign new number formats and fonts to your cells as well as to change their alignment, borders, and patterns. For information on how and when to use the options on the Protection tab, see Chapter 6.

The keystroke shortcut — ⌘+1 — that opens the Format Cells dialog box is one worth learning (as many of you will do almost as much formatting as you do data entry in a worksheet). Just keep in mind that the shortcut is ⌘ plus the number 1 and not the function key F1. Further, you must use the 1 key on the top row of the regular typewriter keyboard, not the 1 located on your numeric keypad. Pressing ⌘ plus the 1 on the numeric keypad doesn't work any better than pressing ⌘+F1.

Getting to know the number formats

As Chapter 2 explains, how you enter values into a worksheet determines the type of number format they get. Here are some examples:

✔ If you enter a financial value complete with the dollar sign and two decimal places, Excel assigns a Currency number format to the cell along with the entry.

✔ If you enter a value representing a percentage as a whole number followed by the percent sign without any decimal places, Excel assigns to the cell the Percentage number format that follows this pattern along with the entry.

✔ If you enter a date (remember that dates are values, too) that follows one of the built-in Excel number formats like 02/19/98 or 19-Feb-98, the program assigns a Date number format that follows the pattern of the date along with a special value representing the date.

Although formatting values in this manner as you go along is fine (and even necessary in the case of dates), you don't have to do it this way. You can always assign a number format to a group of values before or after you enter them. And, in fact, formatting numbers after you enter them is often the most efficient way to go because it's just a two-step procedure:

1. **Select all the cells containing the values that need dressing up.**

2. **Select the number format you want to use either from the Formatting toolbar or the Format Cells dialog box.**

    Many times, you can use one of the tools on the Formatting toolbar — if not, you can select a number format from the Number tab in the Format Cells dialog box (⌘+1).

Even if you're a really good typist and prefer (thank you very much) to enter each value exactly as you want it to appear in the worksheet, you still have to resort to using number formats to make the values that are calculated by formulas match the others you've entered. This is because Excel applies a General number format (which the Format Cells dialog box explains as "General format cells have no specific number format.") to all the values it calculates as well as any you enter that don't exactly follow one of the other Excel number formats. The biggest problem with the General format is that it has the nasty habit of dropping all leading and trailing zeros from the entries, making it very hard to line up numbers in a column on their decimal points.

Figure 3-10 shows this sad state of affairs. The figure shows a sample worksheet with the first-quarter 1998 sales figures for Mother Goose Enterprises before any of the values have been formatted. Notice how the columns of monthly sales figures zig and zag? This is the fault of Excel's General number format; the only cure is to format the values with another, more uniform number format.

Figure 3-10:
First quarter
sales
zigging and
zagging in
Columns B
through E.

Currying your cells with the Currency Style

Given the financial nature of most worksheets, you probably use the Currency format more than any other. This is a really easy format to apply because the Formatting toolbar contains a Currency Style tool that adds a dollar sign, commas between thousands of dollars, and two decimal places to any values in a selected range. If any of the values in the cell selection are negative, the Currency format displays them in parentheses (the way accountants like them) and displays them in red on a color monitor (the way governments like them).

In Figure 3-11, only the cells containing totals are selected for the Currency format (cell ranges E3:E10 and B10:D10). You then format this cell selection with the Currency format by simply clicking the Currency Style button on the Formatting toolbar (the one with the $ icon, naturally).

Figure 3-11:
The totals in
the Mother
Goose sales
table after
clicking the
Currency
Style button
on the
Formatting
toolbar.

Note: Although you can put all the figures in the table into the Currency format to line up the decimal points, this results in a superabundance of dollar signs in a fairly small table. In this example, I decided to format only the monthly and quarterly totals à la Currency.

Fixing the format overflow

You may be wondering if I've lost it altogether, if Excel lost it altogether, or a combination of the two has occurred. Somehow, we have a failure to communicate because there's no way that the pound signs (#######) in the cell ranges E3:E10 and B10:D10 in Figure 3-11 resemble anything close to numbers using the Currency format. Such pound signs where nicely formatted dollar totals should be serve as overflow indicators, declaring that whatever formatting you've given to the value in that cell has added so much to the value's display that Excel can no longer display it within the current column width.

To get rid of the pound signs and bring back the prettied-up values, you simply have to widen the affected columns. Figure 3-12 shows you the Mother Goose Enterprises sales table after widening Columns B through E. (To find out how to widen columns yourself, jump ahead to "Calibrating Columns," later in this chapter.) As you can see, not only are the numbers all there, but they're also sporting dollar signs, commas, and two decimal places.

Those blasted #######s appear in cells whenever any number format you apply (not just the Currency format) adds too much formatting fluff to the values to display them in their cells given the current column width. Be aware that these pound signs also replace perfectly fine-looking formatted values whenever you narrow columns too much. Of course, whenever and wherever this happens in your worksheets, you now know that all you have to do to fix the problem is widen the columns with the affected (infected?) cells.

Figure 3-12:
Monthly sales figures after widening Columns B through E to get rid of the pound-sign overflow indicators.

	File Edit View Insert Format Tools Data Window Help				Wed 3:41:23 PM		

		=SUM(B3:D3)						
	Mother Goose – 1998 Sales							
	A	B	C	D	E	F	G	H
1	Mother Goose Enterprises - 1998 Sales							
2		Jan	Feb	Mar	Qtr 1 Total			
3	Jack Sprat C	80138.58	59389.56	19960.06	$ 159,488.20			
4	Jack and Jill	123456.2	89345.7	25436.84	$ 238,238.74			
5	Mother Hubb	12657.05	60593.56	42300.28	$ 115,550.89			
6	Rub-a-Dub-[	17619.79	40635	42814.99	$ 101,069.78			
7	Georgie Por	57133.56	62926.31	12408.73	$ 132,468.60			
8	Hickory, Dicl	168291	124718.1	41916.13	$ 334,925.23			
9	Little Bo Pee	30834.63	71111.25	74926.24	$ 176,872.12			
10	Total	$ 490,130.81	$ 508,719.48	$ 259,763.27	$ 1,258,613.56			
11								
12	Month/Qtr	0.389421206	0.40419037	0.206388425				
13								
14						✛		
15								

Calming down your cells with the Comma Style format offers a good alternative to the Currency format. Like Currency, the Comma format inserts commas in larger numbers to separate thousands, hundred thousands, millions, and, well, you get the idea.

This format also displays two decimal places and puts negative values in parentheses and in red (on a color monitor). What it doesn't display is dollar signs. This makes it perfect for formatting tables where it's obvious that you're dealing with dollars and cents or for larger values that have nothing to do with money.

The Comma format also works well for the bulk of the values in the sample first-quarter sales worksheet. Figure 3-13 shows this table after the cells containing the monthly sales for each Mother Goose company were formatted with the Comma format. To do this, select the cell range B3:D9 and click the Comma Style button (the one with the , [comma] icon, of course) on the Formatting toolbar.

Figure 3-13 shows how the Comma format takes care of the earlier alignment problem in the quarterly sales figures. Moreover, notice how the Comma-formatted monthly sales figures align perfectly with the Currency-formatted monthly totals in row 10. If you look really closely (you may need a magnifying glass for this one), you see that these formatted values no longer abut the right edges of their cells; they've moved slightly to the left. The gap on the right between the last digit and the cell border is there to accommodate the right parenthesis in negative values, ensuring that they too align precisely on the decimal point.

Figure 3-13: Monthly sales figures after formatting them with the Comma number format.

	A	B	C	D	E	F	G	H
1	Mother Goose Enterprises - 1998 Sales							
2		Jan	Feb	Mar	Qtr 1 Total			
3	Jack Sprat D	80,138.58	59,389.56	19,960.06	$ 159,488.20			
4	Jack and Jill	123,456.20	89,345.70	25,436.84	$ 238,238.74			
5	Mother Hubb	12,657.05	60,593.56	42,300.28	$ 115,550.89			
6	Rub-a-Dub-[	17,619.79	40,635.00	42,814.99	$ 101,069.78			
7	Georgie Por	57,133.56	62,926.31	12,408.73	$ 132,468.60			
8	Hickory, Dic	168,291.00	124,718.10	41,916.13	$ 334,925.23			
9	Little Bo Pee	30,834.63	71,111.25	74,926.24	$ 176,872.12			
10	Total	$ 490,130.81	$ 508,719.48	$ 259,763.27	$ 1,258,613.56			
11								
12	Month/Qtr	0.389421206	0.40419037	0.206388425				
13								
14								
15								

Playing Around with the Percent Style

Many worksheets use percentages in the form of interest rates, growth rates, inflation rates, and so on. To insert a percentage in a cell, place the percent sign (%) after the number. To indicate an interest rate of 12 percent, for example, you type **12%** in the cell. When you do this, Excel assigns a Percent number format and, at the same time, divides the value by 100 (that's what makes it a percentage) and places the result in the cell (0.12 in this example).

Not all percentages in a worksheet are entered by hand in this manner. Some may be calculated by a formula and returned to their cells as raw decimal values. In such cases, you should add a Percent format to convert the calculated decimal values to percentages (done by multiplying the decimal value by 100 and adding a percent sign).

The sample first-quarter sales worksheet just happens to have some percentages calculated by formulas in row 12 that need formatting. (These formulas indicate what percentage each monthly total is of the first-quarter total in cell E10.) Figure 3-14 shows these values after they have been formatted with a Percent format. To accomplish this feat, you simply select the cells and click the Percent Style button on the Formatting toolbar. (Need I point out that it's the tool with a % sign?)

Deciding how many decimal places

You can increase or decrease the number of decimal places used in a number entered with the Currency Style, Comma Style, or Percent Style tool on the Formatting toolbar simply by clicking the Increase Decimal tool or the Decrease Decimal tool also located on this toolbar. (Remember to click these tools while the cell range you just formatted is still selected.)

Figure 3-14: Monthly-to-quarterly sales percentages formatted with the Percent number format.

Each time you click the Increase Decimal tool (the one with the arrow pointing left), Excel adds another decimal place to the number format you applied. Figure 3-15 shows percentages in the cell range B12:D12 after I increased the number of decimal places in the Percent format from none to two (the Percent Style doesn't use any decimal places). I accomplished this by clicking the Increase Decimal tool twice in a row.

The values behind the formatting

Make no mistake about it, all that these fancy number formats do is spiff up the presentation of the values in the worksheet. Like a good illusionist, a particular number format sometimes appears to magically transform some entries, but in reality, the entries are the same old numbers you started with. For example, suppose that a formula returns the following value:

```
25.6456
```

Now suppose that you format the cell containing this value with the Currency Style tool. The value now appears as follows:

```
$25.65
```

This change may lead you to believe that Excel rounded the value up to two decimal places. In fact, the program rounds up only the *display* of the calculated value — the cell still contains the same old value of 25.6456. If you use this cell in another worksheet formula, keep in mind that Excel uses the behind-the-scenes value in its calculation, not the spiffed-up one shown in the cell.

Figure 3-15:
Monthly-to-
quarterly
sales
percentages
after adding
two decimal
places.

But what if you want the values to match their formatted appearance in the worksheet? Well, Excel can do that in a single step. Be forewarned, however, that this is a one-way trip. You can convert all underlying values to the way they are displayed by selecting a single check box, but you can't return them to their previous state by deselecting the check box.

Well, because you insist on knowing this little trick anyway, here goes (just don't write and try to tell me that you weren't warned):

1. **Make sure that all the values in your worksheet are formatted with the right number of decimal places.**

   You must do this step before you convert the precision of all values in the worksheet to their displayed form.

2. **Choose Tools⇨Preferences on the menu bar.**

3. **Select the Calculation tab to bring up the calculation options.**

4. **Select the Precision as Displayed option under Workbook Options to put a check mark in its check box and click the OK button.**

   Excel displays the Data will permanently lose accuracy alert dialog box (or in a question-and-answer balloon if the Office Assistant is open).

5. **Go ahead (live dangerously) and click the OK button or press Return to convert all values to match their display.**

After converting all the values in a worksheet with the Precision as Displayed option, as described in the preceding steps, you may be wise to choose the Save As command on the File menu and edit the filename in the Save as text box (maybe by appending "as Displayed" to the current filename) before you click the Save button or press Return. That way, you still have a disk copy of the original workbook file with the values as entered and calculated by Excel that can act as a backup to your new "as Displayed" version.

Ogling the other number formats

Excel supports a whole bunch more number formats than just the Currency, Comma, and Percent formats. To use them, select the cell range (or ranges) to be formatted and choose Format Cells on the cell shortcut menu (click the secondary mouse button somewhere in the cell selection) or the Cells command on the Format menu (⌘+1) to open the Format Cells dialog box.

After the Format Cells dialog box is open, you then select the Number tab and select the desired format from the Category list box. Some Number format categories — such as Date, Time, Fraction, and Special — give you further formatting choices in a Type list box. Other number formats, such as Number and Currency, have their own particular boxes that give you options for refining their formats. As you select the different formats in these list boxes, Excel shows what effect each format would have on the first of the values in the current cell selection in the Sample area above. When the sample has the format you want to apply to the current cell selection, you just click the OK button or press Return to apply the new number format.

Sorting through the Special number formats

Excel contains a nifty category of number formats called Special. The Special category contains the following four number formats that may be of interest to you:

- ✔ **Zip Code:** Retains any leading zeros in the value (important in zip codes and of absolutely no importance in arithmetic computations) as in 00123.

- ✔ **Zip Code + 4:** Automatically separates the last four digits from the first five digits and retains any leading zeros, as in 00123-5555.

- ✔ **Phone Number:** Automatically encloses the first three digits of the number in parentheses and separates the last four digits from the previous three with a dash, as in (999) 555-1111.

- ✔ **Social Security Number:** Automatically puts dashes in the value to separate its digits into groups of three, two, and four, as in 666-00-9999.

These Special number formats really come in handy when creating databases in Excel, which often deal with stuff like zip codes, telephone numbers, and sometimes even Social Security numbers (see Chapter 9 for more on creating databases).

Creating custom number formats

If none of the predefined number formats of the various types in the different categories fit your bill, you can always resort to creating a custom number format of your very own. To create custom number formats, you must choose Custom as the Category in the Format Cells dialog box and then select the number format code that is closest to what you want from the Type list box and then, most often, edit this number format code in the Type text box.

There's only one problem with doing this: Excel wasn't lying when it called them number format *codes*. All you see in the Type list box when Custom is the Category is a bunch of weird-looking codes composed of lots of #s, 0s, ?s, Ds, Ms, and Ys. Rather than work yourself into a lather (or, heaven forbid, do something nerdy like trying to decipher this gibberish), make life easier and focus your attention on the Sample area above the Type text box as you select various formats from the Format Codes list box. There, Excel shows how the value in the active cell of the selected range will look in the selected format. As soon as you see what you like, go for it by clicking the OK button or pressing Return.

In addition to choosing built-in formats by their number format codes, you can create your own custom codes by doing a little creative editing. Although you do have to use these junky number format codes (ugh) when performing this editing, you really don't have to be a rocket scientist to figure out how to do it. (Not that being a rocket scientist would hurt!)

Rather than bore you with a lot of examples of custom number formats that even a computer nerd would have trouble staying awake through, I just want to introduce you to a custom number format you may actually find quite handy in your worksheets — one that hides the display of any cell entry in the worksheet. (You can continue to see the entry on the formula bar when the cell pointer is in its cell.) You can then use your custom hidden format to temporarily hide certain cell ranges that you don't want printed out or visible in your worksheet on-screen.

To build the custom hidden number format, open the Format Cells dialog box (⌘+1), select Custom in the Category list box in the Number tab of the Format Cells dialog box, and then select General in the Type list box and replace this text with the following number format codes:

```
;;;
```

The custom hidden number format just consists of three semicolons in a row (with no spaces between them). Odd as this looks, these three semicolons tell Excel that it should display nothing for positive values, nothing for negative values, and, while you're at it, nothing for anything else in the cell.

After entering the codes in the Type text box, click the OK button or press Return to apply the custom format to the current cell selection. Custom formats are saved as part of the worksheet the next time you save the workbook file.

When you apply this hidden format to cells, the cell display disappears in the worksheet. (The contents still show up on the formula bar when you select the cell.) To make hidden entries reappear, simply select the hidden cells, open the Format Cells dialog box, and select one of the other visible number formats (the General format, for example) and apply it to cells.

Decoding those darned number format codes

If you just have to know what some of these number format codes mean, here goes. Each number format can control how positive numbers, negative numbers, and everything else looks (that is, zero values and text). These parts are divided by semicolons. (Any format not so divided covers all the other types of entries.) The 0 is a placeholder for a digit and is filled by a zero if the value lacks a digit in that place. The # sign is a placeholder for a digit not to be filled if the value lacks a digit for that place. Ms are used for months in dates or minutes in time, Ds for days, Ys for years, Hs for hours, and Ss for seconds.

Note that Excel adds the custom number formats that you create to the bottom of the Type list box. This means that when you next open the Format Cells dialog box and select Custom in the Category list box of the Number tab, you may have to scroll through the Type list box all the way to the bottom before you can locate and select the number format codes that you're responsible for adding.

Calibrating Columns

For those times when you need to adjust the width of your columns (like when a swarm of #######s appear in the cells you format), Excel makes changing the column widths a breeze. The easiest way to adjust a column is to do a *best-fit* using the AutoFit feature. With this method, Excel automatically determines how much to widen or narrow the column to fit the longest entry currently in the column.

Here's how to use AutoFit to get the best-fit for a column:

1. **Position the mouse pointer on the column frame, on the right border of the column that needs adjusting.**

   The mouse pointer changes to a double-headed arrow pointing left and right.

2. **Double-click the mouse button.**

   Excel widens or narrows the column width to suit the longest entry.

You can do a best-fit for more than one column at a time. Simply select all the columns that need adjusting. (If the columns neighbor one another, drag through their column letters on the frame; if they don't, hold the ⌘ key as you click the individual column letters.) After you select the columns, double-click any of the right borders on the frame.

As I pointed out earlier in this chapter, best-fit à la AutoFit doesn't always produce the expected results. All you have to do is AutoFit a column with a table title to become acquainted with this fact (as the 3D Effects 2 table format did in Figure 3-7). A long title that spills into several columns to the right produces an awfully wide column when you use best-fit.

When AutoFit's best-fit won't do, drag the right border of the column (on the frame) until it's the size you need instead of double-clicking it. This manual technique for calibrating column width also works when more than one column is selected. Just be aware that all selected columns assume whatever size you make the one that you're actually dragging.

You can also set the widths of columns from the Column Width dialog box. When you use the dialog box, you enter the number of characters you want for the column width. To open this dialog box, choose the Column Width command from the column shortcut menu (which you open by clicking any selected column or column letter with the secondary mouse button), or choose Format⇨Column⇨Width on the menu bar.

The Column width text box in the Column Width dialog box shows how many characters are in the standard column width in the worksheet or in the current column width if you previously adjusted it. To change the widths of all the columns you've selected in the worksheet (except those that you already adjusted manually or with AutoFit), enter a new value in the Column width text box and click the OK button.

If you want Excel to size the column to best-fit, choose Format⇨Column⇨ AutoFit Selection on the menu bar. Note that you can use this AutoFit Selection command to apply best-fit to a column based on just some of the cell entries. For example, say that you wanted to use best-fit to make a column just wide enough for a range of headings but not including the worksheet title (that spills over several blank columns to the right). All you have to do is select just the cells in that column that contain the headings on which the new column width should be based before you choose Format⇨Column⇨AutoFit Selection.

If you want to return a column selection to the standard (default) column width by using the pull-down menus, you simply choose Format⇨Column⇨ Standard Width on the menu bar. This opens the Standard Width dialog box containing the value 10 in the Standard column width text box (which happens to be the default width of all columns in a new worksheet). To return all the selected columns to this standard width, click the OK button in this dialog box or simply press Return.

Rambling rows

The story with adjusting the heights of rows is pretty much the same as that with adjusting columns, except that you do a lot less row adjusting than you do column adjusting. That's because Excel automatically changes the height of the rows to accommodate changes to their entries (such as selecting a larger font size or wrapping text in a cell — both of these techniques are coming right up). Most row-height adjustments come about when you want to increase the amount of space between a table title and the table or between a row of column headings and the table of information without actually adding a blank row. (See "From top to bottom" later in this chapter for details.)

To increase the height of a row, drag the bottom border of the row frame down until the row is high enough and then release the mouse button. To shorten a row, reverse this process and drag the bottom row-frame border up. To use AutoFit to create a best-fit for the entries in a row, you double-click the bottom row frame border.

As with columns, you can also adjust the height of selected rows with a dialog box. To open the Row Height dialog box, choose the Row Height command from the row shortcut menu (opened by clicking any selected row or row number with the secondary mouse button) or choose Format⇨ Row⇨Height on the menu bar. To set a new row height for the selected row (or rows), enter the number of characters in the Row height text box and click OK. (The default row height is 13.00 characters, in case you care.) To return to the best-fit for a particular row, choose Format⇨Row⇨AutoFit on the menu bar.

Now you see it, now you don't

A funny thing about narrowing columns and rows: You can get carried away and make a column so narrow or a row so short, that it actually disappears from the worksheet! This can actually come in handy for those times when you don't want part of the worksheet visible. For example, you may have a worksheet that contains a column listing employee salaries — required in calculating the departmental budget figures, but that you would prefer to leave off most printed reports. Rather than waste time moving the column of salary figures outside the area that you want to print, you can just hide the column until after you print the report.

Hiding columns and rows, courtesy of the pull-down and shortcut menus

Although you can hide worksheet columns and rows by just adjusting them out of existence, Excel does offer an easier method of hiding them, via the Format menu or column or row shortcut menus. Suppose that you need to hide Column B in the worksheet because it contains some irrelevant or sensitive information that you don't want to print. To hide this column, you can follow these steps:

1. **Click the letter B on the frame to select the column.**

2. **Choose Format⇨Column⇨Hide on the menu bar.**

That's all there is to it — Column B goes *poof!* All the information in the column disappears from the worksheet. When you hide Column B, notice that the row of column letters in the frame now reads A, C, D, E, F, and so forth.

Note that you can just as well hide Column B by Control+clicking its column letter on the frame and then choosing the Hide command on the column's shortcut menu.

So now, suppose that you've printed the worksheet and need to make a change to one of the entries in Column B. To unhide the column, follow these steps:

1. **Position the mouse pointer on column letter A in the frame and drag the pointer right to select both Columns A and C.**

   You must drag from A to C to include hidden Column B as part of the column selection — don't click with the ⌘ key or you won't get B.

2. **Choose Format⇨Column⇨Unhide on the menu bar.**

Excel brings back the hidden B column and all three columns (A, B, and C) are selected. You can then click the mouse pointer on any cell in the worksheet to deselect the columns.

Note that you can also unhide Column B by selecting Columns A and C and then Control+clicking either one of them and choosing the Unhide command on the column shortcut menu.

Hiding columns and rows with the mouse

I won't lie to you — hiding and redisplaying columns with the mouse can be *very* tricky. It requires a degree of precision that you may not possess (especially if you just recently started using the rodent). However, if you consider yourself a real mouse master, you can hide and unhide columns solely by dragging the mouse pointer as follows:

✔ To hide a column with the mouse, drag the column's right edge to the left until it's on top of the left edge and then release the mouse button.

✔ To hide a row with the mouse, drag the row's bottom border up until it's on top of the upper border.

As you drag a border, Excel displays a screen tip with the current column width or row height measurement in a box near the mouse pointer (just like with the screen tips that appear when using the scroll bars or with the fill handle when using AutoFill to extend a series as explained in Chapter 1). When this Width or Height indicator reaches 0.00, you know that it's time to release the mouse button.

Unhiding a column or row with the mouse is a reversal of the hiding process. This time, you drag the column or row border in between the nonsequential columns or rows in the opposite direction (right for columns and down for rows). The only trick to this is that you must position the mouse pointer just right on the column or row border so that the pointer doesn't just change to a double-headed arrow but changes to a double-headed arrow split in the middle. (Contrast the shapes of the split double-headed arrow pointer with the regular, old double-headed arrow pointer in Table 1-1.)

If you ever manually hide a column or row only to find that you just can't get that blasted split-bar pointer to appear so that you can drag it back into existence, don't get frantic. With columns, just drag through the first and last column or row between those that are hidden and then choose the Unhide command on the columns or rows shortcut menu (see the preceding section)!

Futzing with the Fonts

When you start a new worksheet, Excel assigns a uniform font and type size to all the cell entries you make. This font varies according to the printer you use — for a laser printer like the HP LaserJet or Apple LaserWriter, Excel uses the *Geneva* font in a 9-point size. Although this font is fine for normal entries, you may want to use something with a little more zing for titles and headings in the worksheet.

If you don't especially care for the standard font that Excel uses, modify it by choosing Tools⇨Preferences on the menu bar and then selecting the General tab. When you do this, you see an option called Standard font near the bottom of the Preferences dialog box. Select the new standard font from its pop-up list. If you want a different type size, select the Size option as well and either enter the new point size for the standard font or select it from this option's pop-up list. (You have to restart Excel for standard font changes to take effect.)

With the tools on the Formatting toolbar, you can make most font changes (including selecting a new font style or new font size) without having to resort to the settings on the Font tab in the Format Cells dialog box (⌘+1).

- ✔ To select a new font for a cell selection, click the drop-down button next to the Font drop-down text box on the Formatting toolbar; then select the name of the font that you want to use from the list box.

- ✔ If you want to change the font size, click the drop-down button next to the Font Size drop-down text box on the Formatting toolbar; then select the new font size.

You can also add the attributes of bold, italics, underlining, or strikeout to the font you're using. The Formatting toolbar contains the Bold, Italic, and Underline buttons, which not only add these attributes to a cell selection but remove them as well. After you click one of these attribute tools, notice that the tool changes by losing the shading around its right and bottom edge and becoming a lighter shade of gray. Excel does this to make it appear as though a tool button is pushed in. When you click a "pushed-in" button to remove an attribute, Excel changes the button back to its original form so that it no longer appears pushed in.

Although you'll probably make most font changes with the toolbars, on rare occasions making these changes from the Font tab in the Format Cells dialog box (⌘+1) may be more convenient.

As you can see in Figure 3-16, this Font tab in the Format Cells dialog box brings together under one roof fonts, font styles such as bold and italics, effects like underlining and strikeout, as well as color changes. When you want to make a lot of font-related changes to a cell selection, the Font tab may be your best bet. One of the nice things about using this tab is that it contains a Preview box that shows you how your font changes appear (on-screen at least).

If you change font colors with the Color option on the Font tab in the Format Cells dialog box or with the Font Color button on the Formatting toolbar (the very last button) and then print the worksheet with a black-and-white printer, Excel renders the colors as shades of gray. The Automatic choice in the Font tab Color drop-down list box picks up the color assigned by the Macintosh operating system (usually black).

Figure 3-16:
Use the
Font tab in
the Format
Cells dialog
box to make
lots of font
changes at
one time.

Altering the Alignment

The alignment assigned to cell entries when you first make them is simply a function of the type of entry it is: All text entries are left-aligned, and all values are right-aligned. You can, however, alter this standard arrangement anytime it suits you.

The Formatting toolbar contains three normal alignment tools: the Align Left, Center, and Align Right buttons. These buttons align the current cell selection exactly as you expect them to.

After the Right Align button, you find a special alignment tool called Merge and Center. Despite its rather strange name, you'll want to get to know this button. You can use it to center a worksheet title across the entire width of a table in seconds (or faster, depending upon your machine). Figures 3-17 and 3-18 show how you can use this tool. In Figure 3-17, notice that the title for the 1998 sales worksheet is entered in cell A1. Because it's a long text entry, it spills over to the empty cell to the right (B1). To center this title over the table (which extends from Column A through E), select the cell range A1:E1 (the width of the table) and then click the Merge and Center button on the Formatting toolbar. Figure 3-18 shows the result: The cells in row 1 of Columns A through E are merged into one cell, and now the title is properly centered in this "supercell" and consequently over the entire table.

If you ever need to split up a supercell that you've merged with the Merge and Center button back into its original, individual cells, select the cell, open the Format Cells dialog box (⌘+1), select the Alignment tab, and then deselect the Merge cells check box at the bottom before you click OK or press Return.

Figure 3-17:
Centering
the
worksheet
title over a
table width
with the
Merge and
Center
button.

	A	B	C	D	E	F	G	H
1	Mother Goose Enterprises - 1998 Sales							
2		Jan	Feb	Mar	Qtr 1 Total			
3	Jack Sprat C	80,138.58	59,389.56	19,960.06	$ 159,488.20			
4	Jack and Jill	123,456.20	89,345.70	25,436.84	$ 238,238.74			
5	Mother Hubb	12,657.05	60,593.56	42,300.28	$ 115,550.89			
6	Rub-a-Dub-[	17,619.79	40,635.00	42,814.99	$ 101,069.78			
7	Georgie Por	57,133.56	62,926.31	12,408.73	$ 132,468.60			
8	Hickory, Dic	168,291.00	124,718.10	41,916.13	$ 334,925.23			
9	Little Bo Pee	30,834.63	71,111.25	74,926.24	$ 176,872.12			
10	Total	$ 490,130.81	$ 508,719.48	$ 259,763.27	$ 1,258,613.56			
11								
12	Month/Qtr	38.94%	40.42%	20.64%				
13								
14								
15								

Figure 3-18:
The
worksheet
title after
centering
it across
Columns A
through E.

	A	B	C	D	E	F	G	H
1			Mother Goose Enterprises - 1998 Sales					
2		Jan	Feb	Mar	Qtr 1 Total			
3	Jack Sprat C	80,138.58	59,389.56	19,960.06	$ 159,488.20			
4	Jack and Jill	123,456.20	89,345.70	25,436.84	$ 238,238.74			
5	Mother Hubb	12,657.05	60,593.56	42,300.28	$ 115,550.89			
6	Rub-a-Dub-[	17,619.79	40,635.00	42,814.99	$ 101,069.78			
7	Georgie Por	57,133.56	62,926.31	12,408.73	$ 132,468.60			
8	Hickory, Dic	168,291.00	124,718.10	41,916.13	$ 334,925.23			
9	Little Bo Pee	30,834.63	71,111.25	74,926.24	$ 176,872.12			
10	Total	$ 490,130.81	$ 508,719.48	$ 259,763.27	$ 1,258,613.56			
11								
12	Month/Qtr	38.94%	40.42%	20.64%				
13								
14								
15								

Intent on indents

In Excel 98, you can indent the entries in a cell selection by clicking the
Increase Indent button on the Standard toolbar (the button immediately to
the left of the Borders button with the picture of the arrow pushing the lines
of text to the right). Each time you click this button, Excel indents the
entries in the current cell selection to the right by one character width of
the standard font. (See "Futzing with the Fonts" earlier in this chapter if you
don't know what a standard font is or how to change it.)

Note that you can remove an indent by clicking the Decrease Indent button on the Standard toolbar (the button immediately to the left of the Increase Indent button with the picture of the arrow pushing the lines of text to the left). Also, you can change how many characters an entry is indented (with the Increase Indent button) or outdented (with the Decrease Indent button) by opening the Format Cells dialog box (⌘+1), selecting the Alignment tab, and then altering the value in the Indent text box (either by typing a new value in this text box or by dialing up a new value with its spinner buttons).

From top to bottom

Left, right, and *center* alignment all refer to the placement of a text entry in relation to the left and right cell borders (that is, horizontally). You can also align entries in relation to the top and bottom borders of their cells (that is, vertically). Normally, all entries are vertically aligned with the bottom of the cells (as though they were resting on the very bottom of the cell). You can also vertically center an entry in its cell or align it with the top of its cell.

To change the vertical alignment of a cell selection, open the Format Cells dialog box (⌘+1) and then select the Alignment tab (shown in Figure 3-19) and select Top, Center, Bottom, or Justify in the Vertical pop-up list box.

Figure 3-19:
Changing the vertical alignment by selecting Center on the Vertical pop-up menu.

Figure 3-20 shows the title for the 1998 Mother Goose Enterprises sales worksheet after it was centered vertically in its cell. (This text entry was previously centered across the cell range A1:E1; the height of Row 1 was increased from the normal 12.75 characters to 33.75 characters.)

Figure 3-20:
The
worksheet
title after
centering it
vertically
between
the top and
bottom of
row 1.

| | File Edit View Insert Format Tools Data Window Help | | | | | Wed 3:49:59 PM | | |

| A1 | = Mother Goose Enterprises - 1998 Sales |

Mother Goose - 1998 Sales

	A	B	C	D	E	F	G	H
1			Mother Goose Enterprises - 1998 Sales					
2		Jan	Feb	Mar	Qtr 1 Total			
3	Jack Sprat D	80,138.58	59,389.56	19,960.06	$ 159,488.20			
4	Jack and Jill	123,456.20	89,345.70	25,436.84	$ 238,238.74			
5	Mother Hubb	12,657.05	60,593.56	42,300.28	$ 115,550.89			
6	Rub-a-Dub-l	17,619.79	40,635.00	42,814.99	$ 101,069.78			
7	Georgie Por	57,133.56	62,926.31	12,408.73	$ 132,468.60			
8	Hickory, Dicl	168,291.00	124,718.10	41,916.13	$ 334,925.23			
9	Little Bo Pee	30,834.63	71,111.25	74,926.24	$ 176,872.12			
10	Total	$ 490,130.81	$ 508,719.48	$ 259,763.27	$ 1,258,613.56			
11								
12	Month/Qtr	38.94%	40.42%	20.64%				
13								
14								
15								

Tampering with how the text wraps

Traditionally, column headings in worksheet tables have been a problem because you either had to keep them really short or abbreviate them if you wanted to avoid widening all the columns more than the data warranted. You can get around this problem in Excel by using the Wrap text feature. Figure 3-21 shows a new worksheet in which the column headings containing the various Mother Goose companies use the Wrap text feature to avoid widening the columns as much as these long company names would otherwise require.

Figure 3-21:
A new
worksheet
with the
column
headings
containing
the Mother
Goose
company
names
formatted
with Wrap
Text option.

| | File Edit View Insert Format Tools Data Window Help | | | | | Wed 3:53:35 PM | | |

| B2 | = Jack Sprat Diet Centers |

Workbook2

	A	B	C	D	E	F	G	H	I
1									
2		Jack Sprat Diet Centers	Jack and Jill Trauma Centers	Mother Hubbard Dog Goodies	Rub-a-Dub- Dub Hot Tubs and Spas	Georgie Porgie Pudding Pies	Hickory, Dickory, Dock Clock Repair	Little Bo Peep Pet Detectives	
3									
4									
5									
6									
7									

To create the effect shown in Figure 3-21, select the cells with the column headings (the cell range B2:H2) and then select the Wrap text check box in the Alignment tab in the Format Cells dialog box to turn on text wrap. (You can see this check box in Figure 3-19.)

Text wrap breaks up the long text entries in the selection (that either spill over or are cut off) into separate lines. To accommodate more than one line in a cell, the program automatically expands the row height so that the entire wrapped-text entry is visible.

When you turn on the Wrap text feature, Excel continues to use the horizontal and vertical alignment you specified for the cell. Note that you can use any of the Horizontal alignment options including Left (indent), Center, Right, Justify, or Center Across Selection. You can't, however, use the Fill option. Select the Fill option on the Horizontal pop-up menu only when you want Excel to repeat the entry across the entire width of the cell.

If you want to wrap a text entry in its cell and have Excel justify the text with both the left and right borders of the cell, select the Justify Full option on the Horizontal pop-up menu in the Alignment tab in the Format Cells dialog box.

You can break a long text entry into separate lines by positioning the insertion point in the cell entry (or on the formula bar) at the place where you want the new line to start and pressing ⌘+Control+Return. Excel expands the row containing the cell (and the formula bar above) when it starts a new line. When you press plain old Return to complete the entry or edit, Excel automatically wraps the text in the cell, according to the cell's column width and the position of the line break.

Reordering the orientation

Instead of wrapping text entries in cells, you may find changing the orientation of the text to be more beneficial. Figure 3-22 shows a situation where changing the orientation of the wrapped column headings works much better than just wrapping them in their normal orientation in the cells.

This example shows the same order form introduced in Figure 3-21 after switching the orientation of the column headings with the various Mother Goose companies. Notice that switching the text orientation allows their columns to be narrower than when displayed in the normal orientation.

To make this switch, you select the cell range B2:H2 and then, in the Alignment tab of the Format cells dialog box, click the diamond in the Text Orientation section at the top (at twelve o'clock, so to speak, in the diagram) so that the word "Text" is running up and 90 degrees appears in the Degrees text box below. (You can change the orientation of the entries in your cell selection by entering the number of degrees in this box if you don't want to fool

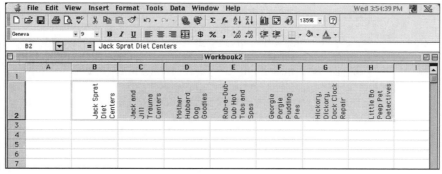

Figure 3-22:
Worksheet
after
rotating the
company
column
headings in
Row 2 up 90
degrees.

around with the diamonds in the diagram in this dialog box.) Note that the Wrap text box is still selected so that the text is both rotated and wrapped (thus avoiding really long, skinny columns).

Figure 3-23 shows the same company headings after using the Text Orientation option on the Alignment tab of the Format Cells dialog box to rotate the company column headings up just 45 degrees from their horizontal orientation. To accomplish this, I clicked the diamond in between the one at the top of the diagram (at twelve o'clock) and the one in the middle of the diagram (at three o'clock). Note that I could have done the same thing just as well by entering 45 in the Degrees text box below the diagram in the Orientation section.

You can set any amount of text rotation from 90 degrees up from horizontal (90 in the Degrees text box) all the way to 90 degrees down from horizontal (–90 in the Degrees text box) either by entering the number of degrees in the Degrees text box, clicking the appropriate place on the semicircular diagram, or by dragging the line extending from the word "Text" in the diagram to the desired angle. To set the text vertically so that each letter is above the other in a single column, click the area of the diagram that shows the word "Text" arranged in this manner (to the immediate left of the diagram that enables you to rotate the text up or down from normal horizontal).

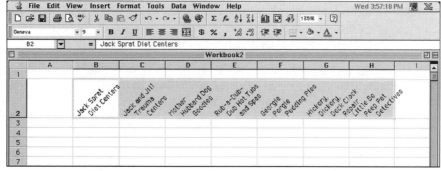

Figure 3-23:
Worksheet
after
rotating the
company
column
headings in
Row 2 up 45
degrees.

Shrink to fit

For those times when you need to prevent Excel from widening the column to fit its cell entries (as may be the case when you need to display an entire table of data on a single screen or printed page), you can use the Shrink to fit text control option on the Alignment tab of the Format Cells dialog box. When you select the Shrink to fit check box, Excel reduces the font size of the entries to the selected cells so that they don't require changing the current column width. Just be aware when using this text control option that, depending on the length of the entries and width of the column, you can end up with some text entries that are so small as to be completely illegible to the human eye!

Bring on the borders!

The gridlines normally displayed in the worksheet to separate the columns and rows are just guidelines to help you keep your place as you build your spreadsheet. You can choose to print them with your data or not. To emphasize sections of the worksheet or parts of a particular table, you can add borderlines or shading to certain cells. Don't confuse the *borderlines* you add to accent a particular cell selection with the *gridlines* normally used to define cell borders in the worksheet — borders you add are printed whether or not you print the worksheet gridlines.

To better see the borders you add to the cells in a worksheet, remove the gridlines normally displayed in the worksheet as follows:

1. **Choose the Tools⇨Preferences command on the menu bar and then select the View tab.**

2. **Select the Gridlines option to remove the check mark from its check box.**

3. **Click OK or press Return.**

Note that the Gridlines check box in the Options dialog box determines whether or not gridlines are displayed in the worksheet on your screen. To determine whether or not gridlines are printed as part of the worksheet printout, choose the File⇨Page Setup command and then select the Sheet tab and select or deselect the Gridlines check box under Print.

To add borders to a cell selection, open the Format Cells dialog box (⌘+1) and then choose the Border tab (shown in Figure 3-24). Select the type of line you want to use in the Style area of the dialog box and then select from the Border section of the dialog box the edge or edges you want this line applied to.

Figure 3-24:
Selecting
borders for
a cell
selection
with the
Border tab
in the
Format
Cells dialog
box.

When selecting where you want the borderlines drawn, keep these things in mind:

- ✔ To have Excel draw borders around only the outside edges of the entire selection, click the Outline button in the Presets section.

- ✔ If you want borderlines to appear around all four edges of each cell in the selection, click the Inside button in the Presets section instead.

When you want to add borderlines to a single cell or around the outer edge of a cell selection, you don't even have to open the Border dialog box; you can simply select the cell or cell range and then click the Borders button pop-up button on the Formatting toolbar and select which type of border-lines to use in the Borders palette that appears.

To get rid of borders, you must select the cells that presently contain them, open the Format Cells dialog box (⌘+1), and click the None button in the Presets section. Note that you can also do the same thing by clicking the first button in the Borders palette (the one showing only dotted lines around and within the rectangle).

Putting on new patterns

You can also add emphasis to particular sections of the worksheet or one of its tables by changing the color and/or pattern of its cells. If you're using a black-and-white printer (as all but a fortunate few of us are), you may want to restrict your color choices to light gray in the color palette. Also, consider restricting your use of patterns to only the very open ones with few dots when enhancing a cell selection that contains any kind of entries. (Otherwise, the entries will be almost impossible to read when printed.)

To choose a new color and/or pattern for part of the worksheet, select the cells you want to pretty up and then open the Format Cells dialog box (⌘+1) and select the Patterns tab (shown in Figure 3-25). To change the color of the cells, click the desired color in the Color palette shown under the Cell shading heading. To change the pattern of the cells (in addition or instead), click the Pattern's pop-up button to open an expanded color palette that contains a number of black-and-white patterns to choose from. Click the desired pattern in this expanded palette. Excel shows what your creation will look like in the worksheet in the Sample box of the Patterns tab of the Format Cells dialog box.

Figure 3-25:
Selecting
new colors
and
patterns
with the
Patterns tab
in the
Format
Cells dialog
box.

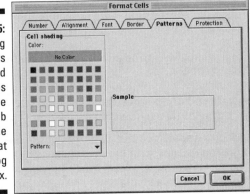

To remove a shading pattern from cells, select the cell range, open the Format Cells dialog box (⌘+1) and select the Patterns tab; then select the No Color option at the top of the Color palette.

You can assign new colors (but not new patterns) to your cell selection from the Fill Color palette opened with the Fill Color button (the button with the paint bucket, second from the end) on the Formatting toolbar. Simply select the cells you want to color, click the Fill Color tool's drop-down list button, and choose the desired color in the color palette that appears. (Remember, too, that the Fill Color palette is one of those that you can tear off and have floating in the worksheet area.)

Although you can't select new patterns (only colors) with the Fill Color tool, you can remove both colors and patterns assigned to a cell selection by selecting the cells and then clicking the Fill Color tool's button and choosing No Fill at the top of the Fill Color palette that appears.

Using those fantastic floating border palettes

Just as you can add certain borders with the Borders palette attached to the Borders pop-up button on the Formatting toolbar, you can remove borders using this palette as well. To remove the borderlines from a cell selection with this button, choose the first border box in the Borders palette. Remember, too, that you can tear the Borders palette (like the Fill Color and Font Color palettes) off of the Formatting toolbar by dragging it completely off the toolbar, thus making it a floating palette that remains open as you work. Then, to close the floating palette later on, you click its Close button in the upper-left corner of its little-bitty window.

If you want the text in a cell range to be a different color from the background you assign, you can change the text color from the Font Color palette by clicking the Font Color button on the Formatting toolbar (the very last one). Change the color of the cells' background by choosing a new color from the Font Color palette by clicking the Font Color button on the Formatting toolbar. To return the text to black in a cell range, select the cells and then choose Automatic at the top of the Font Color palette.

Showing Off in Styles

Cell styles are Excel's way of bringing together under one roof a whole lot of different kinds of formatting (including the number format, font, alignment, borders, patterns, and protection status). Excel includes six built-in cell styles that you can use in any worksheet: Comma, Comma [0], Currency, Currency [0], Normal, and Percent. And when you add hyperlinks (as described in Chapter 10), Excel adds two more built-in styles: Hyperlink and Followed Hyperlink.

The most common of these styles is the Normal style. This is the one automatically used in formatting all cells in a new worksheet. The styles Comma, Comma [0], Currency, Currency [0], and Percent are used to format cell selections with different number formats. (The Followed Hyperlink and Hyperlink styles are used to format hypertext links in the worksheet as described in Chapter 10.)

To apply any of these built-in cell styles (or any others you create on your own) to the current cell selection, simply choose Format⇨Style on the menu bar and then select a new style from the Style name pop-up list box.

Creating new cell styles for a worksheet is as simple as falling off a log. All you do is format one of the cell entries in the worksheet to use all the formatting you want to include in the new style (including the number format, font, alignment, borders, patterns, and protection status — see Chapter 6, if you don't have a clue what that last one is or does).

Then, with the cell pointer located in the sample formatted cell, open the Style dialog box (by choosing Format⇨Style), select the Style name text box, type in the name for your new style before you click the Add button, and click OK or press Return.

The next time you save the workbook, Excel saves the new style as part of the document. To apply the new style to other cells in a worksheet, simply select the cells and then open the Style dialog box and select the style name from the Style name drop-down list box.

Styles are a great way to make custom number formats a lot easier to use in a workbook. For example, you can create a Hidden number style to use the custom number format discussed earlier in this chapter that hides all types of entries. After creating this custom number format (refer to "Creating custom number formats" in this chapter for details on how to go about doing this), apply it to a sample cell in the worksheet and then create a new style named *Hidden* in the Style dialog box and add it to the worksheet. After saving the workbook with this new style, you can thereafter apply it to other cell ranges in the worksheet right from the Style dialog box.

Follow these steps if you want to merge styles that were created for other workbooks saved on disks into the workbook you're currently creating:

1. **Open the workbook that contains the styles you want to copy into the current workbook.**

2. **Choose the Window menu and then select the name of the workbook that is to receive these styles.**

3. **Choose Format⇨Style on the menu bar to open the Style dialog box in the workbook that is to receive a copy of the styles from the other workbook.**

4. **Click the Merge button to open the Merge Styles dialog box, and double-click the name of the workbook from which to copy the styles in the Merge Styles From list box.**

If the workbook you're currently working on contains styles (other than the standard six that are part of every new workbook) with the same names as some of those in the workbook whose styles you're copying, Excel displays an alert dialog box asking you whether you want it to go ahead and merge styles that have the same name. To overwrite the styles in the current workbook whose names are the same, click the Yes button. To merge only the styles with different names, click the No button. To abandon the whole bloody merger of styles, click the Cancel button.

Fooling Around with the Format Painter

Using styles to format worksheet cells is certainly the way to go when you have to apply the formatting over and over again in the workbooks you create. However, there may be times when you simply want to reuse a particular cell format and apply it to select groups of cells in a single workbook without ever bothering to create an actual style for it.

For those occasions when you feel the urge to format on the fly (so to speak), you use the Format Painter tool on the Standard toolbar (the one with the paintbrush icon right next to the Paste tool). This wonderful little tool enables you to take the formatting from a particular cell that you've fancied up and apply its formatting to other cells in the worksheet simply by selecting those cells.

To use the Format Painter to copy a cell's formatting to other worksheet cells, just follow these easy steps:

1. **Format an example cell or cell range in your workbook, selecting whatever fonts, alignment, borders, patterns, and color you want it to have.**

2. **With the cell pointer in one of the cells you just fancied up, click the Format Painter button in the Standard toolbar.**

   The mouse pointer changes from the standard thick, white cross to a thick, white cross with an animated paintbrush by its side, and you see a marquee around the selected cell whose formatting is to be used by the Format Painter.

3. **Drag the white-cross-plus-animated-paintbrush pointer (the Format Painter pointer for short) through all the cells you want to format in the same manner as the example cell you first selected.**

   As soon as you release the mouse button, Excel applies all the formatting used in the example cell to all the cells you just selected!

To keep the Format Painter selected so that you can format a bunch of different cell ranges with the Format Painter pointer, double-click the Format Painter button after you select the sample cell with the desired formatting. To stop formatting cells with the Format Painter pointer, you simply click the Format Painter button (it remains depressed when you double-click it) again to restore the button to its undepressed state and return the mouse pointer to its normal, thick, white-cross shape.

Note that you can use the Format Painter to restore a cell range that you've gussied all up back to its boring default (General) cell format. To do this, you click an empty, previously unformatted cell in the worksheet before you click the Format Painter button and then use the Format Painter pointer to drag through the cells you want returned to the default General format.

Conditional Formatting

Excel 98 introduces the concept of *conditional cell formatting,* which is formatting that is only done when a cell contains a particular value. For example, you can create a conditional format that displays a cell's contents in 14-point, bold type (instead of the normal 9-point, regular type) only when the cell contains a certain value (such as 150,000) or a value that falls into a definite range (between 50,000 and 100,000). You can also have a cell display its contents in red when its value is negative (less than 0).

Figure 3-26 shows an example of conditional formatting in the Jack Sprat Diet Centers - Projected Income for 1999 in the Net earnings (loss) cell (B28). This cell contains the formula that calculates the projected net earnings (or loss, as the case may be).

Figure 3-26:
Formatting
the Net
earnings
(loss) cell
in the
Projected
Income
statement
in the
Conditional
Formatting
dialog box.

In this example, I decided to use the Conditional Formatting feature to display this cell's contents in bold black text on a light gray cell background when the projected net earnings are $500,000 or greater and in bold red text on a black cell background whenever the projected earnings are less than $500,000. In order to make this happen, follow these steps:

1. **Select cell B28 where the conditional formatting is to take place.**

   Prior to using Conditional Formatting, you must select the cells or cell ranges to which this formatting is to be applied.

2. **Choose Format⇨Conditional Formatting on the menu bar to open the Conditional Formatting dialog box.**

3. **Check to make sure that the Cell Value Is option is selected rather than the Formula Is option in the first pop-up list box in the Condition1 area.**

   When creating a conditional format, you can either specify that the cells be formatted when they contain a particular value or range of values (in which case, you use the Cell Value Is option) or when a formula that you specify in the Conditional Formatting is TRUE (in which case, you use the Formula Is option).

4. **Change between in the second pop-up list box to greater than or equal to in the second text box.**

   When using the Cell Value Is option, you can set this second pop-up list box to between, not between, equal to, not equal to, greater than, less than, greater than or equal to, or less than or equal to, as suits the situation.

5. **Type 500000 in the third text box.**

6. **Click the Format button in the Condition 1 area to open the Format Cells dialog box, where you specify format settings for the selected cells.**

   This Format Cells dialog box contains just three tabs: Font, Border, and Patterns, which you can use to format the selected cells when they meet the first condition.

7. **Select the format settings for the first condition on the Font, Border, and Pattern tabs of the Format Cells dialog box; then click the OK button to close the Format Cells dialog box and return to the Conditional Formatting dialog box.**

   For the cell formatting when the value is greater than or equal to $500,000, I chose Bold as the Font style and Automatic as the Color on the Font tab and light blue as Cell Shading Color on the Patterns tab.

8. **Click the Add>> button at the bottom of the Conditional Formatting dialog box to expand the dialog box with a second condition.**

   When using the Conditional Formatting feature, you can set up as many conditions as you need to cover all the circumstances that may arise. In this example, I only need to set up two formatting conditions: One where the value is 500,000 or greater and another where the value is less than 500,000.

9. **Enter the particulars for the second condition in the second set of pop-up list and text boxes.**

   For the second condition, I kept the Cell Value Is option in the first pop-up list box, selected less than in the second pop-up list box, and typed **500000** in the third text box (as shown back in Figure 3-25).

10. **Click the Format button in the Condition 2 area and use the options that appear on the Font, Border, and Patterns tab of the Format Cells dialog box to set up the formatting for the second condition.**

    For the formatting for the second condition, I set the Font Style to Bold and the Color to red on the Font tab and the Cell Shading Color to black on the Patterns tab.

11. **After setting up the formatting for the second condition, click OK in the Format Cells dialog box to close it; then click the OK button in the Conditional Formatting dialog box to close it and apply the conditional formatting to the selected cell.**

Chapter 4

Going through Changes

*P*icture this: You've just finished creating, formatting, and printing a major project with Excel — a workbook with your department's budget for the next fiscal year. Because you finally understand a little bit about how this thing works, you finished the job in crack time. You're actually ahead of schedule.

You turned the workbook over to your boss so that she can check the numbers. There's plenty of time for making those inevitable last-minute corrections — you're feeling on top of this situation.

Then comes the reality check — your boss brings the document back, and she's plainly agitated. "We forgot to include the estimates for the temps and our overtime hours. They've got to go right here. While you're adding them, can you move these rows of figures up and those columns over?"

As she continues to suggest improvements, your heart begins to sink. These modifications are in a different league from "Let's change these column headings from bold to italics and add shading to that row of totals." Clearly, you're looking at a lot more work on this baby than you had contemplated.

Even worse, you're looking at making structural changes that threaten to unravel the very fabric of your beautiful worksheet.

As the preceding fable points out, editing a worksheet in a workbook can occur on different levels:

- ✔ You can make changes that affect the contents of the cells, such as copying a row of column headings or moving a table to a new area in a particular worksheet.

- ✔ You can make changes that affect the structure of a worksheet itself, such as inserting new columns or rows (so that you can enter new data originally left out) or deleting unnecessary columns or rows from an existing table so that you don't leave any gaps.

- ✔ You can even make changes to the number of worksheets in a workbook (either by adding or deleting sheets).

In this chapter, you discover how to safely make all these types of changes to a workbook. As you will see, the mechanics of copying and moving data or inserting and deleting rows are simple to master. It's the impact that such actions have on the worksheet that takes a little more effort to understand. Not to worry! You always have the Undo feature to fall back on for those (hopefully rare) times when you make a little tiny change that throws an entire worksheet into complete and utter chaos.

Opening the Darned Thing Up for Editing

Before you can do any damage — I mean, make any changes — to a workbook, you have to open it up in Excel. To open a workbook, you can click the Open tool on the Standard toolbar (the one second from the left with the picture of a file folder opening up), you can choose File⇨Open on the menu bar, or you can even press the keystroke shortcut ⌘+O (or, if you prefer function keys: Ctrl+F12).

Any way you open it, Excel displays the Select a document dialog box similar to the one shown in Figure 4-1. Then you select the workbook file you want to work on in the list box in the middle of the Select a document dialog box. After clicking the filename in this list box, you can open it by clicking the Open button or pressing the Return key. If you're handy with the mouse, double-click the workbook's filename in the list box to open it.

If the workbook you want to open is in another folder, double-click that folder's name in the list box in the middle or choose the folder in the Select a document pop-up list at the top of the dialog box. If the folder containing the workbook is on another drive, click the Desktop button and then double-click the name of the driver to display its folders and files in the list box in the Select a document dialog box.

Figure 4-1:
You use the
Select a
document
dialog box
to open
workbooks
in Excel.

```
Select a document:
  [ Microsoft Office 98 ▼ ]              ⊟ Macintos...
  ▢ Clipart                      ▲        [   Eject   ]
  ▢ More Help
  ▢ Office                                [ Desktop  ]
  ▢ Readme
  ▢ Sample Files                          [  Cancel  ]
  ▢ Shared Applications
  ▢ Templates                             [   Open   ]
                                ▼
                                          [ Find File... ]
List Files of Type:
[ Readable Files            ▼ ]           ☐ Read Only
```

Opening recently edited workbooks from the File menu

If you know that the workbook you need to edit is one of those that you've had open recently, you don't even have to fool around with the Select a document dialog box. Just open the File pull-down menu and select the filename from the bottom of the File menu. (Excel keeps a running list of the last four files you opened in the program.) If the workbook you want to work with is one of those shown at the bottom of the File menu, you can open it by clicking its filename in the menu or typing its number (1, 2, 3, or 4).

When you don't know where to find them (your files, that is) can't find a workbook

The only problem you can encounter in opening a document from the Select a document dialog box is locating the filename. Everything's hunky-dory as long as you can see the workbook filename listed in its list box. But what about those times when a file seems to have mysteriously migrated and is now nowhere to be found in the list?

File hide-and-seek

The Select a document dialog box has a File Search feature built into it that you can always use to locate a particular file within the open folder. This feature enables you to reduce your search in the Select a document dialog list box to just those files that fall into a specific category (like those files you modified today or sometime this week) or just those files that contain a certain phrase or property (like they were done by a particular author or they contain a particular keyword).

To use the File Search feature, click the Find File button in the Select a document dialog box to open the Search dialog box. In the Search for area of the Search dialog box, you can tell Excel exactly how you want it to conduct its search by using any or all of the following pop-up list boxes:

- ✔ To have Excel restrict the files in the Select a document dialog list box to just those whose filenames contain certain characters, you enter those characters in File name text box of the Search dialog box.

- ✔ To have Excel include certain files with a type different from Microsoft Excel files, open the Files type pop-up list box in the Search dialog box and select that type from the list.

- ✔ To have Excel search for the files on another drive, select the drive you want to search in the Location pop-up list box in the Search dialog box.

To have Excel search for the files using the criteria you specify in these pop-up list boxes, click the OK button or press Return.

Advanced hide-and-seek

If the three Search for pop-up list boxes in the Search dialog box are not enough for the workbook files you've misplaced, Excel offers more searching possibilities on the Summary and Timestamp tabs of the Advanced Search dialog box. To open the Advanced Search dialog box, you click the Advanced Search button near the bottom of the Search dialog box.

The Summary and Timestamp tabs in the Advanced Search dialog box contain criteria options that enable you to narrow the search as follows:

- ✔ **Summary tab:** To have Excel restrict the files displayed in the Select a document list box to just those that contain a certain text or property such as title, author, or keywords entered into a file summary, select the Summary tab, and then enter the text or property in the appropriate text box — Title, Author, Keywords, and Subject. (To create a file summary for a workbook with these types of keywords that you can search for, choose File⇨Properties to open the workbook's Properties dialog box where you select the Summary tab.)

- ✔ **Timestamp tab:** To have Excel restrict the files displayed in the Select a document list box to just those that have been modified within a certain time frame, select the Timestamp tab in the Advanced Search dialog box and then enter the range of dates in the Last saved and/or the Created From and To text boxes.

After you add all the advanced criteria that you can think of for your search, click OK in the Advanced Search dialog box or press Return to close the Advanced Search dialog box and return to the Search dialog box. To conduct the file search using all of the criteria you've specified in the Search and Advanced Search dialog boxes, click OK in the Search dialog box or press Return.

Making a positive ID

After you conduct a file search from the Select a document dialog box, Excel displays the folders and files that match your criteria in the Listed files list box in the Find File dialog box (see Figure 4-2).

Figure 4-2:
The Find File dialog box after conducting a file search.

By default the Find File dialog box shows a preview of each Excel workbook you select in the Listed files list box. You can, if you want, change the file list view from a preview to either a File Info or Summary view by selecting these options in the View pop-up list button.

- Select the File Info view option to display the file size (in kilobytes), author, and the date the file was last saved in columns to the right of each workbook file you select in the File Name column.

- Select the Summary view option to display the file summary information next to the file icon and filename for each file you select in the list. (To create a file summary for a workbook with these types of keywords that you can search for, choose File⇨Properties to open the workbook's Properties dialog box where you click the Summary tab.)

When you locate the workbook you want to work on in the Find File dialog box, make sure that it is selected in the list box and then click the Open button near the bottom or press Return to open the file up in Excel 98.

To open more than one workbook listed in the Find File dialog box, select them in the Find File list box (by holding down the ⌘ key as you select each filename) before you click the Open button.

Doing stuff besides opening files

The Commands button near the bottom of the Find File dialog box contains a pop-up menu that enables you to do stuff besides open the selected file:

✔ **Open Read Only:** This command opens the Excel files that you select in the Find File dialog box's list box in a *read-only* state, which means that you can look but you can't touch. (Actually, you can touch, you just can't save your changes.) To save changes in a read-only file, you must use the Save As command on the Excel File menu and give the workbook file a new filename. (Refer to the section "Making Sure the Data's Safe and Sound" in Chapter 2.)

✔ **Print:** This command sends the files that you select in the Find File dialog box's list box to whatever printer you've installed on your Mac. This command enables you to print a whole bunch of files without having to first open them in Excel (the way you normally print — see Chapter 5).

✔ **Put in Trash:** This command sends the (hopefully, unwanted) files that you select in the Find File dialog box's list box to the Macintosh Trash where you can later delete them in order to free up space on your hard drive.

✔ **Copy:** This command lets you make copies of the files that you select in the Find File dialog box. That way, if you mess up the originals, you always have the copies to fall back on.

✔ **Sorting:** This command enables you to sort the folders and files in the Find File dialog box's list box. Normally, folders and files (with folders preceding files) are alphabetically sorted by name in ascending order. You can use this command to sort the folders and files by their creation date, last saved date, size, or the person who last saved the files.

Much Ado about Undo

Before you start tearing into the workbook that you just opened, you need to get to know the Undo feature and how it can put right many of the things that you can inadvertently mess up. The Undo command on the Edit menu is a regular chameleon command. If you delete the contents of a cell selection with the Clear command on this same menu, Undo changes to Undo Clear. If you move some entries to a new part of the worksheet with the Cut and Paste commands (again, found on the Edit menu), the Undo command changes to Undo Paste.

In addition to choosing Undo (in whatever guise it appears) from the Edit menu, you can also choose this command by pressing ⌘+Z (perhaps for *unZap*) or you can click the Undo tool on the Standard toolbar (the one with the arrow curving to the left).

Undo a bunch

You may have noticed that the Undo tool on the Standard toolbar is now equipped with a pop-up button (marked by the downward pointing triangle to the immediate right of the arrow curving to the left). You can use the pop-up menu attached to this button to undo a whole bunch of actions. Simply click the last action in the Undo list that you want Excel to undo, and the program will undo that action as well as all those listed above in the menu.

For example, say that you've recently done the following series of edits to your worksheet:

- Widened the first column of row headings for a table of data to display all of their text
- Boldfaced and then italicized a row of column headings at the top of a table of data
- Used the Merge and Center tool on the Formatting toolbar to center the table's title over the columns of data

If you then open the pop-up menu attached to the Undo tool on the Standard toolbar, you see the following list:

- Merge Cells
- Italic
- Bold
- Column Width

To undo all of your actions and put the worksheet back to its original state before you started the latest editing sequence, you drag down to and click Column Width in the Undo list. To undo only the centering of the table's title and the formatting of the table's column headings, you drag to and click Bold in the Undo list. To undo only the centering of the table's title with the Merge and Center tool, you drag down to and click Merge Cells in the Undo list.

Undo is Redo the second time around

After you choose the Undo command (by whatever means you find most convenient), Excel 98 adds a new Redo command to the Edit menu. If you delete an entry from a cell with Edit⇨Clear⇨All on the menu bar and then choose Edit⇨Undo Clear (or press ⌘+Z or click the Undo tool on the toolbar), the next time you open the Edit menu, you see the following command at the top of the menu beneath Undo:

```
Redo Clear ⌘+Y
```

When you choose the Redo command, Excel redoes the thing you just undid. Actually, this sounds more complicated than it is. It simply means that you use Undo to switch back and forth between the result of an action and the state of the worksheet just before that action until you decide how you want the worksheet (or until they turn off the lights and lock up the building).

Note that you may find it a heck of a lot easier to just click the Undo and the Redo buttons on the Standard toolbar rather than go through all the rigmarole of choosing their respective commands on the Edit pull-down menu. The Undo button is the one with the picture of the arrow curving to the left; the Redo button is the one with the picture of the arrow curving to the right.

Just as you can undo multiple actions with the pop-up button attached to the Undo tool, you can redo multiple actions in a workbook by clicking the Redo tool's pop-up button (the curved arrow pointing to the right) and clicking the action on the menu that you want redone. Excel then redoes the action that you select as well as all the actions that precede it on the menu.

What ya gonna do when you can't Undo?

Just when you think it is safe to begin gutting the company's most important workbook, I really feel I've got to tell you that (yikes!) Undo doesn't work all the time! Although you can undo your latest erroneous cell deletion, bad move, or unwise copy, you can't undo your latest imprudent save. (You know, like when you meant to choose Save As from the File menu to save the edited worksheet under a different document name but instead chose Save and ended up saving the changes as part of the current document.)

Unfortunately, Excel doesn't let you know when you are about to take a step from which there is no return — until it's too late. After you've gone and done the un-undoable and you open the Edit menu right where you expect the Undo *blah, blah* command to be, it now says

```
Can't Undo
```

To add insult to injury, this extremely unhelpful command appears dimmed to indicate that you can't choose it — as though being able to choose it would change anything!

There is one exception to this rule — a time when Excel gives you advance warning (which you should heed). When you choose a command that is normally undoable but currently — because you're low on memory, or the change will affect so much of the worksheet, or both — Excel knows that it can't undo the change if it goes through with it, the program displays an alert box telling you that there isn't enough memory to undo this action and asking whether you want to go ahead anyway. If you click the Yes button and complete the edit, just realize that you do so without any possibility of pardon. If you find out, too late, that you deleted a row of essential formulas (that you forgot about because you couldn't see them), you can't bring them back with Undo. In such a case, you have to close the file (File⇨Close or ⌘+W) and *NOT save your changes.*

Doing the Old Drag-and-Drop Thing

The first editing technique you need to get under your belt is called *drag and drop.* As the name implies, it's a mouse technique that you can use to pick up a cell selection and drop it into a new place on the worksheet. Although drag and drop is primarily a technique for moving cell entries around a worksheet, you can adapt it to copy a cell selection as well.

To use drag and drop to move a range of cell entries (you can only move one cell range at a time), follow these steps:

1. Select the range as you normally would.

2. Position the mouse pointer on one edge of the selected range.

Your signal that you can start dragging the cell range to its new position in the worksheet is when the pointer changes to the arrowhead.

3. Drag.

You drag by depressing and holding down the mouse button while moving the mouse.

As you drag, you actually move only the outline of the cell range, and Excel keeps you informed of what the new cell range address will be (as a kind of drag-and-drop tooltip) if you release the mouse button. Drag the outline until it's positioned on the new cells in the worksheet where you want the entries to appear (as evidenced by the cell range in the drag-and-drop tooltip).

4. Release the mouse button.

The cell entries within that range reappear in the new location as soon as you release the mouse button.

Figures 4-3 and 4-4 show how you can drag and drop to move a cell range. In Figure 4-3, the cell range A10:E10 (containing the quarterly totals) is selected and is about to be moved to row 12 to make room for sales figures for two new companies: Simple Simon Pie Shoppes and Jack Be Nimble Candlesticks, which hadn't been acquired when this workbook was first created. In Figure 4-4, you see the Mother Goose Enterprises 1998 sales worksheet right after making this move and then selecting cell B12.

Notice in Figure 4-4 that the argument for the SUM function in cell B12 has not kept pace with the change — it continues to sum only the range B3:B9. Eventually, this range must be expanded to include cells B10 and B11, the first-quarter sales figures for the new Simple Simon Pie Shoppes and Jack Be Nimble Candlesticks. (You can find out how to do this in the upcoming section, "Formulas on AutoFill.")

Figure 4-3:
Dragging a selection to its new position in the worksheet.

Figure 4-4:
The
worksheet
after the
drag-and-
drop
operation.

Copies drag-and-drop style

Okay, so the preceding section explained moving a cell range with drag and drop. But what if you want to copy a cell range instead? For example, you need to start a new table in rows further down the worksheet, and you want to copy the cell range with the formatted title and column headings for the new table. To copy the formatted title range in the sample worksheet, follow these steps:

1. **Select the cell range.**

   In the case of Figures 4-3 and 4-4, that's cell range B2:E2.

2. **Hold the Option key as you position the mouse pointer on an edge of the selection.**

   The pointer changes from a thick, shaded cross to an arrowhead with a + (plus) sign to the right of it with the drag-and-drop screen tips right beside it. Keep in mind that the plus sign next to the pointer is your signal that drag and drop will *copy* the selection rather than *move* it.

3. **Drag the cell-selection outline to the place where you want the copy to appear and release the mouse button.**

If, when using drag and drop to move or copy, you position the outline of the selection so that it overlaps any part of cells that already contain entries, Excel displays an alert box with the following question:

Do you want to replace contents of the destination cells?

To avoid replacing existing entries and to abort the entire drag-and-drop mission, click Cancel in this alert box. To go ahead and exterminate the little darlings, click OK or press Return.

Insertions courtesy of drag and drop

Like the Klingons of *Star Trek* fame, spreadsheets such as Excel never take prisoners. When you place or move a new entry into an occupied cell, the new entry completely replaces the old as though the old entry never existed in that cell.

To insert the cell range you're moving or copying within a populated region of the worksheet without wiping out existing entries, hold the Shift key as you drag the selection. (If you're copying, you have to get really ambitious and hold down both the Shift and Option keys at the same time!) With the Shift key depressed as you drag, you get an I-beam shape (instead of a rectangular outline of the cell range) that shows where the selection will be inserted along with the address of the cell range (as a kind of Insertion screen tips) indicating where it would be inserted if you release the mouse button. As you move the I-beam shape, notice that it gloms on to the column and row borders as you move it. When you position the I-beam shape at the column or row border where you want the cell range to be inserted, release the mouse button. Excel inserts the cell range and repatriates the existing entries to neighboring blank cells (out of harm's way).

When inserting cells with drag and drop, it may be helpful to think of the I-beam shape as a pry bar that pulls apart the columns or rows along the axis of the I.

Sometimes, however, getting the I-beam selection indicator to assume this orientation can be tricky. To prepare to drag the cell selection, position the mouse pointer on one of the long edges (either the left or right) of the selection. When you drag the selection, position the mouse pointer slightly in front of the column border (not on it).

Also, keep in mind that sometimes after moving a range to a new place in the worksheet, instead of the data appearing, you may see only #######s in the cells. Remember that the way to get rid of the #######s in the cells is by widening their column enough to display all the data-plus-formatting, and the easiest way to do this kind of widening is by double-clicking the right border of the column.

But I held down the Shift key just like you said . . .

Drag and drop in insert mode is one of Excel's most finicky features. Sometimes, you do everything just right and you still get the alert box indicating that Excel is about to replace existing entries instead of pushing them aside (always click the Cancel button). Fortunately, you can insert things with the Cut and Insert Paste commands (see "Cut and Paste, digital style," later in this chapter) without worrying about which way the I-beam selection goes.

Formulas on AutoFill

Copying with drag and drop (by holding down the Option key) is useful when you need to copy a bunch of neighboring cells to a new part of the worksheet. Frequently, however, you just need to copy a single formula you've just created to a bunch of neighboring cells that need to perform the same type of calculation (such as totaling columns of figures). This type of formula copy, although quite common, can't be done with drag and drop. Instead, use the AutoFill feature (introduced in Chapter 2) or the Copy and Paste commands. (See "Cut and Paste, digital style," later in this chapter.)

Figures 4-5 and 4-6 show how you can use AutoFill to copy one formula to a range of cells. Figure 4-5 shows the Mother Goose Enterprises 1998 Sales worksheet after I added the Simple Simon Pie Shoppes and Jack Be Nimble Candlesticks to the list. Remember that these companies were missing from the original worksheet, so I made room for them by moving the Totals down to row 12 (which you can see back in Figure 4-4).

Unfortunately, Excel doesn't update the sum formulas to include the new rows. (The SUM function still uses B3:B9 when it should be extended to include rows 10 and 11.) To make the SUM function include all the rows, position the cell pointer in cell B12 and click the AutoSum tool on the Standard toolbar. Excel suggests the new range B3:B11 for the SUM function.

Figure 4-6 shows the worksheet after I re-created the SUM formula in cell B12 with the AutoSum tool to include the expanded range. I dragged the fill handle to select the cell range C12:E12 (where this formula should be copied). Notice that I deleted the original formulas from the cell range C12:E12 in this figure to make it easier to see what's going on; normally, you just copy over the original outdated formulas and replace them with new correct copies.

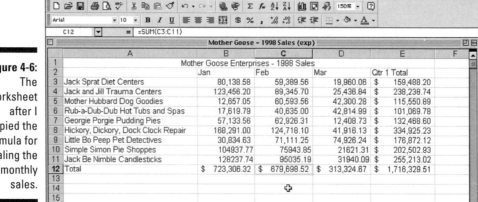

Figure 4-5:
Copying a
formula to a
cell range
with
AutoFill.

Relatively speaking

Check out Figure 4-6 to see the worksheet after the formula in a cell is
copied to the cell range C12:E12 and cell C12 is active. Notice how Excel
handles the copying of formulas. The original formula in cell B12 is as follows:

```
=SUM(B3:B11)
```

When the original formula is copied next door to cell C12, Excel changes the
formula slightly so that it looks like this:

```
=SUM(C3:C11)
```

Figure 4-6:
The
worksheet
after I
copied the
formula for
totaling the
monthly
sales.

Excel adjusts the column reference, changing it from B to C, because I copied from left to right across the rows.

When you copy a formula to a cell range that extends down the rows, Excel adjusts the row numbers in the copied formulas rather than the column letters to suit the position of each copy. For example, cell E3 in the Mother Goose Enterprises 1998 Sales worksheet contains the following formula:

```
=SUM(B3:D3)
```

When you copy this formula down to cell E4, Excel changes the copy of the formula to the following:

```
=SUM(B4:D4)
```

Excel adjusts the row reference to keep current with the new Row 4 position. Because Excel adjusts the cell references in copies of a formula relative to the direction of the copying, the cell references are known as *relative cell references*.

Some things are absolutes!

All new formulas you create naturally contain relative cell references unless you say otherwise. Because most copies you make of formulas require adjustments of their cell references, you rarely have to give this arrangement a second thought. Then, every once in a while, you come across an exception that calls for limiting when and how cell references are adjusted in copies.

One of the most common of these exceptions is when you want to compare a range of different values to a single value. This happens most often when you want to compute what percentage each part is to the total. For example, in the Mother Goose Enterprises 1998 Sales worksheet, you encounter this situation in creating and copying a formula that calculates what percentage each monthly total (in the cell range B14:D14) is of the quarterly total in cell E12.

Suppose that you want to enter these formulas in Row 14 of the Mother Goose Enterprises 1998 Sales worksheet, starting in cell B14. The formula in cell B14 for calculating the percentage of the January-sales-to-first-quarter-total is very straightforward:

```
=B12/E12
```

This formula divides the January sales total in cell B12 by the quarterly total in E12. (What could be easier?) Look, however, at what happens if you drag the fill handle one cell to the right to copy this formula to cell C14:

```
=C12/F12
```

The adjustment of the first cell reference from B12 to C12 is just what the doctor ordered. However, the adjustment of the second cell reference from E12 to F12 is a disaster. Not only do you not calculate what percentage the February sales in cell C12 are of the first quarter sales in E12, but you also end up with one of those horrible #DIV/0! error things in cell C14.

To stop Excel from adjusting a cell reference in a formula in any copies you make, convert the cell reference from relative to absolute. You can do this by typing dollar signs ($) in front of the column letter and row number. A dollar sign placed in front of a cell column and/or row reference in a formula denotes that that part of the cell reference is *absolute* and should not adjusted in any copies made. For example, look at Figure 4-7. Cell B14 in this figure contains the correct formula to copy to the cell range C14:D14:

```
=B12/$E$12
```

Figure 4-8 shows the worksheet after you copy this formula to the range C14:D14 with the fill handle and cell C14 selected. Notice that the formula bar shows that this cell contains the following formula:

Figure 4-7:
Copying the formula for computing the ratio of monthly to quarterly sales with an absolute cell reference.

| | File | Edit | View | Insert | Format | Tools | Data | Window | Help | | | | Thu 11:21:28 AM | | |

| | Arial | | ▼ | 10 | ▼ | **B** | *I* | U | | | | | | |

| | C14 | | ▼ | | = | =C12/$E$12 | | | | |

Mother Goose - 1998 Sales (exp)

	A	B	C	D	E	F
1	Mother Goose Enterprises - 1998 Sales					
2		Jan	Feb	Mar	Qtr 1 Total	
3	Jack Sprat Diet Centers	80,138.58	59,389.56	19,960.06	$ 159,488.20	
4	Jack and Jill Trauma Centers	123,456.20	89,345.70	25,436.84	$ 238,238.74	
5	Mother Hubbard Dog Goodies	12,657.05	60,593.56	42,300.28	$ 115,550.89	
6	Rub-a-Dub-Dub Hot Tubs and Spas	17,619.79	40,635.00	42,814.99	$ 101,069.78	
7	Georgie Porgie Pudding Pies	57,133.56	62,926.31	12,408.73	$ 132,468.60	
8	Hickory, Dickory, Dock Clock Repair	168,291.00	124,718.10	41,916.13	$ 334,925.23	
9	Little Bo Peep Pet Detectives	30,834.63	71,111.25	74,926.24	$ 176,872.12	
10	Simple Simon Pie Shoppes	104937.77	75943.85	21621.31	$ 202,502.93	
11	Jack Be Nimble Candlesticks	128237.74	95035.19	31940.09	$ 255,213.02	
12	Total	$ 723,306.32	$ 679,698.52	$ 313,324.67	$ 1,716,329.51	
13						
14	Month/Qtr		42.14%	39.60%	18.26%	
15			⊕			
16						
17						

Figure 4-8:
The worksheet after copying the formula with the absolute cell reference.

```
=C12/$E$12
```

Because E12 was changed to $E$12 in the original formula, all the copies have this same absolute (unchanging) reference.

If you goof up and copy a formula where one or more of the cell references should have been absolute but you left them all relative, edit the original formula as follows:

1. **Double-click the cell with the formula and click the Edit Formula button on the formula bar or press ⌘+U to edit it.**

2. **Position the insertion point somewhere on the reference you want to convert to absolute.**

3. **Type $ (dollar sign).**

4. **When you finish editing, click the Return button on the formula bar and then copy the formula to the messed-up cell range with the fill handle.**

Cut and Paste, digital style

Instead of drag and drop or AutoFill, you can use the old standby Cut, Copy, and Paste commands to move or copy information in a worksheet. These commands use the Clipboard as a kind of electronic halfway house where the information you cut or copy remains until you decide to paste it somewhere. Because of this Clipboard arrangement, you can use these commands to move or copy information to any other worksheet open in Excel or even to other programs running on your Mac (like a Word 98 document).

To move a cell selection with Cut and Paste, follow these steps:

1. **Select the cells you want to move.**

2. **Click the Cut button on the Standard toolbar.**

   Or, if you prefer, you can choose Cut from the cell shortcut menu (opened by Control+clicking the cell selection) or Edit⇨Cut from the menu bar.

   You can cut out all of this button-and-menu stuff and just press ⌘+X. Whenever you choose the Cut command in Excel, the program surrounds the cell selection with a *marquee* (a dotted line that travels around the cells' outline) and displays the following message on the status bar:

   ```
   Select destination and press ENTER or choose Paste
   ```

3. **Move the cell pointer to, or select, the cell in the upper-left corner of the new range to which you want the information moved.**

4. **Press the Enter key (on the numeric keypad — *not* the Return key) to complete the move operation.**

   Or, if you don't have access to an Enter key (cause your Mac's keyboard doesn't have a numeric keypad), click the Paste button on the Standard toolbar, or choose Paste from the cell shortcut menu, or choose Edit⇨Paste on the menu bar, or press ⌘+V. (Do you think you have enough pasting alternatives in Excel?)

Notice that, when you indicate the destination range, you don't have to select a range of blank cells that matches the shape and size of the cell selection you're moving. Excel only needs to know the location of the cell in the upper-left corner of the destination range to figure out where to put the rest of the cells.

In fact, you can mess yourself up if you select more than the first cell of the destination range and the selected range doesn't exactly match the size and shape of the selection you're moving. When you press Return, Excel displays an alert box with the following message:

```
Cut and paste areas are different shapes
```

If you click OK to get rid of this dialog box, you have to correct the size of the destination range to successfully complete the move operation.

Copying a cell selection with the Copy and Paste commands follows an identical procedure to the one you use with the Cut and Paste commands. After selecting the range to copy, you have even more choices about how to get the information into the Clipboard. Instead of clicking the Copy button on the Standard toolbar or choosing Copy from the cell shortcut menu or Copy from the Edit menu, you can press ⌘+C.

Paste it again, Sam . . .

When copying a selection with the Copy and Paste commands and the Clipboard, you can copy the information multiple times. Just make sure that instead of pressing the Enter key (on the numeric keypad) to complete the first copy operation, you click the Paste button on the Standard toolbar or choose the Paste command (from the cell shortcut menu or the Edit menu) or press ⌘+V.

When you use the Paste command to complete a copy operation, Excel copies the selection to the range you designated without removing the marquee from the original selection. This is your signal that you can select another destination range (either in the same or a different document).

After selecting the first cell of the next range where you want the selection copied, choose the Paste command again. You can continue in this manner, pasting the same selection to your heart's content. When you make the last copy, press Return instead of choosing the Paste command. If you forget and choose Paste, get rid of the marquee around the original cell range by pressing the Esc key.

Note that you can do multiple pasting jobs with the Paste command only after copying stuff to the Clipboard and not after cutting stuff. This means that anytime you use the Cut and Paste commands to move something in the worksheet, you can go ahead and use the Enter key (if you have one) to complete the paste operation because you don't accrue any more pasting benefits from choosing the Paste command.

So what's so special about Paste Special?

Normally, Excel copies all the information in the range of cells you select: formatting as well the formulas, text, and other values you entered. If you want, you can specify that only the entries be copied (without the formatting) or that just the formatting be copied (without the entries). You can even have Excel copy only values in a cell selection, which means that Excel copies all text entries and values entered in a cell selection but does *not* include formulas or formatting. When you paste values, all formulas in the cell selection are discarded and only the calculated values are retained — these values appear in the new cell range just as though you entered them manually.

To paste particular parts of a cell selection while discarding others, you choose the Paste Special command on the cell shortcut menu or on the Edit pull-down menu rather than the standard Paste command (meaning that you don't get the benefit of clicking the Paste button on the Standard toolbar or using the nifty ⌘+V keyboard shortcut). When you choose Paste Special over Paste, Excel displays the Paste Special dialog box shown in Figure 4-9.

Here, you can specify which parts of the current cell selection to use by choosing the appropriate Paste radio button, as follows:

	Paste Special	
Paste		
● All	○ Comments	
○ Formulas	○ Validation	
○ Values	○ All except borders	
○ Formats		
Operation		
● None	○ Multiply	
○ Add	○ Divide	
○ Subtract		
☐ Skip blanks	☐ Transpose	
[Paste Link]	[Cancel] [OK]	

✔ Normally, Excel chooses the All radio button in the Paste section to paste all the stuff in the cell selection (formulas, formatting, you name it).

✔ Click the Formulas radio button in the Paste section to paste all the text, numbers, and formulas in the current cell selection while at the same time omitting all of the current formatting applied to their cells.

✔ Click the Values radio button in the Paste section to convert formulas in the current cell selection to their calculated values.

✔ Click the Formats radio button in the Paste section to paste only the formatting from the current cell selection and leave the cell entries in the dust.

✔ Click the Comments radio button in the Paste section to paste only the notes that you've attached to their cells (kinda like electronic sticky notes — see Chapter 6 for details).

✔ Click the Validation radio button in the Paste section to paste only the data validation rules into the cell range that you've set up with the new Data⇨Validation command.

✔ Click the All except borders radio button in the Paste section to paste all the stuff in the cell selection except any borders used there.

✔ Normally, the None radio button in the Operation section of the Paste Special dialog box is selected, indicating that Excel will perform no operation between the data entries you've cut or copied to the Clipboard and the data entries in the cell range where you paste.

✔ Click the Add radio button in the Operation section to add the data you've cut or copied to the Clipboard and the data entries in the cell range where you paste.

✔ Click the Subtract radio button in the Operation section to subtract the data you've cut or copied to the Clipboard from the data entries in the cell range where you paste.

✓ Click the Multiply radio button in the Operation section to multiply the data you've cut or copied to the Clipboard by the data entries in the cell range where you paste.

✓ Click the Divide radio button in the Operation section to divide the data you've cut or copied to the Clipboard by the data entries in the cell range where you paste.

✓ Select the Skip Blanks check box when you want Excel to paste everywhere except for any empty cells in the incoming range. In other words, a blank cell cannot overwrite your current cell entries.

✓ Select the Transpose check box when you want Excel to change the orientation of the pasted entries (for example, if the original cell entries ran down the rows of a single column of the worksheet, the transposed pasted entries will run across the columns of a single row).

✓ Click the Paste Link button when you're copying cell entries and you want to establish a link between copies you're pasting and the original entries so that changes to the original cells are automatically updated in the pasted copies.

Let's Be Clear about Deleting Stuff

No discussion about editing in Excel would be complete without a section on getting rid of the stuff you put into cells. You can perform two kinds of deletions in a worksheet.

✓ **Clearing a cell:** just deletes or empties the cell's contents without removing the cell from the worksheet, which would alter the layout of the surrounding cells.

✓ **Deleting a cell:** gets rid of the whole kit and caboodle — cell structure along with all its contents and formatting. When you delete a cell, Excel has to shuffle the position of entries in the surrounding cells to plug up any gaps made by the demise.

Sounding the all clear!

To get rid of just the contents of a cell selection rather than delete the cells along with their contents, select the range of cells to be cleared and press Delete or ⌘+B, or choose Edit⇨Clear⇨Contents on the menu bar.

If you want to get rid of more than just the contents of a cell selection, choose Edit⇨Clear and then choose from among the submenu commands:

- Choose All to get rid of all formatting and notes as well as entries in the cell selection.
- Choose Formats to delete only the formatting from the current cell selection without touching anything else.
- Choose Comments if you only want to remove the notes in the cell selection but leave everything else behind.

Get these cells outta here!

To delete the cell selection rather than just clear out its contents, select the cell range and choose Delete from the cell shortcut menu or Edit⇨Delete from the menu bar or press ⌘+K. Excel displays the Delete dialog box. You use the radio button options in this dialog box to indicate how Excel should shift the cells left behind to fill in the gaps when the cells currently selected are blotted out of existence:

- Normally, the Shift cells left radio button is selected, meaning that Excel moves entries from neighboring columns on the right to the left to fill in gaps created when you delete the cell selection by clicking OK or pressing Return.
- If you want Excel to move entries up from neighboring rows below, click the Shift cells up radio button.
- If you decide to remove all the rows in the current cell selection, click the Entire row radio button in the Delete dialog box.
- If you decide to delete all the columns in the current cell selection, click the Entire column radio button.

If you know ahead of time that you want to delete an entire column or row from the worksheet, you can select the column or row on the workbook window frame and then choose Delete from the column or row shortcut menu or choose Edit⇨Delete. You can remove more than one column or row at a time by dragging through their column letters or row numbers or ⌘+clicking them if they are not adjacent.

Deleting entire columns and rows from a worksheet is risky business unless you are sure that the columns and rows in question contain nothing of value. Remember, when you delete an entire row from the worksheet, you delete *all information from Column A through IV* in that row (and you can see only a very few columns in this row). Likewise, when you delete an entire column from the worksheet, you delete *all information from Row 1 through 65,536* in that column.

Kindly Step Aside . . .

For those inevitable times when you need to squeeze new entries into an already populated region of the worksheet, you can insert new cells in the area rather than go through all the trouble of moving and rearranging several individual cell ranges. To insert a new cell range, select the cells (many of which are already occupied) where you want the new cells to appear and then choose Insert on the cell shortcut menu or the Insert⇨Cells command on the menu bar or you can press ⌘+I. Doing any of these displays the Insert dialog box with the following radio button options:

- ✔ Click the Shift cells right radio button to shift existing cells to the right to make room for the ones you want to add before clicking OK or pressing Return.

- ✔ To instruct the program to shift existing entries down instead, use the default Shift cells down radio button before clicking OK or pressing Return.

- ✔ As when you delete cells, when you insert cells with the Insert dialog box, you can insert complete rows or columns in the cell range by clicking either the Entire row or the Entire column radio button. You can also select the row number or column letter on the frame before you choose the Insert command.

Stamping Out Your Spelling Errors

To check the spelling in a worksheet, choose Tools⇨Spelling on the menu bar or click the Spelling button (the one with a check mark under ABC) on the Standard toolbar or press F7. Any way you do it, Excel begins checking the spelling of all text entries in the worksheet. When the program comes across an unknown word, it displays the Spelling dialog box, similar to the one shown in Figure 4-10.

Figure 4-10:
Checking
your
spelling in
the Spelling
dialog box.

Excel suggests replacements for the unknown word, with a likely replacement in the Suggestions list box appearing in the Change to list box of the Spelling dialog box. If that replacement is incorrect, you can scroll through the Suggestions list and click the correct replacement. Use the Spelling dialog box options as follows:

- To replace the word listed after the Not in Dictionary prompt with the word listed in the Change to list box, click the Change button.

- To change all occurrences of this misspelled word in the worksheet to the word listed in the Change to list box, click the Change All button.

- If you want to add the unknown word (such as your name) to a custom dictionary so that it won't be flagged when you check the spelling in the worksheet later on, click the Add button.

- If you want Excel from then on to automatically correct this spelling error with the suggestion shown in the Change to text box (by adding the misspelling and suggestion to the AutoCorrect dialog box — refer to "You really AutoCorrect that for me" in Chapter 2), click the AutoCorrect button.

- If you think that the word is fine as is, then click the Ignore button (or the Ignore All button if you don't want the spell checker to bother you with this word again).

Notice that the Excel spell checker not only flags words not found in its built-in or custom dictionary but also flags occurrences of double words in a cell entry (such as *total total*) or words with unusual capitalization (such as *NEw York* instead of *New York*).

Keep in mind that you can check the spelling of just a particular group of entries by selecting the cells before you choose Tools⇔Spelling on the menu bar, click the Spelling button on the Standard toolbar, or press F7.

Chapter 5

Printing the Masterpiece

· ·

· ·

*W*hen all is said and done, for most people, getting the data down on paper is really what spreadsheets are all about (all the talk about the "paperless" office to the contrary). All the data entry, all the formatting, all the formula checking, all the things you do to get a spreadsheet ready are really just preparation for printing its information.

In this chapter, you find out just how easy it is to print reports with Excel 98. And you discover that just by following a few simple guidelines, you can produce top-notch reports the first time you send the document to the printer (instead of the second or even the third time around).

The only trick to printing a worksheet is getting used to the paging scheme and figuring out how to control it. Many of the worksheets you create with Excel are not only longer than one printed page but also wider. Unlike a word processor, such as Word 98, which only pages the document vertically (because it doesn't let you create a document wider than the page size you're using), spreadsheet programs like Excel 98 often have to break up pages both vertically and horizontally to print a worksheet document (a kind of tiling of the print job, if you will).

When breaking a worksheet into pages, Excel first pages the document vertically down the rows in the first columns of the print area (just like a word processor). After paging the first columns, the program pages down the rows of the second set of columns in the print area. Excel pages down and then over until all the document included in the print area (which can include the entire worksheet or just sections) is paged.

When paging the worksheet, keep in mind that Excel does not break up the information within a row or column. If all the information in a row doesn't fit at the bottom of the page, the program moves the entire row to the following page. So, too, if all the information in a column doesn't fit at the right edge of the page, the program moves the entire column to a new page. (Because Excel pages down and then over, chances are that the column will not appear on the next page of the report.)

You have several ways of dealing with such paging problems — and, in this chapter, you're going to be exposed to them all! After you have these page problems under control, printing, as you will shortly see, is a proverbial piece of cake.

Starting the Show with Print Preview

Do the world a favor and save a forest or two by using the Print Preview feature before you print any worksheet, section of worksheet, or entire workbook. Because of the peculiarities in paging worksheet data, you should check the page breaks for any report that requires more than one page. Print Preview mode not only shows you exactly how the worksheet data will be paged when printed but also enables you to modify the margins, change the page settings, and even go ahead and print the report when everything looks okay.

To switch to Print Preview mode, click the Print Preview button on the Standard toolbar (it's the one with the magnifying glass on the page, right next to the Print button) or choose File➪Print Preview on the menu bar. Excel displays all the information on the first page of the report in a sepa-rate window with its own toolbar. The mouse pointer becomes a magnifying glass. Figure 5-1 shows the Print Preview window with the first page of a four-page sample report.

When Excel displays a full page in the Print Preview window, you can barely read its contents; increase the view to actual size if you need to verify some of the information. You can zoom up to 100 percent by clicking the previewed page with the magnifying-glass mouse pointer or by clicking the Zoom button at the top of the Print Preview window. Figure 5-2 shows the first page of the four-page report after you zoom in by clicking the Zoom pointer (with the magnifying-glass icon) on the top central portion of the page.

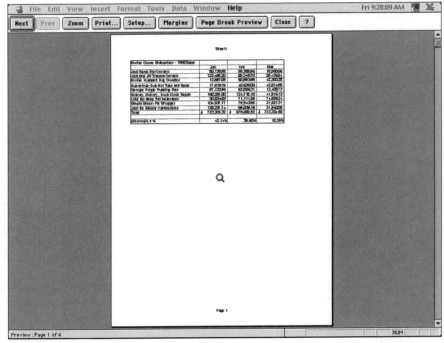

Figure 5-1:
The first
page of a
four-page
report,
shown in
Print
Preview
mode.

Figure 5-2:
The first
page of a
previewed
report after
clicking the
top of the
page with
the Zoom
tool.

After a page is enlarged to actual size, use the scroll bars to bring new parts of the page into view in the Print Preview window. If you prefer to use the keyboard, press the ↑ and ↓ keys or Page Up and Page Down to scroll up or down the page; press ← and → or ⌘+Page Up and ⌘+Page Down to scroll left and right.

To return to the full-page view, click the mouse pointer (in its arrowhead form) anywhere on the page or click the Zoom button on the Print Preview toolbar a second time. Excel indicates the number of pages in a report on the status bar of the Print Preview window. If your report has more than one page, you can view pages that follow the one you're previewing by clicking the Next command button at the top of the window. To review a page you've already seen, back up a page by clicking the Previous button. You can also advance to the next page by pressing the Page Down or ↓ key or move back to the previous page by pressing the Page Up or ↑ key when the page view is full-page rather than actual size.

When you finish previewing the report, you have the following options:

- ✔ If the pages look okay, you can click the Print button to display the Print dialog box and start printing the report from there. (See "Printing it your way" later in this chapter.)

- ✔ If you notice some paging problems that you can solve by choosing a new paper size, page order, orientation, or margins, or if you notice a problem with the header or footer in the top or bottom margin of the pages, you can click the Setup button and take care of these problems in the Page Setup dialog box.

- ✔ If you notice some paging problems that you can solve by modifying the page breaks, click the Page Break Preview button. This takes you back to the workbook window with a reduced view of the worksheet where you can change the page breaks by dragging the borders with the mouse. After you've got the borders adjusted the way you want them, return to the normal view by choosing View⇨Normal on the Excel menu bar. You can then print the report by choosing File⇨Print on the menu bar or by clicking the Print button on the Standard toolbar.

- ✔ If you notice some problems with the margins or with the column widths and you want to adjust them in Print Preview mode, you can click the Margins button and drag the margin markers into place. (See "Massaging the margins" later in this chapter for details.)

- ✔ If you notice any other kind of problem, such as a typo in a heading or a wrong value in a cell, click the Close button and return to the normal worksheet document window; you cannot make any text editing changes in the Print Preview window.

✔ After you make corrections to the worksheet, you can print the report from the normal document window by choosing File⇨Print on the menu bar (or pressing ⌘+P). Alternatively, you can switch back to Print Preview mode to make a last-minute check and click the Print button, or use the Print button on the Standard toolbar (fourth from left with the printer icon on it).

The Page Stops Here

Excel automatically displays the page breaks in the normal document window after you preview the document. Page breaks appear on-screen as dotted lines between the columns and rows that will print out on different pages.

To get rid of page breaks in the document window, choose Tools⇨Preferences on the menu bar, select the View tab, clear the check mark from the Page breaks check box, and click OK or press Return.

Printing it right away

As long as you want to use Excel's default print settings to print all the cells in the current worksheet, printing in Excel 98 is a breeze. Simply click the Print button on the Standard toolbar (the fourth tool from the left, with the printer icon). The program then prints one copy of all the information in the current worksheet, including any charts and graphics — but not including comments you added to cells. (See Chapter 6 for details about adding comments to your worksheet and Chapter 8 for details about charts and graphics.)

After you click the Print tool, Excel routes the print job to the Macintosh print queue, which acts like a middleman to send the job to the printer. While Excel is sending the print job to the print queue, Excel displays a Printing dialog box to keep you informed of its progress (such as Printing Page 2 of 3). After this dialog box disappears, you are free to go back to work in Excel. To abort the print job while it's being sent to the print queue, press ⌘+. (period) or click the Cancel button in the Printing dialog box.

Printing it your way

Printing with the Print tool on the Standard toolbar is fine, provided that all you want is a single copy of all the information in the current worksheet. If you want more copies, more or less data (such as all the worksheets in the workbook or just a cell selection within a particular worksheet), or you need to change some of the page settings (like the size of the page or the orientation of the printing on the page), then you need to print from the Print dialog box (shown in Figure 5-3).

Figure 5-3:
The Print
dialog box.

Excel provides a number of ways to open the Print dialog box:

- ✔ Press ⌘+P.
- ✔ Choose the File⇨Print command on the menu bar.
- ✔ Press ⌘+Shift+F12.

Printing in particular

Within the Print dialog box you can specify General print settings such as the printer to use (if you have access to more than one, say on an AppleTalk or Ethernet network), the number of copies to print, and the source of the paper (if you want to manually feed a front page and then have the remaining pages come from the printer's cassette). You can also stipulate Excel-specific print settings which let you decide between printing just the cells that are currently selected, the worksheets that are currently selected, or every worksheet in the entire workbook.

The General print settings for most types of printers (like laser and ink jet printers) include:

- ✔ **Printer:** To select a new printer to use in printing your worksheet (when you have access to more than one), click this button and select the printer's name on the pop-menu that appears.
- ✔ **Destination**: To save the print job in a PostScript file (the language that many types of printers understand) rather than send it to the printer (displayed on the Printer pop-up button) so that you can take it to another Mac and print it out there, click this button and select the File

option on the pop-up menu. With File selected on the Destination button, Excel opens a Save As dialog box where you specify the name and folder location for the PostScript file. If you want to take the file to a copy shop to print it with one of their fancy laser printers, save it on a $3^1/_2$-inch floppy disk.

✔ **Copies:** To print more than one copy of the report, enter the number of copies you want to print in the Copies text box.

✔ **Collated:** When you *collate* pages, you simply make separate stacks of each complete report, rather than print all copies of page one, and then all copies of page two, and so on. To have Excel collate each copy of the printed report for you, select the Collated check box.

✔ **Pages:** Normally, Excel selects the All radio button that prints all the pages required to produce the information in the areas of the workbook that you want printed. Sometimes, however, you may need to reprint only a page or range of pages that you've modified within this section. To reprint a single page, enter its page number in both the From and To text boxes.

To change the Excel-specific printer settings, click the pop-up button that reads General and select Microsoft Excel on the pop-up menu. When you select Microsoft Excel, you can choose between the following three options:

✔ **Selection:** Click this radio button to have Excel print just the cells that you've currently selected in your workbook. (Yes, you must remember to select these cells before opening the Print dialog box and clicking this radio button!)

✔ **Active sheets:** Excel automatically selects this radio button and prints all the information in whatever worksheets are active in your workbook. Normally, this means printing just the data in the current worksheet. To print other worksheets in the workbook when this radio button is selected, hold down ⌘ as you click the sheet's tab. To include all the sheets between two sheet tabs, click the first one and then hold Shift as you click the second tab (Excel selects all the tabs in between).

✔ **Entire workbook:** Click this radio button to have Excel print all the data in each and every one of the worksheets in your workbook.

After you finish selecting new print options, you can send the job to the printer by clicking the Print button or pressing Return.

Setting and clearing the Print Area

Excel includes a special printing feature called the *Print Area*. You can use the File⇨Print Area⇨Set Print Area command to define any cell selection on a worksheet as the Print Area. After you define the Print Area, Excel 98 then prints this cell selection anytime you print the worksheet (either with the Print button on the Standard toolbar or from the Print dialog box, using the File⇨Print command or one of its shortcuts). Whenever you fool with the Print Area, you need to keep in mind that after you define the Print Area, its cell range is the only one you can print (regardless of what options you select in the Print dialog box) until you clear the Print Area.

To clear the Print Area (and therefore go back to the printing defaults established in the Print dialog box — see "Printing in particular," which precedes this section, for details), you just have to choose File⇨Print Area⇨Clear Print Area on the menu bar.

You can also define and clear the Print Area from the Sheet tab of the Page Setup dialog box (see the next section). To define the Print Area from this dialog box, insert the cursor in the Print area text box on the Sheet tab and then select the cell range or ranges in the worksheet (remembering that you can reduce the Page Setup dialog box to just this text box by clicking its minimize box). To clear the Print Area from this dialog box, select the cell addresses in the Print area text box and press the Delete key.

My Page Was Setup!

As I said at the beginning of this chapter, about the only thing that's the slightest bit complex in printing a worksheet is figuring out how to get the page breaks right. Fortunately, the options in the Page Setup dialog box give you a great deal of control over what goes on which page. To open the Page Setup dialog box, choose File⇨Page Setup on the menu bar or click the Setup button if the Print Preview window is open. The Page Setup dialog box contains four tabs: Page, Margins, Header/Footer, and Sheet.

The particular options in the Page tab of the Page Setup dialog box may vary slightly with the type of printer you use. Figure 5-4 shows the Page Setup dialog box when the Apple LaserWriter is the current printer. (All the options you see here are also present when using other laser printers such as the HP LaserJet printer.)

For most types of printers, the Page tab of the Page Setup dialog box includes options for changing the orientation, scaling the printing, and choosing a new paper size and print quality:

> ✔ **Orientation:** Portrait positions the paper so that the short side is on the top and bottom. Landscape positions the printing with the long side of the paper on top and bottom. (See "Getting the lay of the landscape," which follows.)

Figure 5-4:
The Page
Setup
dialog box.

✔ **Adjust to:** Lets you increase or decrease the size of the print by a set percentage (much like using the Zoom feature to zoom in and out on worksheet data on-screen). When entering values in the Adjust to text box, keep in mind that 100 percent represents normal size and that any percentage below that reduces the size of the print (and puts more on each page), whereas any percentage above increases the size of the print (and puts less on each page).

✔ **Fit to:** Lets you fit all the printing on a single page (by default) or on a set number of pages wide by a set number of pages tall. (See "Packing it all on one page," later in this chapter.)

✔ **First page number:** Lets you change the starting page number when you want the first number to be higher than 1. You use this numbering option only when you're printing page numbers in the header or footer. (See "From header to footer," later in this chapter.)

✔ **Print quality:** Some printers let you change the quality of the printing depending upon whether you're producing a first rough draft or a final printout.

✔ **Options:** Opens a Setup dialog box for the specific printer you've selected. This dialog box lets you change stuff like the paper size, orientation of the page, and the scale of the printing (which duplicate the work of the Orientation and Adjust to options on the Page tab of the Page Setup dialog box).

Getting the lay of the landscape

For many printers (including most of the dot-matrix, laser, or inkjet persuasion), the Page tab of the Page Setup dialog box includes an Orientation section for changing the printing from the more normal *portrait* (where the printing runs parallel to the short edge of the paper) to *landscape* (where the printing runs parallel to the long edge of the paper). With these types of printers, you can usually use the Adjust to or Fit to options (see "Packing it all on one page," which follows) to scale the size of the printing, enabling you to enlarge or reduce the printing by a particular percentage or to force all the information on a single page or a set number of pages.

Because many worksheets are far wider than they are tall (like budgets or sales tables that track expenditures over all 12 months), if your printer supports changing the orientation of the page, you may find that such worksheets look better if you switch the orientation from the normal portrait mode (which accommodates fewer columns on a page) to landscape mode.

Figure 5-5 shows the Print Preview window with the first page of a report in landscape mode. For this report, Excel can get three more columns of information on this page in landscape mode than it can in portrait mode. However, because this page orientation accommodates fewer rows, the total page count for this report increases from two pages in portrait mode to four pages in landscape mode.

Figure 5-5:
A report
shown in
landscape
mode in the
Print
Preview
window.

Packing it all on one page

If your printer supports scaling options, you're in luck. You can always get a worksheet to fit on a single page simply by clicking the Fit to radio button. When you click this radio button, Excel figures out how much to reduce the size of the information you're printing to get it all on one page.

If you preview this one page and find that the printing is just too small to read comfortably, reopen the Page tab of the Page Setup dialog box and try changing the number of pages in the page(s) wide by tall text boxes (to the immediate right of the Fit to radio button). For example, instead of trying to stuff everything on one page, check out how the worksheet looks on two pages across: Type **2** in the page(s) wide text box and leave **1** in the pages tall text box. Alternatively, see how the worksheet looks on two pages down: Leave the **1** in the page(s) wide text box and type **2** in the pages tall text box.

After using the Fit to option, you may find that you don't want to scale the printing. Cancel scaling by clicking the Adjust to radio button right above the Fit to button and type **100** in the % normal size text box (or select 100 with the up- and down-arrow buttons).

Massaging the margins

Excel uses a standard top and bottom margin of 1 inch on each page of the report and a standard left and right margin of $^3/_4$ inch.

Frequently, you find that you can squeeze the last column or the last few rows of the worksheet data you're printing on a page just by adjusting the margins for the report. To get more columns on a page, try reducing the left and right margins. To get more rows on a page, try reducing the top and bottom margins.

You can change the margins in two ways:

  ✔ Open the Page Setup dialog box (either by choosing File➪Page Setup on the menu bar or by clicking the Setup button in the Print Preview window) and then select the Margins tab (see Figure 5-6) and enter the new settings in the Top, Bottom, Left, and Right text boxes — or select the new margin settings with their respective spinner buttons.

  ✔ Open the Print Preview window, click the Margins button, and drag the margin markers to their new positions (see Figure 5-7).

Figure 5-6:
The Margins tab in the Page Setup dialog box.

Top Margin Marker　　Header Margin Marker　　Column Markers

Figure 5-7:
The Print Preview window after clicking the Margins button.

Bottom Margin Marker　　　　Footer Margin Marker

Left Margin Marker　　　　Right Margin Marker

You can use the Center on page options in the Margins tab of the Page Setup dialog box to center a selection of data (that takes up less than a full page) between the current margin settings. Select the Horizontally check box to center the data between the left and right margin. Select the Vertically check box to center the data between the top and bottom margins.

If you use the Margins button in the Print Preview window to change the margin settings, you can modify the column widths as well as the margins. (Figure 5-7 shows the margin and column markers that appear when you click the Margins button in the Print Preview window.) To change one of the margins, position the mouse pointer on the desired margin marker (the pointer shape changes to a double-headed arrow) and drag the marker in the appropriate direction. When you release the mouse button, Excel redraws the page using the new margin setting. You may gain or lose columns or rows, depending on what kind of adjustment you make. Changing the column widths is the same story: Drag the column marker to the left or right to decrease or increase the width of a particular column.

From header to footer

Headers and footers are simply standard text that appears on every page of the report. The *header* prints in the top margin of the page, and the *footer* prints — you guessed it — in the bottom margin. Both are centered vertically in the margins. Unless you specify otherwise, Excel does not bother to add either a header or footer to your workbook printouts.

You can use a header and footer in a report to identify the document used to produce the report and display the page numbers and the date and time of printing.

Getting a standard job

To add a header or footer, open the Header/Footer tab in the Page Setup dialog box and select the header and/or footer information in the Header and/or Footer pop-up list box found there (see Figure 5-8). Both the Header and Footer pop-up list boxes in this tab contain a wide number of stock pieces of information for your header and footer, including the name of the worksheet (picked up from the sheet tab — see Chapter 6 to find out how to rename a sheet tab), who prepared the worksheet (picked up from the User name text box in the General tab of the Preferences dialog box — see Chapter 12), the page number, the current date, the name of the workbook document, or various combinations of these pieces of information.

Figure 5-8:
The
Header/
Footer tab
of the Page
Setup
dialog box
with a stock
header and
footer.

Figure 5-8 shows the Header/Footer tab of the Page Setup dialog box after choosing

```
mind over media Confidential, Sheet1, Page 1
```

in the Header pop-up list box (mind over media is the company to which Excel is registered [this name is the same as the one listed as the registered user on the About Microsoft Excel dialog box], Sheet1 is the name of the worksheet, and Page 1 is, of course, the current page number) and also choosing

```
Page 1 of ?
```

in the Footer drop-down list box (which puts in the current page number, along with the total number of pages, in the report). You can select this paging option in either the Header or Footer pop-up list box.

Figure 5-9 shows the first page of the report in Print Preview mode. Here, you can see the header and footer as they will print. (Fortunately, you can verify in the Print Preview window that the header information won't all print on top of each other as it appears in the header preview area in the Page Setup dialog box.) You can also see how the Page 1 of ? works in the footer: On the first page, you see the centered footer, Page 1 of 2; on the second page, you would see the centered footer, Page 2 of 2.

If you no longer want a header or footer printed in your report, you simply open the Header/Footer tab in the Page Setup dialog box and then select the (none) option at the very top of the Header and Footer pop-up list box.

Little Bo-Peep Pet Detectives - Client List

Case No	Last Name	First Name	Street	City	State	Zip	Status	Hours	Rate	Total Due
101-920	Harvey	Scott	12 Elm Street	Scholar	MN	58764	Active	250	75.00	$18,750
101-014	Andersen	Hans	341 The Shadow	Scholar	MN	58764	Closed	175	75.00	$13,125
103-023	Appleseed	Johnny	6789 Fruitree Tr	Along The Way	SD	66017	Active	321	125.00	$40,125
102-013	Baggins	Bingo	99 Hobbithole	Shire	ME	04047	Active	100	125.00	$12,500
103-007	Baum	L. Frank	447 Toto Too Rd	Oz	KS	65432	Closed	421	125.00	$52,625
104-026	Brown	Charles	59 Flat Plains	Saltwater	UT	84001	Active	575	125.00	$71,875
101-001	Bryant	Michael	326 Chefs Lane	Paris	TX	78705	Active	600	100.00	$60,000
101-028	Cassidy	Butch	Sundance Kidde	Hole In Wall	CO	80477	Closed	345.5	75.00	$25,913
102-006	Cinderella	Poore	8 Lucky Maiden Way	Oxford	TN	07557	Closed	800	75.00	$60,000
103-004	Cupid	Eros	97 Mount Olympus	Greece	CT	03331	Active	123.5	75.00	$9,263
103-022	Dragon	Kai	2 Pleistocene Era	Ann's World	ID	00001	Active	450.2	75.00	$33,765
104-031	Eaters	Big	444 Big Pigs Court	Dogtown	AZ	85257	Closed	780	125.00	$97,500
106-022	Foliage	Red	49 Maple Syrup	Waffle	VT	05452	Active	205	125.00	$25,625
102-020	Franklin	Ben	1789 Constitution	Jefferson	WV	20178	Active	189.5	75.00	$14,213
104-019	Fudde	Elmer	8 Warner Way	Hollywood	CA	33461	Active	463.5	125.00	$57,938
102-002	Gearing	Shane	1 Gunfighter's End	LaLa Land	CA	90069	Active	902.5	125.00	$112,813
102-012	Gondor	Aragorn	2956 Gandalf	Midearth	WY	80342	Closed	157	125.00	$19,625
104-005	Gookin	Polly	4 Feathertop Hill	Hawthorne	MA	01824	Active	169.5	125.00	$21,188
105-008	Harvey	Chauncey	60 Lucky Starr Pl	Shetland	IL	60080	Active	226.5	125.00	$28,313
106-021	Horse	Seabisquit	First Place Finish	Raceway	KY	23986	Active	300	125.00	$37,500
101-015	Humperdinck	Engelbert	6 Hensel+ Gretel Tr	Gingerbread	MD	20815	Active	705.5	125.00	$88,188
103-017	Jacken	Jill	Up the Hill	Pail of Water	OK	45678	Closed	200	75.00	$15,000
105-027	Laurel	Stan	2 Oliver Hardy	Celluloyde	NM	82128	Closed	352	125.00	$44,000
101-030	Liberty	Statuesque	31 Gotham Centre	Big Apple	NY	10011	Active	236.5	125.00	$29,563
103-016	Oakenshield	Rex	Mines of Goblins	Everest	NJ	07639	Closed	400	125.00	$50,000
103-024	Oakley	Anney	Six Shooter Path	Target	ND	66540	Active	502.5	125.00	$62,813
101-029	Oow	Lu	888 Sandy Beach	Honolulu	HI	99909	Active	732	125.00	$91,500
104-018	Ridinghoode	Crimson	232 Cottage Path	Wulfen	PA	15201	Active	125.5	125.00	$15,688

Page 1 of 4

Figure 5-9:
The first page of a preview report showing the header and footer as they will print.

Getting a custom job

Most of the time, the stock headers and footers available in the Header and Footer pop-up list boxes are sufficient for your report needs. Every once in a while, however, you may want to insert information not available in these list boxes or in an arrangement not offered in the stock headers and footers. For those times, you need to turn to the Custom Header and Custom Footer buttons in the Header/Footer tab of the Page Setup dialog box and go about creating your header or footer by inserting your own information.

Figure 5-10 shows the Header dialog box that appears when you click the Custom Header button after selecting the stock header shown in Figure 5-8.

Notice that in the custom Header dialog box, the header is divided into three sections: Left Section, Center Section, and Right Section. All header text you enter in the Left Section of this dialog box is justified with the left margin of the report. All header text you enter in the Center Section box is centered between the left and right margins, and (you guessed it) all text you enter in the Right Section box is justified with the right margin of the report.

Total Pages   Sheet Tab
Font   Time

Page   Date   Filename

Figure 5-10:
Creating a
custom
header in
the Header
dialog box.

You can use the Tab key to advance to the next section in the header and to select the contents of that section and Shift+Tab to go to and select the previous section. If you want to break the header text in one of the sections, press Return to start a new line. If you want to clear the contents of a section, select the items and press Delete.

As Figure 5-10 shows, Excel puts some pretty weird codes with lots of ampersands (&[Page] and &[Date]) in the center and right sections of this stock header. When creating a custom header (or footer), you too can mix these weird ampersand codes with your own text. To insert such codes in a section of the header (or footer), click the appropriate button:

 ✔ **Page button:** inserts the &[Page] code that puts in the current page number.

 ✔ **Total page button:** inserts the &[Pages] code that puts in the total number of pages. Thus, you can have Excel display the Page 1 of 4 kind of thing by typing the word **Page** and pressing the spacebar, clicking the Page button, pressing the spacebar again, typing **of**, pressing the spacebar a third time, and, finally, clicking the Total Page button to insert Page &[Page] of &[Pages] in the custom header (or footer).

 ✔ **Date button:** inserts the &[Date] code that puts in the current date.

 ✔ **Time button:** inserts the &[Time] code that puts in the current time.

 ✔ **Filename button:** inserts the &[File] code that puts in the name of the workbook file.

 ✔ **Sheet Tab button:** inserts the &[Tab] code that puts in the name of the worksheet as shown on the sheet tab.

In addition to inserting ampersand codes in the custom header (or footer), you can select a new font, font size, or font attribute for any of its sections by clicking the Font button. When you click the Font button, Excel opens the Font dialog box where you can select a new font, font style, font size, or special effects (like strikethrough, superscript, or subscript).

When you finish creating your custom header (or footer), click the OK button to close the Header (or Footer) dialog box and return to the Header/Footer tab of the Page Setup dialog box (where you can see the fruits of your labor in the sample boxes).

Sorting out the sheet settings

The Sheet tab of the Page Setup dialog box (similar to the one shown in the following section in Figure 5-11) contains a variety of printing options that may come in handy from time to time:

- **Print area:** This text box shows you the cell range of the current Print Area that you've selected with the File⇨Print Area⇨Set Print Area command on the menu bar. Use this text box to make changes to the range of cells that you want to print. To change the Print Area range, select this text box and then drag through the cell range in the worksheet or type in the cell references or range names (as explained in Chapter 6). Separate individual cell ranges with a comma (as in A1:G72, K50:M75) when designating nonadjacent areas. If, in selecting the cell range, you find that you need to, you can reduce the Page Setup dialog box to just the Print area text box by clicking its minimize button.

  Use the Print area option when your workbook contains a section that you routinely need to print so that you don't have to keep selecting the range and then clicking the Selection radio button in the Microsoft Excel-specific print options in the Print dialog box every blasted time you print it.

- **Rows to repeat at top:** Use this option to designate rows of a worksheet as *print titles* to be printed across the top of each page of the report. (See "Putting out the print titles," which follows this section.) Select this text box and then drag down the rows or enter the row references (such as 2:3). If, in selecting the rows to use as print titles, you find it necessary, you can reduce the Page Setup dialog box to just the Rows to repeat at top text box by clicking its minimize button.

- **Columns to repeat at left:** Use this option to designate columns of a worksheet as print titles to be printed at the left edge of each page of the report. (See "Putting out the print titles," which follows this section.) Select this text box and then drag across the columns or enter the column references (such as A:B). If, in selecting the columns to use as print titles, you find you need to, you can reduce the Page Setup dialog box to just the Columns to repeat at left text box by clicking its minimize button.

✓ **Gridlines:** Hides or shows the cell gridlines in the printed report.

✓ **Black and white:** When you select this check box, Excel prints the different colors assigned to cell ranges in black and white. Select this option when you've used colors for text and graphics in a workbook on a color monitor but want to print them in monochrome on a black-and-white printer. (Otherwise, they become shades of gray on a black-and-white printer.)

✓ **Draft quality:** When you select this check box, Excel doesn't print cell gridlines (regardless of the status of the Gridlines check box) and omits some graphics from the printout. Select this option when you want to get a fast and dirty copy of the report and are only concerned with checking the text and numbers.

✓ **Row and column headings:** When you select this check box, Excel includes the worksheet frame with the column letters and row numbers on each page of the report. Select this option when you want to be able to identify the location of the printed information. (See "Letting Your Formulas All Hang Out," later in this chapter, for an example.)

✓ **Comments:** When you select the At end of sheet or As displayed on sheet options on the Comments pop-up menu, Excel prints the text of comments attached to cells that are included in the report. When you select the At end of sheet option, the program prints the notes in a series all together at the end of the report. When you select the As displayed on sheet, the program prints only the notes that are currently displayed in the worksheet. (See "Electronic Sticky Notes" in Chapter 6 for details.)

✓ **Down, then over:** Normally, Excel selects this radio button, which tells the program to number and page a multipage report by proceeding down the rows and then across the columns to be printed.

✓ **Over, then down:** Select this radio button to alter the way a multipage report is numbered and paged. When you select this option, Excel proceeds to number and page across the columns and then down the rows to be printed.

Putting out the print titles

The Print titles section of the Sheet tab of the Page Setup dialog box enables you to print particular row and column headings on each page of the report. Excel refers to such row and column headings in a printed report as *print titles.* Don't confuse print titles with the header of a report. Even though both are printed on each page, header information appears in the top margin of the report; print titles always appear in the body of the report — at the top, in the case of rows used as print titles, and on the left, in the case of columns.

To designate print titles for a report, follow these steps:

1. **Open the Page Setup dialog box by choosing File⇨Page Setup on the menu bar.**

   The Page Setup dialog box appears, as shown in Figure 5-11.

2. **Select the Sheet tab.**

   To designate worksheet rows as print titles, go to Step 3a. To designate worksheet columns as print titles, go to Step 3b.

3a. **Select the Rows to repeat at top text box and then drag through the rows whose information is to appear at the top of each page in the worksheet below. If, in selecting the rows, you find it necessary, you can reduce the Page Setup dialog box to just the Rows to repeat at top text box by clicking the text box's minimize button.**

Figure 5-11:
Setting the
print titles
for the
sample
report.

In the example shown in Figure 5-11, I clicked the minimize button associated with the Rows to repeat at top text box and then dragged through Rows 1 and 2 in Column A of the Bo Peep Pet Detectives — Client List worksheet, and the program entered the row range $1:$2 in the Rows to repeat at top text box.

Note that Excel indicates the print-title rows in the worksheet by placing a dotted line (that moves like a marquee) on the border between the titles and the information in the body of the report.

3b. Select the Columns to repeat at left and then drag through the range of columns whose information is to appear at the left edge of each page of the printed report in the worksheet below. If, in selecting the columns, you find it necessary, you can reduce the Page Setup dialog box to just the Columns to repeat at left text box by clicking its minimize button.

Note that Excel indicates the print-title columns in the worksheet by placing a dotted line (that moves like a marquee) on the border between the titles and the information in the body of the report.

4. Click OK or press Return.

After you close the Page Setup dialog box, the dotted line showing the border of the row and/or column titles disappears from the worksheet.

In Figure 5-11, Rows 1 and 2 containing the worksheet title and column headings for the Bo Peep Pet Detectives clients database are designated as the print titles for the report. Figure 5-12 shows the Print Preview window with the second page of the report. In this figure, you can see how these print titles appear on all pages of the report.

To clear print titles from a report when you no longer need them, open the Sheet tab of the Page Setup dialog box and then delete the row and column ranges from the Rows to repeat at top and the Columns to repeat at left text boxes before you click OK or press Return.

When Ya Gonna Give Your Page a Break?

Sometimes, as you preview a report, you see that Excel split onto different pages information that you know should always appear together on the same page.

Figure 5-13 shows a worksheet in Page Break Preview with an example of a bad vertical page break that you can remedy by adjusting the location of the page break between Page 2 and Page 3. Given the page size, orientation, and margin settings for this report, Excel breaks the page between Columns L and M. This break separates the sales figures for July, August, and September in Columns J, K, and L from the Quarter 3 Totals in Column M.

Figure 5-12:
The second
preview page
of the sample
report
showing the
print titles
defined in
Figure 5-11.

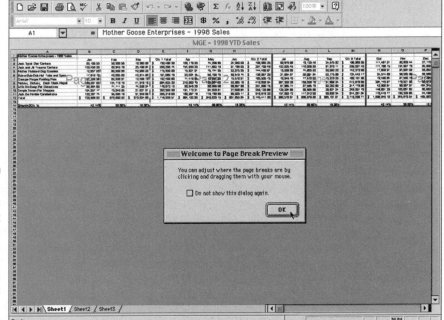

Figure 5-13:
Displaying a
worksheet
to be
printed in
the Page
Break
Preview
mode.

To keep all the third-quarter figures on the same page, you need to move the page break to the left so that the break between Page 2 and Page 3 occurs between Columns I and J. That way, all the third quarter sales (for July, August, and September) will be printed together with the Quarter 3 totals on Page 3 of the report. Figure 5-13 shows how you can create the vertical page break in Page Break Preview mode by following these steps:

1. **Choose View⇨Page Break Preview on the menu bar.**

   This takes you into a page break preview window that shows your worksheet data at a reduced magnification (60 percent of normal in Figure 5-13) with the page numbers displayed in large light type and the page breaks shown by heavy lines between the columns and rows of the worksheet.

2. **Click OK or press Return to get rid of the Welcome to Page Break Preview alert dialog box that appears when you first get into Page Break Preview.**

3. **Position the mouse pointer somewhere on the page break indicator (one of the heavy lines surrounding the representation of the page) that you need to adjust; when the pointer changes to a double-headed arrow, drag the page indicator to the desired column or row and release the mouse button.**

   For the example shown in Figure 5-13, I drag the page break indicator between Page 2 and Page 3 to the left so that it's between Columns I and J. Excel then inserts a new page break between Columns Q and R (which adds a Page 4 to the report). I then drag this page break indicator to the left so that it's between Columns M and N (so that all the fourth quarter sales are together on the fourth page with the fourth quarter and year-to-date totals, as shown in Figure 5-14).

4. **After you finish adjusting the page breaks in Page Break Preview (and, presumably, printing the report), choose View⇨Normal on the menu bar to return the worksheet to its regular view of the data.**

Keep in mind that you can also modify the page breaks with the Insert⇨Page Break command on the menu bar in the regular worksheet. When inserting a manual page break with this command, you use the top and left edges of the cell pointer to determine where to place the manual page break. The top edge of the cell pointer determines where the page break occurs horizontally; the left edge of the cell pointer determines where the page break occurs vertically. Then, after placing the cell pointer, you choose the Insert⇨Page Break command and Excel inserts dotted lines between the columns and rows that indicate the limits of the new page break.

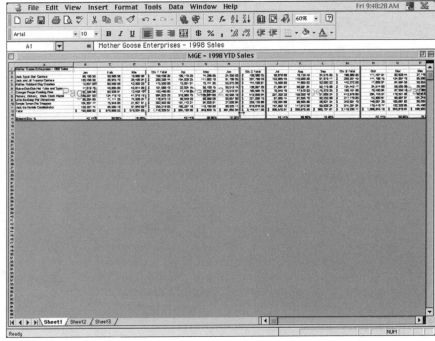

To remove a manual page break from a worksheet, position the cell pointer somewhere in the row below a horizontal page break or somewhere in the column to the right of a vertical page break. (Manual page breaks are indicated in the worksheet by dotted lines that are indistinguishable from automatic page breaks.) Then choose Insert⇨Remove Page Break on the menu bar. (The Page Break command changes to the Remove Page Break command on the Insert menu, depending on where you place the cell pointer.) If you inserted both a vertical and a horizontal page break at the same time, you must position the cell pointer in the same cell you used to create the two page breaks in order to get rid of them both in a single operation.

Letting Your Formulas All Hang Out

One more basic printing technique you may need every once in a while is how to print the formulas in a worksheet instead of printing the calculated results of the formulas. You can check over a printout of the formulas in your worksheet to make sure that you haven't done anything stupid (like replace a formula with a number or use the wrong cell references in a formula) before you distribute the worksheet company-wide — which can be really embarrassing.

Before you can print a worksheet's formulas, you have to display the formulas, rather than their results, in the cells.

1. **Choose Tools⇨Preferences on the menu bar.**
2. **Select the View tab.**
3. **Select the Formulas check box to put a check mark in it.**
4. **Click the OK button or press Return.**

When you follow these steps, Excel displays the contents of each cell in the worksheet as they normally appear only in the formula bar or when you're editing them in the cell. Notice that value entries lose their number formatting, formulas appear in their cells (Excel widens the columns with best-fit so that the formulas appear in their entirety), and long text entries no longer spill over into neighboring blank cells.

Excel allows you to toggle between the normal cell display and the formula cell display by pressing ⌘+~, (that is, press ⌘ and the tilde key). The *tilde key* is the one (usually found in the upper-left corner of your keyboard) that does double-duty above the weird backward accent key, `, which is not to be confused with the apostrophe that appears on a key below the quotation mark.

After Excel displays the formulas in the worksheet, you're ready to print it as you do any other report. You can include the worksheet column letters and row numbers as headings in the printout so that, if you *do* spot an error, you can pinpoint the cell reference right away. To include the row and column headings in the printout, click the Row and column headings check box in the Sheet tab of the Page Setup dialog box before you send the report to the printer.

After you print the worksheet with the formulas, return the worksheet to normal by opening the Page Setup dialog box and selecting the View tab and then deselecting the Formulas check box before clicking OK, or pressing Return, or by just pressing ⌘+~.

Part III

Getting Organized and Staying That Way

The 5th Wave   By Rich Tennant

"MY GIRLFRIEND RAN A SPREADSHEET OF MY LIFE, AND GENERATED THIS CHART. MY BEST HOPE IS THAT SHE'LL CHANGE HER MAJOR FROM 'COMPUTER SCIENCES' TO 'REHABILITATIVE SERVICES.'"

In this part . . .

In today's business world, we all know how vital it is to stay organized — as well as how difficult it is. Needless to say, keeping straight the spreadsheets you create in Excel 98 is no less important and, in some cases, no less arduous.

Part III helps you tackle this conundrum by giving you the inside track on how to keep on top of all the stuff in every single worksheet you create or edit. Not only do you discover in Chapter 6 how to keep track of the information in one worksheet, but also, in Chapter 7, how to juggle the information from one worksheet to another and even from one workbook to another.

Chapter 6

Oh, What a Tangled Worksheet We Weave!

• •

• •

*Y*ou already know that each Excel worksheet offers an awfully big place in which to store information (and that each workbook you open offers you three of these babies). Because your computer monitor lets you see only a tiny bit of any of the worksheets in a workbook at any one time, the issue of keeping on top of information is not a small one (pun intended).

Although the Excel worksheet employs a coherent cell-coordinate system that you can use to get anywhere in the great big worksheet, you've got to admit that this A1, B2 stuff — although highly logical — remains fairly alien to human thinking. (I mean, saying "Go to cell IV88" just doesn't have anywhere near the same impact as saying "Go to the corner of Hollywood and Vine.") Consider for a moment how hard it is to come up with a meaningful association between the 1998 depreciation schedule and its location in the cell range AC50:AN75 so that you can remember where to find it.

In this chapter, I cover some of the more effective techniques for keeping on top of information. You find out how to change the perspective on a worksheet by zooming in and out on the information, how to split the document window into separate panes so that you can display different sections of the worksheet at the same time, and how to keep particular rows and columns on the screen at all times.

And, as if that weren't enough, you also see how to add comments to cells, assign descriptive, English-type names to cell ranges (like Hollywood and Vine!), and use the Find and Replace commands to locate and, if necessary, replace entries anywhere in the worksheet. Finally, you see how to control when Excel recalculates the worksheet and how to limit where changes can be made.

Zeroing In with Zoom

So what are you gonna do now that the boss won't spring for that 21-inch monitor for your computer? All day long, you're either straining your eyes to read all the information in those little, tiny cells, or you're scrolling like mad trying to locate a table you can't seem to find today. Never fear, the Zoom feature is here. You can use Zoom like a magnifying glass to blow up part of the worksheet or shrink it down to size.

Figure 6-1 shows a blowup of a client list worksheet after increasing it to 200-percent magnification (twice normal size). To blow up a worksheet like this, select the 200% option at the top of the Zoom button's pop-up menu — the button second from the end on the Standard toolbar. (You can also do this by choosing View➪Zoom on the menu bar and then clicking the 200% radio button in the Zoom dialog box, if you really want to go to all that trouble.) One thing's for sure, you don't have to go after your glasses to read the names in those cells! The only problem with 200-percent magnification is that you can see only a few cells at one time.

Figure 6-2 shows the same worksheet, this time at 25-percent magnification (roughly one-quarter normal size). To reduce the display to this magnification, you select the 25% setting on the Zoom button's pop-up menu on the Standard toolbar (unless you're just dying to open the Zoom dialog box so that you can accomplish this via its 25% radio button).

Whew! At 25 percent of normal screen size, the only thing you can be sure of is that you can't read a thing! However, notice that with this bird's-eye view, you can see at a glance how far over and down the data in this worksheet extends.

The Zoom pop-up menu and dialog box offer five precise magnification settings: 200%, 100% (normal screen magnification), 75%, 50%, and 25%. To use other percentages besides these, you have the following options:

✔ If you want to use other precise percentages in between the five preset percentages (such as 150% or 85%) or settings greater or less than the highest or lowest (such as 400% or 10%), select the Zoom button's text box on the Standard toolbar, type the new percentage, and press Return. (You can also do this by opening the Zoom dialog box and entering the percentage in its Custom text box.)

Figure 6-1:
Zooming in:
A sample
worksheet
at 200-
percent
magnifi-
cation.

Figure 6-2:
Zooming
out: A
sample
worksheet
at 25-
percent
magnif-
ication.

> ✔ If you don't know what percentage to enter in order to display a par-
> ticular cell range on the screen, select the range, choose Selection at
> the very bottom of the Zoom button's pop-up menu or open the Zoom
> dialog box, click the Fit Selection radio button, and then click OK or
> press Return. Excel figures out the percentage necessary to fill up your
> screen with just the selected cell range.

You can use the Zoom feature to locate and move to a new cell range in the
worksheet. First, select a small magnification, such as 50%. Then locate the
cell range you want to move to and select one of its cells. Finally, use the
Zoom feature to return the screen magnification to 100% again. When Excel
returns the display to normal size, the cell you selected and its surrounding
range appear on-screen.

Getting the Full Screen View

Excel 98 includes a Full Screen view command that can give you a lot more
screen real estate by removing the display of all the docked toolbars that
you have displayed.

To put a worksheet into Full Screen mode and get rid of all those space-
guzzling toolbars, choose View⇨Full Screen on the Excel menu bar. Excel
then removes all the docked toolbars, leaving only the menu bar, workbook
title bar, and status bar displayed. In exchange for removing the docked
toolbars, Excel displays a floating Full Screen toolbar. This toolbar contains
only one button: Close Full Screen. So when you finish perusing your
worksheet data in Full Screen mode, you click the Close Full Screen button.
Clicking this button closes the Full Screen toolbar, while at the same time
restoring all the docked toolbars that were temporarily put away.

Splitting the Difference

Although zooming in and out on the worksheet can help you get your
bearings, it can't bring together two separate sections so that you can
compare their data on-screen (at least not at a normal size where you can
actually read the information). To manage this kind of trick, split the document window into separate panes and then scroll the worksheet in each
pane so that they display the parts you want to compare.

Splitting the window is easy. Figure 6-3 shows a projected income statement
for the Jack Sprat Diet Centers at 125% magnification after splitting its
worksheet window horizontally into two panes and scrolling up Rows 18
through 29 in the second pane. Each pane has its own vertical scroll bar,
which enables you to scroll different parts of the worksheet into view.

Figure 6-3:
The
worksheet
in a split
document
window
after
scrolling up
the income
statement in
the lower
pane.

Split Bar

To split a worksheet into two (upper and lower) horizontal panes, you can drag the *split bar,* the black bar located right above the scroll arrow at the very top of the vertical scroll bar, down until the window is divided as you want it. Use the following steps:

1. **Click the vertical split bar and hold down the mouse button.**

   The mouse pointer changes to a double-headed arrow with a split in its middle (like the one used to display hidden rows).

2. **Drag downward until you reach the row at which you want the document window divided.**

   A gray dividing line appears in the workbook document window as you drag down, indicating where the document window will be split.

3. **Release the mouse button.**

   Excel divides the window into horizontal panes at the pointer's location and adds a vertical scroll bar to the new pane.

You can also split the document window into two vertical (left and right) panes by following these steps:

1. **Click the split bar located at the right edge of the horizontal scroll bar.**

2. **Drag to the left until you reach the column at which you want the document window divided.**

3. **Release the mouse button.**

   Excel splits the window at that column and adds a second horizontal scroll bar to the new pane.

Don't confuse the tab split bar to the left of the horizontal scroll bar with the horizontal split bar at its right. You drag the tab split bar to increase or decrease the number of sheet tabs displayed at the bottom of the workbook window; you use the horizontal split bar to divide the workbook window into two vertical panes.

Note that you can make the panes in a workbook window disappear by double-clicking anywhere on the split bar that divides the window rather than having to drag the split bar all the way to one of the edges of the window to get rid of it.

Instead of dragging split bars, you can divide a document window with the Window⇨Split command on the menu bar. When you choose this command, Excel uses the position of the cell pointer to determine where to split the window into panes. The program splits the window vertically at the left edge of the pointer and horizontally along the top edge. If you want the workbook window split into just two horizontal panes, do this: Using the top of the cell pointer as the dividing line, position the cell pointer in the first column of the desired row that is displayed on your screen. If you want the workbook window split into just two vertical windows, do this: Using the left edge of the cell pointer as the dividing line, position the cell pointer in the first row of the desired column that's displayed on your screen.

When the left edge of the cell pointer is right up against the left edge of the workbook window (as it is when the pointer is in any cell in the very first column shown on-screen), the program doesn't split the window vertically — it splits the window horizontally along the top edge of the cell pointer. When the top edge of the pointer is right up against the top edge of the document window (as it is when the pointer is in a cell in the very first row displayed on-screen), the program doesn't split the window horizontally — it splits the window vertically along the left edge of the cell pointer.

If you position the cell pointer somewhere in the midst of the cells displayed on-screen when you choose the Window⇨Split command, Excel splits the window into four panes along the top and left edge of the cell pointer. For example, if you position the cell pointer in cell C6 of the Little Bo Peep Client List worksheet and then choose Window⇨Split, the window splits into four panes: A horizontal split occurs between Rows 5 and 6, and a vertical split occurs between Columns B and C (as shown in Figure 6-4).

After you split the window into panes, you can move the cell pointer into a particular pane either by clicking one of its cells or by pressing Shift+F6 (which moves the pointer to the last occupied cell or the top-left cell in each pane in the workbook window in a counterclockwise direction). To remove the panes from a window, choose Window⇨Remove Split on the menu bar.

Fixed Headings Courtesy of Freeze Panes

Window panes are great for viewing different parts of the same worksheet that you normally can't see together. You can also use window panes to freeze headings in the top rows and first columns so that the headings stay in view at all times, no matter how you scroll through the worksheet. Frozen headings are especially helpful when you work with a table that contains information that extends beyond the rows and columns shown on-screen.

Figure 6-4: The client-list worksheet window split into four panes with the cell pointer in cell C6.

Figure 6-5 shows just such a table. The client-list worksheet contains many more rows than you can see at one time (unless you decrease the magnification to 25% with Zoom, which makes the data too small to read). As a matter of fact, this worksheet continues down to Row 34.

By splitting the document window into two horizontal panes between Rows 2 and 3 and then freezing the top pane, you can keep the column headings in Row 2 that identify each column of information on the screen as you scroll the worksheet up and down to review information on different employees. If you further split the window into vertical panes between Columns B and C, you can keep the case numbers and last names on the screen as you scroll the worksheet left and right.

Figure 6-5 shows the client list after splitting the window into four panes and freezing them. To create and freeze these panes, follow these steps:

1. Position the cell pointer in cell C3.

2. Choose Window⇨Freeze Panes on the menu bar.

In this example, Excel freezes the top and left window pane above Row 3 and left of Column C.

Figure 6-5: Use frozen panes to keep the column headings and last names on the screen at all times.

	Case No	Last Name	First Name	Street	City	State	Zip	Status	Hours	Rat
1				**Little Bo-Peep Pet Detectives - Client List**						
3	101-920	Harvey	Scott	12 Elm Street	Scholar	MN	58764	Active	250	75.0
4	101-014	Andersen	Hans	341 The Shadow	Scholar	MN	58764	Closed	175	75.0
5	103-023	Appleseed	Johnny	6789 Fruitree Tr	Along The Way	SD	66017	Active	321	125.0
6	102-013	Baggins	Bingo	99 Hobbithole	Shire	ME	04047	Active	100	125.0
7	103-007	Baum	L. Frank	447 Toto Too Rd	Oz	KS	65432	Closed	421	125.0
8	104-026	Brown	Charles	59 Flat Plains	Saltewater	UT	84001	Active	575	125.0
9	101-001	Bryant	Michael	326 Chef's Lane	Paris	TX	78705	Active	600	100.0
10	101-028	Cassidy	Butch	Sundance Kidde	Hole In Wall	CO	80477	Closed	345.5	75.0
11	102-006	Cinderella	Poore	8 Lucky Maiden Way	Oxford	TN	07557	Closed	800	75.0
12	103-004	Cupid	Eros	97 Mount Olympus	Greece	CT	03331	Active	123.5	75.0
13	103-022	Dragon	Kai	2 Pleistocene Era	Ann's World	ID	00001	Active	450.2	75.0
14	104-031	Eaters	Big	444 Big Pigs Court	Dogtown	AZ	85257	Closed	780	125.0
15	106-022	Foliage	Red	49 Maple Syrup	Waffle	VT	05452	Active	205	125.0
16	102-020	Franklin	Ben	1789 Constitution	Jefferson	WV	20178	Active	189.5	75.0
17	104-019	Fudde	Elmer	8 Warner Way	Hollywood	CA	33461	Active	463.5	125.0
18	102-002	Gearing	Shane	1 Gunfighter's End	LaLa Land	CA	90069	Active	902.5	125.0
19	102-012	Gondor	Aragorn	2956 Gandalf	Midearth	WY	80342	Closed	157	125.0
20	104-005	Gookin	Polly	4 Feathertop Hill	Hawthorne	MA	01824	Active	169.5	125.0
21	105-008	Harvey	Chauncey	60 Lucky Starr Pl	Shetland	IL	60080	Active	226.5	125.0
22	106-021	Horse	Seabisquit	First Place Finish	Raceway	KY	23986	Active	300	125.0
23	101-015	Humperdinck	Engelbert	6 Hansel+Gretel Tr	Gingerbread	MD	20815	Active	705.5	125.0
24	103-017	Jacken	Jill	Up the Hill	Pail of Water	OK	45678	Closed	200	75.0
25	105-027	Laurel	Stan	2 Oliver Hardy	Celluloyde	NM	82128	Closed	352	125.0

When Excel sets up the frozen panes, the borders of frozen panes are represented by a single line rather than a thin bar, as is the case with unfrozen panes.

Figure 6-6 shows what happens when you scroll the worksheet up after freezing the window panes. In this figure, I scrolled the worksheet up so that Rows 12 through 34 appear under Rows 1 and 2. Because the vertical pane with the worksheet title and column headings is frozen, it remains on-screen. (Normally, Rows 1 and 2 would be the first to disappear as you scroll the worksheet up.)

Figure 6-7 shows what happens when you scroll the worksheet to the left. In this figure, I scrolled the worksheet so that Columns E through L appear after Columns A and B. Because the first two columns are frozen, they remain on-screen, helping you identify who belongs to what information.

To unfreeze the window panes in a worksheet, choose Window⇨Unfreeze Panes. Choosing this command removes the window panes, indicating that Excel has unfrozen them.

	A	B	C	D	E	F	G	H	I	J
1				**Little Bo-Peep Pet Detectives - Client List**						
2	Case No	Last Name	First Name	Street	City	State	Zip	Status	Hours	Rat
12	103-004	Cupid	Eros	97 Mount Olympus	Greece	CT	03331	Active	123.5	75.
13	103-022	Dragon	Kai	2 Pleistocene Era	Ann's World	ID	00001	Active	450.2	75.
14	104-031	Eaters	Big	444 Big Pigs Court	Dogtown	AZ	85257	Closed	780	125.
15	106-022	Foliage	Red	49 Maple Syrup	Waffle	VT	05452	Active	205	125.
16	102-020	Franklin	Ben	1789 Constitution	Jefferson	WV	20178	Active	189.5	75.
17	104-019	Fudde	Elmer	8 Warner Way	Hollywood	CA	33461	Active	463.5	125.
18	102-002	Gearing	Shane	1 Gunfighter's End	LaLa Land	CA	90069	Active	902.5	125.
19	102-012	Gondor	Aragorn	2956 Gandalf	Midearth	WY	80342	Closed	157	125.
20	104-005	Gookin	Polly	4 Feathertop Hill	Hawthorne	MA	01824	Active	169.5	125.
21	105-008	Harvey	Chauncey	60 Lucky Starr Pl	Shetland	IL	60080	Active	226.5	125.
22	106-021	Horse	Seabisquit	First Place Finish	Raceway	KY	23996	Active	300	125.
23	101-015	Humperdinck	Engelbert	6 Hansel+Gretel Tr	Gingerbread	MD	20815	Active	705.5	125.
24	103-017	Jacken	Jill	Up the Hill	Pail of Water	OK	45678	Closed	200	75.
25	105-027	Laurel	Stan	2 Oliver Hardy	Celluloyde	NM	82129	Closed	352	125.
26	101-030	Liberty	Statuesque	31 Gotham Centre	Big Apple	NY	10011	Active	236.5	125.
27	103-016	Oakenshield	Rex	Mines of Goblins	Everest	NJ	07639	Closed	400	125.
28	103-024	Oakley	Anney	Six Shooter Path	Target	ND	66540	Active	502.5	125.
29	101-029	Oow	Lu	888 Sandy Beach	Honolulu	HI	99909	Active	732	125.
30	104-018	Ridinghoode	Crimson	232 Cottage Path	Wulfen	PA	15201	Active	125.5	125.
31	106-009	Sunnybrook	Rebecca	21 Last Week	Portland	OR	97210	Closed	245	75.
32	102-025	Washington	George	8 Founders Diamond	Hamilton	DC	01776	Closed	365.4	100.
33	106-010	White	Snow	552 Magic Mirror Ct	Dwarf Place	WA	98063	Active	762.5	75.
34	102-003	Wolfe	Big Bad	3 West End Blvd	London	AZ	85251	Closed	500	125.

Figure 6-6:
The Bo Peep Client List scrolled up to display the last rows in the database.

| File | Edit | View | Insert | Format | Tools | Data | Window | Help | | Fri 11:43:59 AM | |

C3 = Scott

Bo-Beep Client List

	A	B	E	F	G	H	I	J	K	L	M
1			**Pet Detectives - Client List**								
2	Case No	Last Name	City	State	Zip	Status	Hours	Rate	Total Due	Paid	
12	103-004	Cupid	Greece	CT	03331	Active	123.5	75.00	$9,263	No	
13	103-022	Dragon	Ann's World	ID	00001	Active	450.2	75.00	$33,765	No	
14	104-031	Eaters	Dogtown	AZ	85257	Closed	780	125.00	$97,500	Yes	
15	106-022	Foliage	Waffle	VT	05452	Active	205	125.00	$25,625	Yes	
16	102-020	Franklin	Jefferson	WV	20178	Active	189.5	75.00	$14,213	Yes	
17	104-019	Fudde	Hollywood	CA	33461	Active	463.5	125.00	$57,938	Yes	
18	102-002	Gearing	LaLa Land	CA	90069	Active	902.5	125.00	$112,813	Yes	
19	102-012	Gondor	Midearth	WY	80342	Closed	157	125.00	$19,625	Yes	
20	104-005	Gookin	Hawthorne	MA	01824	Active	169.5	125.00	$21,188	Yes	
21	105-008	Harvey	Shetland	IL	60080	Active	226.5	125.00	$28,313	No	
22	106-021	Horse	Raceway	KY	23996	Active	300	125.00	$37,500	No	
23	101-015	Humperdinck	Gingerbread	MD	20815	Active	705.5	125.00	$88,188	Yes	
24	103-017	Jacken	Pail of Water	OK	45678	Closed	200	75.00	$15,000	No	
25	105-027	Laurel	Celluloyde	NM	82128	Active	352	125.00	$44,000	No	
26	101-030	Liberty	Big Apple	NY	10011	Active	236.5	125.00	$29,563	No	
27	103-016	Oakenshield	Everest	NJ	07639	Closed	400	125.00	$50,000	No	
28	103-024	Oakley	Target	ND	66540	Active	502.5	125.00	$62,813	No	
29	101-029	Oow	Honolulu	HI	99909	Active	732	125.00	$91,500	No	
30	104-018	Ridinghoode	Wulfen	PA	15201	Active	125.5	125.00	$15,688	Yes	
31	106-009	Sunnybrook	Portland	OR	97210	Closed	245	75.00	$18,375	No	
32	102-025	Washington	Hamilton	DC	01776	Closed	365.4	100.00	$36,540	No	
33	106-010	White	Dwarf Place	WA	99063	Active	762.5	75.00	$57,188	Yes	
34	102-003	Wolfe	London	AZ	85251	Closed	500	125.00	$62,500	Yes	

Client List

Ready   NUM

Figure 6-7: The Bo Peep Client List scrolled left to display Columns G through L.

Electronic Sticky Notes

Excel lets you add text comments to particular cells in a worksheet. *Comments* act kind of like electronic pop-up versions of sticky notes. For example, you can add a comment to yourself to verify a particular figure before printing the worksheet or to remind yourself that a particular value is only an estimate (or even to remind yourself that it's your anniversary and to pick up a little something special for your spouse on the way home!).

In addition to using notes to remind yourself of something you've done or that still remains to be done, you can also use a note to mark your current place in a large worksheet. You can then use the note's location to quickly find your starting place the next time you work with that worksheet.

Adding a comment to a cell

To add a comment to a cell, follow these steps:

1. **Select the cell to which you want to add the comment.**

2. **Choose Insert⇨Comment on the menu bar.**

A new text box appears (similar to the one shown in Figure 6-8). This text box contains the name of the user (as it appears in the User name text box on the General tab of the Preferences dialog box) and an insertion point located at the beginning of a new line right below the user name.

3. **Type the text of your comment in the text box.**

4. **When finished entering the comment text, click somewhere outside of the text box.**

   Excel marks the location of a comment in a cell by adding a tiny red triangle in the upper-right corner of the cell. (This triangular note indicator appears in red on a color monitor.)

5. **To display the comment in a cell, position the thick white-cross mouse pointer somewhere in the cell with the note indicator.**

Comments in review

When you have a workbook whose sheets contain a bunch of different comments, you probably don't want to take the time to position the mouse pointer over each of its cells in order to be able to read each comment. For those times, you need to choose View⇨Comments on the menu bar.

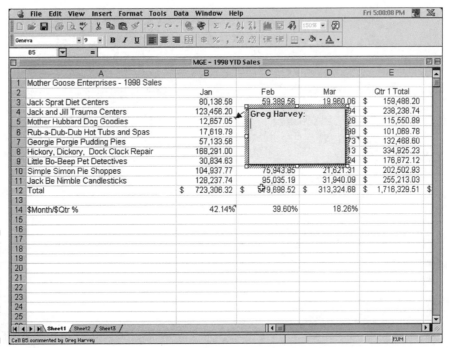

Figure 6-8:
Adding a
comment to
a cell in a
new text
box.

When you choose this command, Excels displays all the comments in the workbook while at the same time displaying the Reviewing toolbar (shown in Figure 6-9).

With the Reviewing toolbar open, you can then move back and forth from comment to comment by clicking the Next Comment and Previous Comment buttons. When you reach the last comment in the workbook, you receive an alert box asking you whether you want to continue reviewing the comments from the beginning (which you can do by simply clicking the OK button). After you finish reviewing the comments in your workbook, you can hide their display by clicking the Hide All Comments button (which does double-duty with the Show All Comments) on the Reviewing toolbar (or by again choosing View⇨Comments on the menu bar, if the Reviewing toolbar is no longer open).

Editing the comments in a worksheet

You have a couple of different methods for editing the contents of a comment, depending upon whether or not the comment is already displayed on the screen. If the comment is displayed in the worksheet, you can edit its contents by clicking the I-beam mouse pointer in its text box. Clicking the I-beam pointer locates the insertion point, while at the same time selecting

Figure 6-9:
The
Reviewing
toolbar.

the comment's text box (indicated by the appearance of a thick cross-hatched line with sizing handles around the text box). After making your editing changes, just click somewhere outside the comment's text box to deselect the comment.

If the comment is not displayed in the worksheet, you need to display the Reviewing toolbar and then select its cell. After the cell pointer is in the cell whose comment needs editing, click the Edit Comment. If the Reviewing toolbar is not displayed and you don't want to take the time to open it, you can edit a cell's comment by choosing the Edit Comment command on the cell's shortcut menu (opened by Control+clicking the cell).

To change the screen position of the comment you're editing, you select the comment by clicking somewhere on it and then position the mouse pointer on one of the edges of its text box. When a four-headed arrow appears at the tip of the mouse pointer, you can drag the text box to a new place in the worksheet. Note that when you release the mouse button, Excel redraws the arrow connecting the comment's text box to the note indicator in the upper-right corner of the cell.

To change the size of a comment's text box, you select the comment and then position the mouse pointer on one of its sizing handles and then drag in the appropriate direction (away from the center of the box to increase its size or toward the center to decrease its size). When you release the mouse button, Excel redraws the comment's text box with the new shape and size.

To change the font of the comment text, you need to Control+click the comment and then choose Format⇨Comment on the comment text box's shortcut menu or, with the comment's text box selected, simply press ⌘+1 like you do to open the Format Cells dialog box. Excel opens the Format Comment dialog box that contains a lone Font tab (with the same options as the Font tab of the Format Cells dialog box shown in Figure 3-16). You can then use the options on the Font tab to change the font, font style, font size, or color of the text displayed in the selected comment.

To delete a comment, you need to select its cell in the worksheet and then choose Edit⇨Clear⇨Comments on the menu bar or choose Delete Comment on the cell's shortcut menu. Excel removes the comment along with the note indicator from the selected cell.

Note that you can change the background color of a comment's text box or select a new shape or shading for the text box by using the buttons on the Drawing toolbar. For information on how to identify and use its buttons, see "Telling all with a text box" in Chapter 8.

Getting your comments in print

When printing a worksheet, you can print the comments along with the selected worksheet data by selecting either the At end of sheet or As displayed on sheet option from the Comments pop-up list box located on the Sheet tab of the Page Setup dialog box. (Refer to "Sorting out the sheet settings" in Chapter 5 for details on choosing between the At end of sheet and As displayed on sheet settings.)

The Cell Name Game

By assigning descriptive names to cells and cell ranges, you can go a long way toward keeping on top of the location of important information in a worksheet. Rather than trying to associate random cell coordinates with specific information, you just have to remember a name. And, best of all, after you name a cell or cell range, you can use this name with the Go To feature.

If I only had a name . . .

When assigning range names to a cell or cell range, you need to follow a few guidelines:

✔ Range names must begin with a letter of the alphabet, not a number. For example, instead of *98Profit,* use *Profit98.*

✔ Range names cannot contain spaces. Instead of a space, use the underscore (Shift+hyphen) to tie the parts of the name together. For example, instead of *Profit 98,* use *Profit_98.*

✔ Range names cannot correspond to cell coordinates in the worksheet. For example, you can't name a cell *Q1* because this is a valid cell coordinate. Instead, use something like *Q1_sales.*

To name a cell or cell range in a worksheet:

1. **Select the cell or cell range that you want to name.**

2. **Click the cell address in the Name Box on the formula bar.**

   Excel selects the cell address in the Name Box.

3. **Type the name for the selected cell or cell range in the Name Box.**

   When typing the range name, you must follow Excel's naming conventions: Refer to the bulleted list of cell-name do's and don'ts, earlier in this section for details.

4. **Press the Return key.**

To select a named cell or range in a worksheet, click the range name on the Name Box pop-up menu. To open this pop-up menu, click the pop-up button that appears to the right of the cell address on the formula bar.

Note that you can also accomplish the same thing by pressing F5 or choosing Edit⇨Go To on the menu bar. The Go To dialog box appears (see Figure 6-10). Double-click the desired range name in the Go to list box. (Alternatively, select the name and click OK or press Return.) Excel moves the cell pointer directly to the named cell. If you selected a cell range, all the cells in that range are selected.

Name that formula!

Cell names are not only a great way to identify and find cells and cell ranges in your spreadsheet but also a great way to make out the purpose of your formulas. For example, say that you have a simple formula in cell K3 that calculates the total due by multiplying the hours you worked for the client (in cell I3) by the client's hourly rate (in cell J3). Normally, this formula would be entered in cell K3 as

```
=I3*J3
```

Figure 6-10:
Selecting
a cell by
choosing its
range name
in the Go To
dialog box.

However, if you assign the name Hours to cell I3 and the name Rate to cell J3, you can then enter the formula as

```
=Hours*Rate
```

in cell K3. I don't think anyone would dispute that the formula =Hours*Rate is much easier to understand than =I3*J3.

To enter a formula using cell names rather than cell references, follow these steps (see Chapter 2 if you need to brush up on how to create formulas):

1. **Name your cells as described earlier in this section.**

   For this example, give the name Hours to cell I3 and the name Rate to cell J3.

2. **Place the cell pointer in the cell where the formula is to appear.**

   For this example, put the cell pointer in cell K3.

3. **Type = (equal sign) to start the formula.**

4. **Choose Insert⇨Name⇨Paste on the menu bar, and then in the Paste Name dialog box, double-click the name of the cell or cell range you want to insert into the formula.**

   For this example, you select cell I3 by double-clicking its cell name, Hours, in the list box of the Paste Name dialog box.

5. **Type the arithmetic operator used in the formula.**

   For this example, you type * (asterisk) for multiplication. (Refer to Chapter 2 for a list of the other arithmetic operators.)

6. **Choose Insert⇨Name⇨Paste on the menu bar again, this time then double-clicking the name of the next cell or cell range to be inserted into the formula.**

   For this example, you select cell J3 by double-clicking its cell name, Rate, in the Paste Name dialog box.

7. **Click the Enter box or press Return to complete the formula.**

   In this example, Excel enters the formula =Hours*Rate in cell K3.

The only problem with creating an original formula from cell range names is that you can't use the fill handle to copy the formula to blank cells where the same calculation is performed on a slightly different set of cells. (See "Formulas on AutoFill" in Chapter 4.) This is because the names given to cells and cell ranges function like absolute cell addresses in a formula so that instead of adjusting each copy to the cell references in a new row or column, Excel makes an exact duplicate of the original copy. See the next section, "Naming formulas with data table headings" for a way around this problem.

Naming formulas with data table headings

In Excel 98, when working with a traditional data table that contains row and columns headings (like the one shown in Figure 6-11), you can use the table's row and column headings in place of cell addresses to identify the cells used in your formulas. This feature not only eliminates the need for assigning range names to the cells but also ensures that these row- and column-heading labels appear in the copies you make of the original formula!

Figures 6-11 and 6-12 illustrate how easily you can create a descriptive formula using the row and column headings from the data table and then copy that formula (and its use of the row and column headings) to other cells in the table. Figure 6-11 shows a simple data table that computes the sales price for a number of pies sold by the Georgie Porgie Pudding Pies company. The first column of the table contains the row headings that identify each type of pie that is to be put on sale. The second column contains the retail prices for each type of pie, and the third column contains discount percentages. The fourth column of this data table contains the sale price of each type of pie. To compute the sales price of each type of pie, you need to create a formula that subtracts the discount amount (calculated by multiplying the retail price of the pie by the discount percentage) from the retail price.

Figure 6-11: Creating a formula that uses the row and column headings in the data table.

To create the first sale price formula in cell D5 using the row and column headings, I had to type in the entire formula. (There's no way you can point to the labels in the data table — you only succeed in selecting cell addresses.) In place of the address of the cell containing the retail price value (cell B5 in this example) and the cell with the discount percentage (C5), I entered the column heading followed by the row heading for each cell, as in:

```
=Retail Price Blackberry Pie--(Retail Price Blackberry
Pie*Discount Blackberry Pie)
```

Note that in using the row and column names in place of the cell address, I could have just as well preceded the column heading for each cell with the row, as in:

```
=Blackberry Pie Retail Price--(Blackberry Pie Retail
Price*Blackberry Pie Discount)
```

Figure 6-12 shows the data table after copying this original formula for calculating the sales price in cell D5 down to the cell range D6:D8 and then selecting cell D6. Note the contents of the formula copied to cell D6:

```
=Retail Price Cherry Pie--(Retail Price Cherry Pie*Discount
Cherry Pie)
```

Figure 6-12: Copying the formula that uses the row and column headings in the data table.

When you create a formula using the row and column headings in a data table, these row and column headings are copied and automatically adjusted to suit the cells actually used in the new formula. So there you have it: an easy method for creating descriptive formulas (both in the original and its copies) without having to go to the trouble of "formally" naming the cells!

"Seek and Ye Shall Find . . ."

When all else fails, you can use Excel's Find feature to locate specific information in the worksheet. When you choose Edit⇨Find on the menu bar, or press ⌘+F or Shift+F5, Excel opens the Find dialog box (see Figure 6-13). In the Find what text box, enter the text or values you want to locate and then click the Find Next button or press Return to start the search.

When you search for a text entry with the Find feature, be mindful of whether the text or number you enter in the Find what text box is separate in its cell or occurs as part of another word or value. For example, if the characters "ca" are in the Find what text box and the Find entire cells only check box is not selected, Excel finds the following:

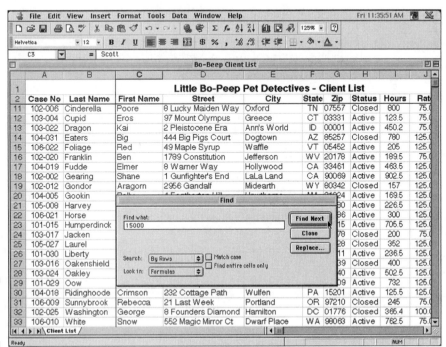

Figure 6-13: The Find dialog box.

   ✔ The field name *Ca* in *Case No* cell A2

   ✔ The state code *CA* (for California) in cells F17 and F18.

   ✔ The *ca* that occurs in *Rebecca* in cell C31

If you checked the Find entire cells only check box in the Find dialog box before starting the search, Excel does not consider the *Ca* in *Case No* or the *ca* in *Rebecca* to be a match because both of these cases have other text surrounding the text you are searching for.

When you search for text, you can also specify whether or not you want Excel to match the case you use (upper- or lowercase) when entering the search text in the Find what text box. By default, Excel ignores case differences between text in cells of your worksheet and the search text you enter in the Find what text box. To conduct a case-sensitive search, you need to select the Match case check box.

When you search for values in the worksheet, be mindful of the difference between formulas and values. For example, cell K24 of the Bo Peep Client List (refer to Figure 6-7) contains the value $15,000. However, if you type **15000** in the Find what text box and press Return to search for this value, Excel displays an alert box with the following message

```
Cannot find matching data
```

instead of finding the value 15000 in cell K24. Excel does this because the value in this cell is calculated by the following formula

```
=I24*J24
```

and nowhere in that formula does the value 15000 show up. To get Excel to find the 15000s displayed in the cells of the worksheet, you need to choose Values in the Look in pop-up menu of the Find dialog box in place of the normally used Formulas option.

If you want to restrict the search to just the text or values in the text of the comments in the worksheet, you need to select the Comments option in this pop-up menu.

If you don't know the exact spelling of the word or name, or the precise value or formula you're searching for, you can use *wildcards,* which are symbols that stand for missing or unknown text. Use the question mark (?) to stand for a single unknown character; use the asterisk (*) to stand for any number of missing characters. Suppose that you enter the following in the

Find what text box and select the Values option in the Look in pop-up menu:

```
7*4
```

Excel stops at cells that contain the values *74, 704,* and *7,5234,* and even finds the text entry *782 4th Street.*

If you actually want to search for an asterisk in the worksheet rather than use the asterisk as a wildcard, precede it with a tilde (~), as follows:

```
~*4
```

This arrangement enables you to search the formulas in the worksheet for one that multiplies by the number 4. (Remember that Excel uses the asterisk as the multiplication sign.)

The following entry in the Find what text box finds cells that contain *Jan, January, June, Janet,* and so on.

```
J?n
```

Normally, Excel searches only the current worksheet for the search text. You you must select all the worksheets prior to entering the search text in the Find dialog box and starting the search. To select all the worksheets in a workbook, Control+click one of the tabs at the bottom of the document window and choose the Select All Sheets command on the shortcut menu that appears. (See Chapter 7 for more on working with more than one worksheet in a workbook.)

When Excel locates a cell in the worksheet that contains the text or values you're searching for, it selects that cell while at the same time leaving the Find dialog box open (remember that you can move the Find dialog box if it obscures your view of the cell). To search for the next occurrence of the text or value, click the Find Next button. (The simplest way to do this is by pressing Return.)

Excel normally searches down the worksheet by rows. To search across the columns first, select the By Columns option in the Search pop-up menu. To reverse the search direction and revisit previous occurrences of matching cell entries, press the Shift key as you click the Find Next button in the Find dialog box.

You Can Be Replaced!

If your purpose for finding a cell with a particular entry is so that you can change it, you can automate this process by choosing Edit⇨Replace instead of Edit⇨Find on the menu bar (⌘+H). After entering the text or value you want to replace in the Find what text box, enter the text or value you want to enter as the replacement in the Replace with text box.

When you enter replacement text, enter it exactly as you want it to appear in the cell. In other words, if you replace all occurrences of *Jan* in the worksheet with *January,* enter the following in the Replace with text box:

```
January
```

Make sure that you use the capital J in the Replace with text box, even though you can enter the following in the Find what text box (providing you don't check the Match Case check box):

```
jan
```

After specifying what to replace and what to replace it with, you can have Excel replace occurrences in the worksheet on a case-by-case basis or globally. To replace all occurrences in a single operation, click the Replace All button.

Be careful with global search-and-replace operations; they can really mess up a worksheet in a hurry if you inadvertently replace values, parts of formulas, or characters in titles and headings that you hadn't intended to change. With this in mind, always follow one rule:

Never undertake a global search-and-replace operation on an unsaved worksheet.

Also, verify whether or not the Find entire cells only check box is selected before you begin. You can end up with a lot of unwanted replacements if you leave this check box unselected when you really want to replace only entire cell entries (rather than matching parts in cell entries).

If you do make a mess, choose the Edit⇨Undo Replace command (⌘+Z) to restore the worksheet.

To see each occurrence before you replace it, click the Find Next button or press Return. Excel selects the next cell with the text or value you entered in the Find what text box. To have the program replace the selected text, click the Replace button. To skip this occurrence, click the Find Next button to continue the search. When you finish replacing occurrences, click the Close button to close the Replace dialog box.

You Can Be So Calculating

Locating information in a worksheet — although admittedly extremely important — is only a part of the story of keeping on top of the information in a worksheet. In really large workbooks that contain many completed worksheets, you may want to switch to manual recalculation so that you can control when the formulas in the worksheet are calculated. You need this kind of control when you find that Excel's recalculation of formulas each time you enter or change information in cells slows the program's response to a crawl. By holding off recalculations until you're ready to save or print the workbook, you find that you can work with Excel's worksheets without interminable delays.

To put the workbook on manual recalculation, choose Tools⇨Preferences on the menu bar and select the Calculation tab. Then select the Manual radio button in the Calculation area. When doing this, you probably don't want to remove the check mark from the Recalculate before save check box (not generally a very smart idea) so that Excel still automatically recalculates all formulas before saving the workbook. By keeping this setting active, you are assured of saving only the most up-to-date values.

After switching to manual recalculation, Excel displays the message

```
Calculate
```

on the status bar whenever you make a change to the worksheet that somehow affects the current values of its formulas. Whenever you see Calculate on the status bar, this is the signal that you need to bring the formulas up-to-date before saving the workbook (as you would before printing its worksheets).

To recalculate the formulas in a workbook when calculation is on manual, press ⌘+= (equal sign) or click the Calc Now (Cmd+=) button in the Calculation tab of the Preferences dialog box.

Excel then recalculates the formulas in all the worksheets in your workbook. If you've only made changes to the current worksheet and don't want to wait around for Excel to recalculate every other worksheet in the workbook, you can restrict the recalculation to the current worksheet by clicking the Calc Sheet button on the Calculation tab of the Preferences dialog box.

Putting On the Protection

After you've more or less finalized a worksheet by checking out its formulas and proofing its text, you often want to guard against any unplanned changes by protecting the document.

Each cell in the worksheet can be *locked* or *unlocked*. By default, Excel locks all the cells in a worksheet so that, when you follow these steps, Excel locks the whole thing up tighter than a drum.

1. **Choose Tools⇨Protection⇨Protect Sheet on the menu bar.**

   Excel opens the Protect Sheet dialog box where the Contents, Objects, and Scenarios check boxes are all selected.

2. **If you want to assign a password that must be supplied before you can remove the protection from the worksheet, type the password in the Password (optional) text box.**

3. **Click OK or press Return.**

   If you type a password in the Password (optional) text box, Excel opens the Confirm Password dialog box. Reenter the password in the Reenter password to proceed text box exactly as you typed it into the Password (optional) text box in the Protect Sheet dialog box and click OK or press Return.

If you want to go a step further and protect the layout of the worksheets in the workbook, you protect the entire workbook as follows:

1. **Choose Tools⇨Protection⇨Protect Workbook on the menu bar.**

   Excel opens the Protect Workbook dialog box where the Structure check box is selected and the Windows check box is not selected. With the Structure check box selected, Excel won't let you mess around with the sheets in the workbook (by deleting them or rearranging them). If you want to protect any windows that you've set up (as described at the beginning of this chapter), you need to select the Windows check box as well.

2. **If you want to assign a password that must be supplied before you can remove the protection from the worksheet, type the password in the Password (optional) text box.**

3. **Click OK or press Return.**

   If you type a password in the Password (optional) text box, Excel opens the Confirm Password dialog box. Reenter the password in the Reenter password to proceed text box exactly as you typed it into the Password (optional) text box in the Protect Sheet dialog box and click OK or press Return.

If you're using Excel 98 on a network, you can use the Tools⇨Protection⇨ Protect and Share Workbook to protect a workbook that many users have access so that none of them can disable the Track Changes feature (which gives you an audit trail of who made what change). When you use this command, you select the Sharing with track changes check box and then enter a password in the Password (optional) text box. (In this case, the password is not really optional as you need a way to prevent unauthorized co-workers from turning off the track changes feature.)

Selecting the Protect Sheet command makes it impossible to make further changes to the contents of any of the locked cells in that worksheet. Select- ing the Protect Workbook command makes it impossible to make further changes to the layout of the worksheets in that workbook.

Excel displays an alert dialog box with the following message when you try to edit or replace an entry in a locked cell:

```
The cell or chart you are trying to change is protected and
therefore read-only
```

Usually, your intention in protecting a worksheet or an entire workbook is not to prevent *all* changes but to prevent changes in certain areas of the worksheet. For example, in a budget worksheet, you may want to protect all the cells that contain headings and formulas but allow changes in all the cells where you enter the budgeted amounts. That way, you can't inadvert- ently wipe out a title or formula in the worksheet simply by entering a value in the wrong column or row (not an uncommon occurrence).

To leave certain cells unlocked so that you can still change them after protecting the worksheet or workbook, follow these steps:

1. **Select the cells you still want to be able to change after turning on the worksheet or workbook protection.**

2. **Open the Format Cells dialog box by choosing Format⇨Cells on the menu bar (⌘+1); then select the Protection tab.**

3. **Remove the check mark from the Locked check box in the Protection tab of the Format Cells dialog box; then click OK or press Return.**

4. **Turn on protection in the worksheet by choosing Tools⇨Protection⇨ Protect Sheet on the menu bar and then click OK or press Return in the Protect Sheet dialog box.**

You can advance from one unlocked cell to the next in a protected worksheet by pressing the Tab key. To advance to the previous unlocked cell, you press Shift+Tab. By using the Tab key, you can speed through the data entry in a worksheet form where many, if not most, of the cells are protected and therefore strictly off-limits.

To remove protection from the current worksheet or workbook document so that you can once again make changes to its cells (be they locked or unlocked), choose Tools⇨Protection and then choose either the Unprotect Sheet or the Unprotect Workbook command on the submenu. If you assigned a password when protecting the worksheet or workbook, you must then reproduce the password exactly as you assigned it (including any case differences) in the Password text box of the Unprotect Sheet or Unprotect Workbook dialog box.

Be very careful with passwords. If you forget the password for a worksheet, you cannot ever again change any locked cells, and you cannot unlock any more cells in the worksheet. If you forget the password for a workbook, you can make no further changes to the layout of its worksheets.

Chapter 7

Maintaining Multiple Worksheets

· ·

In This Chapter

▶ Moving from sheet to sheet in your workbook

▶ Adding more sheets to a workbook

▶ Deleting sheets from a workbook

▶ Selecting a bunch of sheets for editing as a group

▶ Naming sheet tabs something else besides Sheet1, Sheet2, and so on

▶ Putting the sheets in a different order in a workbook

▶ Displaying parts of different sheets on the same screen

▶ Copying or moving sheets from one workbook to another

▶ Creating formulas that refer to values on different worksheets in a workbook

· ·

*W*hen you're brand-new to spreadsheets, you have enough trouble keeping track of a single worksheet — let alone three worksheets — and the very thought of working with more than one is a little more than you can take. However, as soon as you get a little experience under your belt, you find that working with more than one worksheet in a workbook is no more taxing than working with just a single worksheet.

Don't confuse the term *workbook* with *worksheet.* The workbook forms the document (file) that you open and save as you work. Each workbook (file) normally contains three blank worksheets. These worksheets are like the loose-leaf pages in a notebook binder from which you can delete or to which you can add as you need. To help you keep track of the worksheets in your workbook and navigate between them, Excel provides sheet tabs (Sheet1 through Sheet3) that are kinda like tab dividers in a loose-leaf notebook.

Juggling Worksheets

You need to see *how* to work with more than one worksheet in a workbook, but it's also important to know *why* you'd want to do such a crazy thing in the first place. The most common situation is, of course, when you have a bunch of worksheets that are somehow related to each other and, therefore, naturally belong together in the same workbook. For example, take the case of Mother Goose Enterprises with its different companies: Jack Sprat Diet Centers, Jack and Jill Trauma Centers, Mother Hubbard Dog Goodies, Rub-a-Dub-Dub Hot Tubs and Spas, Georgie Porgie Pudding Pies, Hickory, Dickory, Dock Clock Repair, Little Bo Peep Pet Detectives, Simple Simon Pie Shoppes, and Jack Be Nimble Candlesticks. To keep track of the annual sales for all these companies, you can create a workbook containing a worksheet for each of the nine different companies.

By keeping the sales figures for each company in a different sheet of the same workbook, you gain all the following benefits:

- You can enter the stuff that's needed in all the sales worksheets (if their sheet tabs are selected) just by typing it once into the first worksheet. (See "Editing en masse," later in this chapter.)

- In order to help you build the worksheet for the first company's sales, you can attach *macros* to the current workbook so that they are readily available when you create the worksheets for the other companies. (See Chapter 12 for details on creating macros that record your actions in the current workbook.)

- You can quickly compare the sales of one company to the sales of another. (See "Opening Windows on Your Worksheets," later in this chapter.)

- You can print all the sales information for each store as a single report in one printing operation. (Refer to Chapter 5 for specifics on printing an entire workbook or particular worksheets in a workbook.)

- You can easily create charts that compare certain sales data from different worksheets. (See Chapter 8 for details.)

- You can easily set up a summary worksheet with formulas that total the quarterly and annual sales for all nine companies. (See "To Sum Up . . ." later in this chapter.)

- You can add hyperlinks to the worksheet that you can click to go from one worksheet to the next or immediately to a summary worksheet. (See Chapter 10 for details.)

Sliding between the sheets

Each workbook that you create contains three worksheets, rather predictably named Sheet1 through Sheet3. In typical Excel fashion, these names appear on tabs at the bottom of the workbook window. To go from one worksheet to another, you simply click the tab that contains the name of the sheet you want to see. Excel then brings that worksheet to the top of the stack, displaying its information in the current workbook window. You can always tell which worksheet is current because its name is displayed in bold type on the tab and its tab appears without any dividing line as an extension of the current worksheet.

The only problem with moving to a new sheet by clicking its sheet tab occurs when you add so many worksheets to a workbook (as described later in this chapter in the section called "Don't Short-Sheet Me!") that not all the sheet tabs are visible at any one time and the sheet tab you want to click is not visible in the workbook. To deal with this problem, Excel provides tab scrolling buttons (see Figure 7-1) that you can use to bring new sheet tabs into view.

🖝 Click the tab scroll button with the triangle pointing right to bring the next unseen tab of the sheet on the right into view.

🖝 Click the tab scroll button with the triangle pointing left to bring the next unseen tab of the sheet on the left into view.

Figure 7-1: Using the sheet tab scrolling buttons to bring new sheet tabs into view.

Active Sheet Tab
Ready Tab Scrolling Buttons

✔ Click the tab scroll button with the triangle pointing right to the vertical bar to bring the last group of sheet tabs, including the very last tab, into view.

✔ Click the tab scroll button with the triangle pointing left to the vertical bar to bring the first group of sheet tabs, including the very first tab, into view.

Just don't forget that scrolling the sheet tab you want into view is not the same thing as *selecting* it: You still need to select the tab for the desired sheet to bring it to the front of the stack.

To make it easier to find the sheet tab you want to select without having to do an inordinate amount of tab scrolling, you can drag the tab split bar (see Figure 7-2) to the right to reveal more sheet tabs (consequently making the horizontal scroll bar shorter). If you don't care at all about using the horizontal scroll bar, you can maximize the number of sheet tabs in view by actually getting rid of this scroll bar. To do this, you drag the tab split bar to the right until it's right up against the vertical split bar, which gives you a view of about 12 sheet tabs at a time (on a standard 14-inch monitor in a resolution of 640 by 480 pixels).

Figure 7-2:
Using the
tab split bar
to display
more sheet
tabs by
making the
horizontal
scroll bar
shorter.

	A	B	C	D	E	F	G	H	I	J	K	L
1	Mother Goose Enterprises - Projected Income 1999											
2												
3	Revenues	6,681,450.78										
4	Costs and Revenues											
5	Equipment	882,387.00										
6	Rent	1,287,923.88										
7	Personnel	346,452.79										
8	Maintenance	618,404.88										
9	Marketing and Sales	892,958.06										
10	General and Adminstrative	219,925.60										
11	Total Costs and Expenses	4,245,950.21										
12												
13	Operating Income (loss)	2,435,500.57										
14												
15	Other Income											
16	Interest Income	218,430.60										
17	Other	103,769.00										
18	Total Other Income (expenses)	322,199.60										
19												
20	Income (loss) before Taxes	2,757,700.17										
21	Provision for Taxes	689,425.04										
22	Net Earnings (loss)	2,068,275.13										

Total Income / Sprat Diet Ctr / J&J Trauma Ctr / Hubbard Dog Goodies / R-D-D Hot Tubs / Porgie Puddi

Tab Split Bar

Going sheet to sheet via the keyboard

You can forget all about the darned tab scrolling buttons and sheet tabs and just go back and forth through the sheets in a workbook with the keyboard. To move to the next worksheet in a workbook, press ⌘+PgDn. To move to the previous worksheet in a workbook, press ⌘+PgUp. The nice thing about ⌘+PgDn and ⌘+PgUp is that these keystroke shortcuts work whether or not the next or previous sheet tab is currently displayed in the workbook window!

When you decide that you then want to restore the horizontal scroll bar to its normal length, you can either manually drag the tab split bar to the left or simply double-click it.

Editing en masse

Each time you click a sheet tab, you select that worksheet and make it active, enabling you to make whatever changes are necessary to its cells. There are times, however, when you want to select bunches of worksheets so that you can make the same editing changes to all of them simultaneously. When multiple worksheets are selected, any editing change you make to the current worksheet, such as entering information in cells or deleting stuff from them, affects the same cells in all the selected sheets in exactly the same way.

In other words, say you need to set up three worksheets in a new workbook, all of which contain the names of the 12 months in Row 3 starting in Column B. Prior to entering January in cell B3 and then using the AutoFill handle to fill in the rest of the 11 months across Row 3, you would select all three worksheets (say Sheet1, Sheet2, and Sheet3 for argument's sake). That way, Excel inserts the names of the 12 months in Row 3 of all three selected worksheets just by your entering them once in the third row of the first sheet (pretty slick, huh?).

Likewise, say you have another workbook where you need to get rid of Sheet2 and Sheet3. Instead of selecting Sheet2, choosing Edit⇨Delete Sheet, and then selecting Sheet3 and repeating the Edit⇨Delete Sheet command, you can select both worksheets and then zap them out of existence in one fell swoop by choosing the Edit⇨Delete Sheet command.

To select a bunch of worksheets in a workbook, you have the following choices:

- ✔ To select a group of neighboring worksheets, click the first sheet tab and then scroll the sheet tabs until you see the tab of the last worksheet you want to select. Hold the Shift key as you click the last sheet tab to select all the tabs in between — the old shift-click method applied to worksheet tabs.

- ✔ To select a group of non-neighboring worksheets, click the first sheet tab and then hold down the ⌘ key as you click the tabs of the other sheets to be selected.

Excel shows you which worksheets are selected by turning their sheet tabs white (although only the active sheet's tab name appears in bold) and displaying [Group] after the filename of the workbook on the Excel window's title bar.

To deselect the group of worksheets when you finish your "group editing," you simply click a nonselected (that is, gray) worksheet tab. You can also deselect all the selected worksheets by Shift+clicking the active sheet or by choosing the Ungroup Sheets command on any tab's shortcut menu (opened by Control+clicking the sheet tab).

Don't Short-Sheet Me!

For some of you, the three worksheets automatically put into each new workbook that you start are as many as you will ever, ever need (or want) to use. For others of you, a measly three worksheets may seldom, if ever, be sufficient for the workbooks you create. (For instance, say your company operates in ten locations, or you routinely create budgets for 20 different departments or track expenses for 40 account representatives.)

Excel makes it easy to insert additional worksheets in a workbook or remove those that you don't need. To insert a new worksheet in the workbook, follow these steps:

1. **Select the tab of the sheet where you want Excel to insert the new worksheet.**

2. **Choose Insert⇨Worksheet on the menu bar or choose Insert on the sheet tab's shortcut menu.**

   If you choose the Insert⇨Worksheet command, Excel inserts a new worksheet and gives its tab the next available number (like Sheet4). If you choose the Insert command on the sheet tab's shortcut menu,

Excel opens the Insert dialog box where you can specify the type of sheet to insert (such as Worksheet, Chart, MS Excel 4.0 Macro, or MS Excel 5.0 dialog) on the General tab before you click OK and proceed to Step 3.

3. **Make sure that the Worksheet icon on the General tab of the Insert dialog box is selected and then click OK or press Return.**

To insert a bunch of new worksheets in a row in the workbook, select a group with the same number of tabs as the number of new worksheets you want to add, starting with the tab where you want to insert the new worksheets. Next, choose Insert⇨Worksheet on the menu bar or choose Insert on the tab's shortcut menu and Worksheet on the General tab. Then click OK in the Insert dialog box or press Return.

To delete a worksheet from the workbook, follow these steps:

1. **Select the tab of the worksheet you want to delete.**

2. **Choose Edit⇨Delete Sheet on the menu bar or choose Delete on the tab's shortcut menu.**

   Excel then displays a scary message in an alert box about how you're going to permanently delete the selected sheets.

3. **Go ahead and click the OK button or press Return if you're really sure that you want to zap the entire sheet.**

   Just keep in mind that this is one of those situations where Undo is powerless to put things right by restoring the deleted sheet to the workbook.

To delete a bunch of worksheets from the workbook, select all the worksheets you want to delete and choose Edit⇨Delete Sheet on the menu bar or choose Delete on the tab's shortcut menu. Then, if you're sure that you won't miss any of the worksheets, click OK or press Return when the alert dialog box appears.

If you find that you're constantly having to monkey around with the number of worksheets in a workbook, either by adding new worksheets or deleting a bunch, you may want to think about changing the default number of worksheets in a workbook. To change the magic number of three sheets to a more realistic number for your needs, choose Tools⇨Preferences to open the Preferences dialog box, select the General tab, and enter a new number in the Sheets in new workbook text box or select a new number with the spinner buttons before you click OK.

A sheet by any other name . . .

Let's be honest: The sheet names that Excel comes up with for the tabs in a workbook (Sheet1 through Sheet3) are, to put it mildly, not very original — and are certainly not descriptive of their function in life! Luckily, you can easily rename a worksheet tab to whatever helps you remember what you put on the worksheet (provided that this descriptive name is no longer than 31 characters).

To rename a worksheet tab, just follow these steps:

1. **Control+click the sheet tab and then choose the Rename command on the sheet tab's shortcut menu.**

   This selects the current name on the sheet tab.

2. **Replace the current name on the sheet tab by typing in the new sheet name.**

3. **Press Return.**

   Excel displays the new sheet name on its tab at the bottom of the workbook window.

Getting your sheets in order

Sometimes, you may find that you need to change the order in which the sheets appear in the workbook. Excel makes this possible by letting you drag the tab of the sheet you want to arrange in the workbook to the place where it should be inserted. As you drag the tab, the pointer changes to a sheet icon with an arrowhead on it, and the program marks your progress among the sheet tabs (see Figures 7-3 and 7-4 for an example). When you release the mouse button, Excel reorders the worksheets in the workbook by inserting the sheet at the place where you dropped the tab off.

If you hold down the Option key as you drag the tab, Excel inserts a *copy* of the worksheet at the place where you release the mouse button. You can tell that Excel is copying the sheet, rather than just moving it in the workbook, because the pointer shows a plus on the sheet icon containing the arrowhead. When you release the mouse button, Excel inserts the copy in the workbook, which is designated by the addition of (2) after the tab name. For instance, if you copy Sheet3 to another place in the workbook, the sheet tab of the copy is named Sheet3 (2). You can then rename the tab to something civilized. (See "A sheet by any other name . . ." earlier in this chapter for details.)

Figure 7-3:
Reordering
the sheets
in the
MGE-1999
Projected
Income
workbook
by dragging
the Total
Income
sheet tab to
the front.

Figure 7-4:
The
worksheet
after
moving the
Total
Income
sheet to the
front of the
workbook.

Short and sweet (sheet names)

Although Excel allows up to 31 characters (including spaces) for a sheet name, you're gonna want to keep your sheet names much briefer for two reasons:

✔ First, the longer the name, the longer the sheet tab. And the longer the sheet tab, the fewer tabs that can be displayed. And the fewer the tabs, the more tab scrolling you have to do to select the sheets you want to work with.

✔ Second, should you start creating formulas that use cells in different worksheets (see "To Sum Up. . .," later in this chapter,

for an example of this), Excel uses the sheet name as part of the cell reference in the formula. (How else can Excel keep straight the value in cell C1 on Sheet1 from the value in cell C1 on Sheet2?) Therefore, if your sheet names are long, you end up with unwieldy formulas in the cells and on the formula bar even when you're dealing with simple formulas that only refer to cells in a couple of different worksheets.

So remember: As a general rule, the fewer characters in a sheet name, the better.

Opening Windows on Your Worksheets

Just as you can split up a single worksheet into window panes so that you can view and compare different parts of that same sheet on the screen (see Chapter 6), you can split up a single workbook into worksheet windows and then arrange the windows so that you can view different parts of each worksheet on the screen.

To open up the worksheets that you want to compare in different windows, you simply insert new workbook windows (in addition to the one that Excel automatically opens when you open the workbook file itself) and then select the worksheet that you want displayed in the new window. You can accomplish this with the following steps:

1. **Choose Window➪New Window on the menu bar to create a second worksheet window; then select the tab of the worksheet that you want displayed in this second window (indicated by the :2 added to the end of the filename in the title bar).**

2. **Choose the Window➪New Window command again to create a third worksheet window; then select the tab of the worksheet that you want displayed in this third window (indicated by the :3 added to the end of the filename in the title bar).**

3. **Continue in this manner, using the Window⇨New Window command to create a new window and then selecting the tab of the worksheet to be displayed in that window for each worksheet that you want to compare.**

4. **Choose the Window⇨Arrange command and select one of the Arrange options (as described next); then click OK or press Return.**

When you open the Arrange Windows dialog box, Excel presents you with the following options:

- ✔ **The Tiled radio button:** To have Excel arrange and size the windows so that they all fit side by side on the screen in the order in which they were opened.

- ✔ **The Horizontal radio button:** To have Excel size the windows equally and then place them one above the other.

- ✔ **The Vertical radio button:** To have Excel size the windows equally and then place them next to each other.

- ✔ **The Cascade radio button:** To have Excel arrange and size the windows so that they overlap one another with only their title bars showing.

- ✔ **The Windows of active workbook check box:** To have Excel show only the windows that you've opened in the current workbook. (Otherwise, the program also displays all the windows in any other workbooks you have open — yes, it is possible to open more than one workbook as well as more than one window within each open workbook, provided that your computer has enough memory and you have enough stamina to keep track of all that information.)

After you place the windows in one arrangement or another, you can activate the one you want to use (if it's not already selected) by clicking it. (In the case of the cascade arrangement, you need to click the window's title bar.)

When you select a worksheet window that has been tiled or placed in the horizontal or vertical arrangement, Excel indicates that the window is selected by highlighting its title bar and adding scroll bars to the window. When you click the title bar of a worksheet window that has been placed in the cascade arrangement, the program displays the window on the top of the stack as well as highlighting its title bar and adding scroll bars.

You can temporarily zoom the window up to full size by clicking the Zoom button on the window's title bar (the button the second from the right). When you finish the work you need to do in the full-size worksheet window, return it to its previous arrangement by clicking the Zoom button again.

To select the next tiled, horizontal, or vertical window on the screen or display the next window in a cascade arrangement with the keyboard, press ⌘+F6. To select the previous tiled, horizontal, or vertical window or display the previous window in a cascade arrangement, press ⌘+Shift+F6. Note that these keystrokes work to select the next and previous worksheet window even when the windows are maximized in the Excel program window.

If you close one of the windows you've arranged by its Close button (the one in the upper-left corner) or by pressing ⌘+W, Excel does not automatically resize the other open windows to fill in the gap. Likewise, if you create another window with the Window⇨New Window command, Excel does not automatically arrange it in with the others. (In fact, the new window just sits on top of the other open windows.)

To fill in the gap created by closing a window or to integrate a newly opened window into the current arrangement, open the Arrange Windows dialog box and click the OK button or press Return. (The same radio button you clicked last time is still selected; if you want to choose a new arrangement, click the new radio button before you click OK.)

Don't try to close a particular worksheet window with the File⇨Close command on the menu bar because you'll only succeed in closing the entire workbook file, while at the same time getting rid of all the worksheet windows you've created.

When you save your workbook, Excel saves the current window arrangement as part of the file along with all the rest of the changes. If you don't want the current window arrangement saved, close all but one of the windows (by double-clicking their Control-menu buttons or selecting their windows and then pressing ⌘+W); then click that last window's Zoom button and select the tab of the worksheet that you want displayed the next time you open the workbook before saving the file.

Passing Sheets in the Night

In some situations, you need to move a particular worksheet or copy it from one workbook to another. To move or copy worksheets between workbooks, follow these steps:

1. **Open both the workbook with the worksheet(s) you want to move or copy and the workbook that is to contain the moved or copied worksheet(s).**

   Use the Open tool on the Standard toolbar or choose the File⇨Open command (⌘+O) to open the workbooks.

2. **Select the workbook that contains the worksheet(s) that you want to move or copy.**

   To select the workbook with the sheet(s) that you want to move or copy, choose its name on the Window menu.

3. **Select the worksheet(s) you want to move or copy.**

   To select a single worksheet, click its sheet tab. To select a group of neighboring sheets, click the first tab and then hold down Shift as you click the last tab. To select various nonadjacent sheets, click the first tab and then hold down the ⌘ key as you click each of the other sheet tabs.

4. **Choose the Edit⇨Move or Copy Sheet command on the menu bar or choose the Move or Copy command on a tab's shortcut menu.**

   Excel opens up the Move or Copy dialog box (similar to the one shown in Figure 7-5) in which you indicate whether you want to move or copy the selected sheet(s) and where to move or copy them to.

Figure 7-5:
The Move
or Copy
dialog box.

5. **In the To book drop-down list box, select the name of the workbook you want to copy or move the worksheets to.**

   If you want to move or copy the selected worksheet(s) to a new workbook rather than to an existing one that you have open, select the (new book) option that appears at the very top of the To book drop-down list box.

6. **In the Before sheet list box, select the name of the sheet that the worksheet(s) you're about to move or copy should precede.**

7. **Select the Create a copy check box to copy the selected worksheet(s) to the designated workbook (rather than move them).**

8. **Click the OK button or press Return to complete the move or copy operation.**

If you prefer a more direct approach, you can move or copy sheets between open workbooks by dragging their sheet tabs from one workbook window to another. Note that this method works with a bunch of sheets as well as with a single sheet; just be sure that you select all their sheet tabs before you begin the drag-and-drop procedure.

To drag a worksheet from one workbook to another, you must open both workbooks and then use the Window⇨Arrange command on the menu bar and select an arrangement (such as Horizontal or Vertical to put the workbook windows either on top of each other or side by side). Before you close the Arrange Windows dialog box, be sure that the Windows of active workbook check box does *not* contain a check mark.

After arranging the workbook windows, drag the worksheet tab from one workbook to another. If you want to copy rather than move the worksheet, hold down the Option key as you drag the sheet icon(s). To locate the worksheet in the new workbook, position the downward pointing triangle that moves with the sheet icon in front of the worksheet tab where it's to be inserted and then release the mouse button.

Figures 7-6 and 7-7 illustrate how easily you can move or copy a worksheet from one workbook to another using this drag-and-drop method.

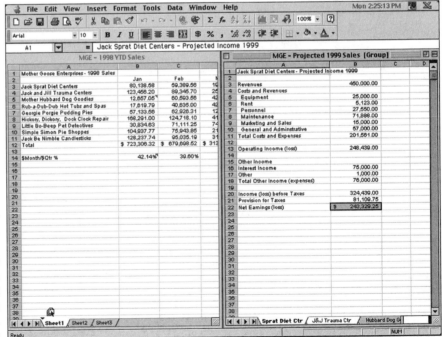

Figure 7-6: Copying the Sprat Diet Ctr and J&J Trauma Ctr worksheets to the MGE - 1998 YTD Sales workbook via drag and drop.

In Figure 7-6, you see two workbook windows: the workbook named MGE -
1998 YTD Sales in the left pane and the workbook named MGE - Projected
1999 Sales in the right pane (arranged with the Tiled option in the Arrange
Windows dialog box). To copy the Sprat Diet Ctr and the J&J Trauma Ctr
sheets from the MGE - Projected 1999 Sales workbook to the MGE - 1998 YTD
Sales workbook, you simply select both the Sprat Diet Ctr and J&J Trauma
Ctr tabs and then hold down the Option key as you click the Sprat Diet Ctr
tab and drag the sheet icons to their new position right before Sheet2 of the
MGE - 1998 YTD Sales workbook.

Figure 7-7 shows the workbooks after releasing the mouse button. As you
can see, Excel inserts the copy of the Sprat Diet Ctr and the J&J Trauma Ctr
worksheets into the MGE - 1998 YTD Sales workbook at the place indicated
by the triangle that accompanies the sheet icon (in between Sheet1 and
Sheet2 in this example).

Figure 7-7:
The screen
after
inserting a
copy of the
Sprat Diet
Ctr and J&J
Trauma Ctr
worksheets
between
Sheet1 and
Sheet2 of
the MGE -
1998 YTD
Sales
workbook.

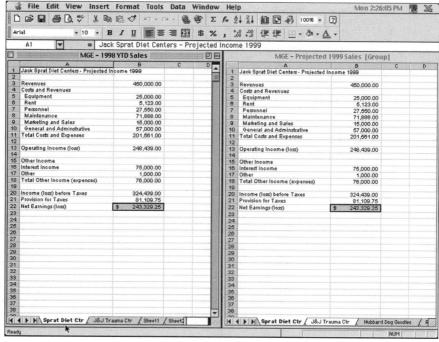

To Sum Up . . .

I now want to introduce you to the fascinating subject of creating a *summary worksheet* that recaps or totals the values stored in a bunch of other worksheets in the workbook.

The best way that I can show you how to create a summary worksheet is to walk you through the procedure of making one (entitled Total Income) for the MGE - Projected 1999 Sales workbook, which totals the projected revenue and expenses for all the companies owned by Mother Goose Enterprises.

Because the MGE - Projected 1999 Sales workbook already contains nine worksheets, each with the 1999 projected revenue and expenses for one of these companies, and these worksheets are all laid out in the same arrangement, creating this summary worksheet is a breeze.

1. **I start by inserting a new worksheet in front of the other worksheets in the MGE - Projected 1999 Sales workbook and renaming its sheet tab from Sheet1 to Total Income.**

   To find out how to insert a new worksheet, refer to "Don't Short-Sheet Me!" To find out how to rename a sheet tab, refer to "A sheet by any other name . . ." earlier in this chapter.

2. **Next, I enter the worksheet title Mother Goose Enterprises - Projected 1999 Income in cell A1.**

   Do this by selecting cell A1 and then typing the text.

3. **Finally, I copy the rest of the row headings for Column A (containing the revenue and expense descriptions) from the Sprat Diet Ctr worksheet to the Total Income worksheet.**

   To do this, select cell A3 in the Total Income sheet; then select the Sprat Diet Ctr tab and select the cell range A3:A22 in this sheet before pressing ⌘+C, selecting the Total Income tab again, and pressing Return.

Now, after widening Column A to accommodate the copied row headings, I am ready to create the "master" SUM formula that totals the revenues of all nine companies in cell B3 of the Total Income sheet.

1. **I start by selecting cell B3 and then clicking the AutoSum tool on the Standard toolbar.**

   Excel then puts =SUM( ) in the cell with the insertion point placed between the two parentheses.

2. Then I select the Sprat Diet Ctr sheet tab and then its cell B3 to select the projected revenues for the Jack Sprat Diet Centers.

The formula bar now reads =SUM('Sprat Diet Ctr'!B3) after selecting this cell.

3. Next I type , (the comma starts a new argument) and then select the J&J Trauma Ctr sheet tab followed by clicking its cell (B3) to select projected revenues for the Jack and Jill Trauma Centers.

The formula bar now reads =SUM('Sprat Diet Ctr'!B3,'J&J Trauma Ctr'!B3) after selecting this cell.

4. I then continue in this manner, typing a comma and then selecting cell B3 with the projected revenues for all the other companies in the following seven sheets.

At the end of this procedure, the formula bar now appears with the whopping SUM formula shown on the formula bar in Figure 7-8.

5. To complete the SUM formula in cell B3 of the Total Income worksheet, I then click the Enter box in the formula bar. (I can press the Return key as well.)

Figure 7-8 shows you the result after using AutoFit to widen Column B. As you can see in the formula bar, the master SUM formula that returns 6,681,450.78 to cell B3 of the Total Income worksheet gets its result by summing the values in B3 in all nine of the supporting worksheets.

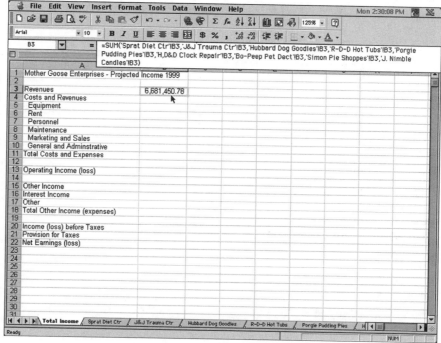

Figure 7-8:
The Total Income worksheet after creating the SUM formula in cell B3 that totals the projected revenues for all nine Mother Goose companies.

All that's left to do now is to use AutoFill to copy the master formula in cell B3 down to row 22 as follows:

1. **With cell B3 still selected, I drag the AutoFill handle in the lower-right corner of cell B3 down to cell B22 to copy the formula for summing the values for the nine companies down this column.**

2. **Then I delete the SUM formulas from cells B4, B12, B14, B15, and B19 (all of which contain zeros because these cells have no income or expenses to be totaled).**

In Figure 7-9, you see the first section of the final summary projected income worksheet after copying the formula created in cell B3 and deleting the formulas from the cells that should be blank (all those that came up 0 in Column B).

Although this Total Income summary worksheet looks like it's a lot of work to create at first glance, it's really quite simple to put together. And the best part is that, because the values in the summary worksheet are tied by formula to the values entered in the income statement worksheet for each company, any update or correction made to these figures is automatically reflected in the summary values in the Total Income sheet, giving you 100 percent accuracy in your totals without requiring any extra work on your part!

Figure 7-9:
The first part of the Total Income worksheet after copying the SUM formula in cell B3 down the worksheet and then deleting the copied formulas that returned zero as the result.

Part IV
Life beyond the Spreadsheet

The 5th Wave   By Rich Tennant

"NIFTY CHART, FRANK, BUT NOT ENTIRELY NECESSARY."

In this part . . .

*D*on't let anybody kid you: Spreadsheets are the bread and butter of Excel 98. And for many of you, creating, editing, and printing spreadsheets is the be-all and end-all of Excel and "who could ask for anything more?" But don't get the wrong impression. Just because Excel is a whiz at spreadsheets doesn't mean that it's a one-trick pony, and just because spreadsheets may be the only thing that you churn out in your present job doesn't mean that someday you won't be moving into a job where you need to chart spreadsheet data, create and maintain Excel databases, and, who knows, even publish your worksheet data on the World Wide Web.

Part IV is here just in case you need to stray beyond the confines of the spreadsheet into such exotic areas as creating charts and adding graphic images, creating, sorting, and filtering databases, and publishing worksheets on the Internet or company intranet. Between the entertaining information in Chapter 8 about making charts, the fact-filled information in Chapter 9 on working with Excel databases, and the tips and tricks in Chapter 10 on creating hyperlinks and converting worksheet data into HTML documents, you'll be more than ready should the day arise (or already be here) when you are forced to go beyond the pale of the good old Excel spreadsheet.

Chapter 8

The Simple Art of Making Charts

In This Chapter

▶ Creating great-looking charts with the Chart Wizard

▶ Changing a chart with the Chart toolbar

▶ Formatting a chart's axes

▶ Adding a text box and arrow to a chart

▶ Changing the orientation of a 3-D chart

▶ Using the drawing tools to add graphics to charts and worksheets

▶ Adding QuickTime movies to a worksheet

▶ Printing a chart without printing the rest of the worksheet data

As Confucius said, "A picture's worth a thousand words" (or, in our case, numbers). By adding charts to worksheets, you not only heighten interest in the otherwise boring numbers but also illustrate trends and anomalies that may not be apparent from just looking at the values alone. Because Excel 98 makes it so easy to chart the numbers in a worksheet, you can also experiment with different types of charts until you find the one that best represents the data — in other words, the picture that best tells the particular story.

Just a word about charts before you find out how to make them in Excel. Remember your high-school algebra teacher valiantly trying to teach you how to graph equations by plotting different values on an x-axis and a y-axis on graph paper? Of course, you were probably too busy with more important things like cool cars and rock 'n' roll to pay too much attention to an old algebra teacher. Besides, you probably told yourself, "I'll never need this junk when I'm out on my own and get a job!"

Well, see, you just never know. It turns out that even though Excel automates almost the entire process of charting worksheet data, you may need to be able to tell the x-axis from the y-axis, just in case Excel doesn't draw the chart the way you had in mind. To refresh your memory, the x-axis is the horizontal axis, usually located along the bottom of the chart; the y-axis is the vertical one, usually located on the left side of the chart.

In most charts that use these two axes, Excel plots the categories along the x-axis at the bottom and their relative values along the y-axis on the left. The x-axis is sometimes referred to as the *time axis* because the chart often depicts values along this axis at different time periods such as months, quarters, years, and so on.

Conjuring Up Charts with the Chart Wizard

Well, that's enough background on charts. Now let's get on with the charting itself. Excel makes the process of creating a new chart in a worksheet as painless as possible with the Chart Wizard. The Chart Wizard walks you through a four-step procedure, at the end of which you have a complete and beautiful new chart.

Before you start the Chart Wizard, it's a good idea to first select the cell range that contains the information that you want charted. Keep in mind that to end up with the chart you want, the information should be entered in standard table format. With the information in this format, you can select it all as a single range.

If you create a chart that uses an x-axis and y-axis (as most do), the Chart Wizard naturally uses the row of column headings in the selected table for the category labels along the x-axis. If the table has row headings, the Chart Wizard uses these as the headings in the legend of the chart (if you choose to include one). The *legend* identifies each point, column, or bar in the chart that represents the values in the table.

After you select the information to chart, follow these steps to create the chart:

1. **Click the Chart Wizard button on the Standard toolbar to open the Chart Wizard - Step 1 of 4 - Chart Type dialog box.**

   The Chart Wizard button is the fifth tool from the right and has a picture of a column chart. When you click the Chart Wizard button as described in Step 1, Excel opens the Chart Wizard - Step 1 of 4 - Chart Type dialog box shown in Figure 8-1.

2. **If you want to use a chart other than the default Clustered Column, select the new chart type and/or chart sub-type on the Standard Types or Custom Types tabs in the Chart Wizard - Step 1 of 4 - Chart Type dialog box.**

Figure 8-1:
The Chart
Wizard -
Step 1 of 4 -
Chart Type
dialog box.

To select another chart type, click its sample chart in the Chart type list box. To select a chart sub-type, click its representation in the Chart sub-type portion of the dialog box. To see how your data will look using the chart type and chart sub-type you've selected on the Standard Types tab, click and hold down the Press and Hold to View Sample button that's right below the area showing the name of the chart type and chart sub-type.

3. **Click the Next button or press Return to open the Chart Wizard - Step 2 of 4 - Chart Source Data dialog box.**

The Chart Wizard - Step 2 of 4 - Chart Source Data dialog box (similar to the one shown in Figure 8-2) lets you change the data range that is to be charted (or select it from scratch, if you haven't already done so), as well as define how the series within that data range are defined.

When this dialog box is displayed, any cell range selected prior to selecting the Chart Wizard is surrounded by the marquee in your worksheet and specified in formula form (with absolute cell references) in the Data range text box. To modify this range (perhaps to include the row of column headings or the column of row headings), either reselect the range with the mouse or edit the cell references in the Data range text box. Remember that if the Chart Wizard - Step 2 of 4 - Chart Source Data dialog box is in the way of the cells you need to select, you can reduce this dialog box to just this text box by clicking the text box's minimize button.

Figure 8-2:
The Chart
Wizard -
Step 2 of 4 -
Chart
Source
Data dialog
box.

4. **Check the cell range shown in the Data range text box and, if necessary, adjust the range address (either by typing or selecting the cell range in the worksheet itself).**

   Normally, the Chart Wizard makes each column of values in the selected table into a separate *data series* on the chart. The *legend* (the boxed area with samples of the colors or patterns used in the chart) identifies each data series in the chart.

   In terms of worksheet data selected in Mother Goose Enterprises 1998 first quarter sales worksheet (partially shown in Figure 8-1), this means that Excel uses each bar in the column chart to represent a different month's sales and clusters these sales together by the nine different companies. If you want, you can switch the data series from columns to rows by clicking the Rows radio button. Clicking the Rows radio button in this example makes each bar represent the sales of one of the nine different companies and causes them to be clustered together by month.

   When the chart forms the data series by columns, the Chart Wizard uses the entries in the first column (the row headings in cell range A3:A11) to label the x-axis (the so-called *category labels*). The Chart Wizard uses the entries in the first row (the column labels in cell range B2:D2) as the headings in the legend.

5. **If you want the Chart Wizard to use the rows of the selected data range as the data series of the chart (rather than the columns), click the Rows radio button next to the Series in heading.**

   If you need to make individual changes to either the names or cells used in the data series, you can do so by selecting the Series tab in the Chart Wizard - Step 2 of 4 - Chart Source Data dialog box.

6. **Click the Next button or press Return to open the Chart Wizard - Step 3 of 4 - Chart Options dialog box.**

The Chart Wizard - Step 3 of 4 - Chart Options dialog box (shown in Figure 8-3) lets you assign a whole bunch of options, including the titles to appear in the chart, whether or not gridlines are used, where the legend is displayed, whether or not data labels appear next to their data series, and whether or not the Chart Wizard draws a data table showing the values that are being charted right below the data series in the chart.

Figure 8-3:
The Chart
Wizard -
Step 3 of 4 -
Chart
Options
dialog box.

7. **Select the tab for the options you want to change (Titles, Axes, Gridlines, Legend, Data Labels, or Data Table) and then change the option settings as necessary. (See "Changing the Chart Options" later in this chapter for more information.)**

8. **Click the Next button in the dialog box or press Return to open the Chart Wizard - Step 4 of 4 - Chart Location dialog box.**

The Chart Wizard - Step 4 of 4 - Chart Location dialog box (shown in Figure 8-4) lets you place your new chart either on its own chart sheet in the workbook or as a new graphic object on one of the worksheets in your workbook.

9a. **To place the chart on its own sheet, click the As new sheet radio button; then, if you want, enter a new name for the sheet (besides Chart1, Chart2, and so on) in the text box to its right.**

9b. **To place the chart somewhere on one of the worksheets in your workbook, make sure that the As object in radio button is selected and then select the name of the worksheet in the pop-up menu to its right. (If you want to rename the worksheet at the same time, you can do so by typing in a new sheet name — which replaces the original sheet name because it's already highlighted.)**

Figure 8-4:
The Chart
Wizard -
Step 4 of 4 -
Chart
Location
dialog box.

10. Click the Finish button or press Return to close the last Chart Wizard dialog box.

If you selected the As new sheet option, your new chart appears on its own chart sheet, and the Chart toolbar magically appears floating in the workbook document window. If you selected the As object in radio button, your chart appears as a selected graphic — along with the floating Chart toolbar — on the designated worksheet (similar to the one shown in Figure 8-5, which shows the column chart created for the Mother Goose Enterprises 1998 first quarter sales).

Figure 8-5:
The
completed
Cluster
Column
chart
representing
Qtr. 1 sales
as it
appears
in the
worksheet.

Instant charts with F11!

If you just don't have time for the Chart Wizard and its four-step process outlined earlier, you can create a finished chart in an instant by doing these two steps:

1. Select the cells with the labels and values to be charted.

2. Press the function key F11.

Excel then creates a new Clustered Column chart using the selected data on its own chart sheet.

After creating a new chart as a graphic object in a worksheet, you can easily move or resize the chart right after creating it because the chart is still selected. (You can always tell when a graphic object like a chart is selected because you see *selection handles* — those tiny squares — around the edges of the object.) Immediately after creating the chart, the Chart toolbar appears floating above in the workbook document window.

- To move the chart, position the mouse pointer somewhere inside the chart and drag the chart to a new location.

- To resize the chart (you may want to make it bigger if it seems distorted in any way), position the mouse pointer on one of the selection handles. When the pointer changes from the arrowhead to a double-headed arrow, drag the side or corner (depending on which handle you select) to enlarge or reduce the chart.

When the chart is properly sized and positioned in the worksheet, set the chart in place by deselecting it. (Simply click the mouse pointer in any cell outside the chart.) As soon as you deselect the chart, the selection handles disappear, as does the Chart toolbar, from the document window. To reselect the chart (to edit, size, or move it), click anywhere on the chart with the mouse pointer.

When you select a chart embedded in a worksheet, Excel automatically selects the charted data in the worksheet as follows: Category labels are enclosed in a pink border, legend labels are enclosed in a green border, and cells with the charted data (the data series) are enclosed in blue.

Changing the chart with the Chart toolbar

After you create a chart, you can use the buttons on the Chart toolbar (shown in Figure 8-6) to make all kinds of changes to it.

✔ **Chart Objects:** To select the part of the chart you want to change, click the Chart Objects drop-down button and click the object's name on the pop-up menu or click the object directly in the chart itself with the mouse pointer. When you click a new object in a chart, its name automatically appears in the Chart Objects text box.

✔ **Format:** To change the formatting of the selected chart object (whose name is shown in the text box of the Chart Objects button), click the Format button to open a dialog box with the formatting options you can modify. Note that the name of this button (as shown with screen tips) changes to match the chart object that you've selected: If Chart Area appears in the Chart Objects' text box, the button is called Format Chart Area; if Legend appears as the selected chart object in this text box, the button's name changes to Format Legend.

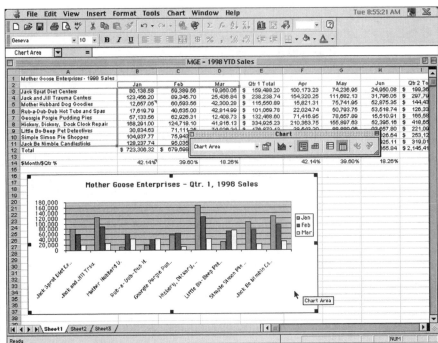

Figure 8-6: Editing an embedded chart with the Chart toolbar.

✔ **Chart Type:** To change the type of chart, click the Chart Type drop-down button and then click the new chart type in the pop-up palette.

✔ **Legend:** Click the Legend button to hide or display the chart's legend.

✔ **Data Table:** Click the Data Table button to add or remove a data table that encapsulates the values that are represented by the chart's graphics (Figure 8-7 shows an example of a data table added to the Clustered Column chart added to the 1998 Sales worksheet).

✔ **By Row:** Click the By Row button to have the data series in the chart represent the rows of values in the selected data range.

✔ **By Column:** Click the By Column button to have the data series in the chart represent the columns of values in the selected data range.

✔ **Angle Text Downward:** Click the Angle Text Downward button when the Category Axis or Value Axis objects are selected to have the text of their labels slanted down 45 degrees as shown with the _ab_ that appears on this button.

✔ **Angle Text Upward:** Click the Angle Text Upward button when the Category Axis or Value Axis objects are selected to have the text of their labels appear slanted up 45 degrees as shown with the _ab_ that appears on this button.

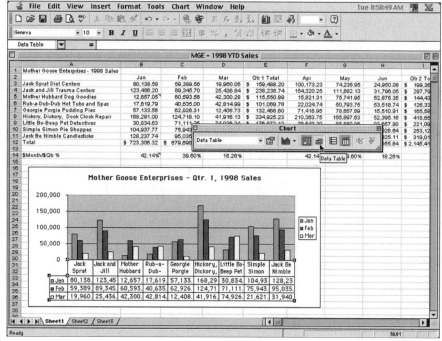

Figure 8-7: A Clustered Column chart with a data table containing the Qtr. 1 sales figures.

Editing the chart directly in the worksheet

At times, you may want to make changes to specific parts of a chart that you've embedded in a worksheet (for example, selecting a new font for titles or repositioning the legend). To make these kinds of changes, you can double-click the particular object (such as the title, legend, plot area, and so on) in the worksheet. When you double-click a chart object, Excel selects it and displays a format dialog box specific to the part of the chart you double-clicked. For example, if you double-click somewhere on the legend of a chart, the Format Legend dialog box with its three tabs (Patterns, Font, and Placement) as shown in Figure 8-8 appears. You can then use the options on any of these tabs to spruce up the legend's appearance.

Note that you can also edit a chart by selecting the part you want to change as follows:

✔ To select one of these chart objects, simply click it.

✔ You can tell when an object is selected because selection handles appear around it. (Figure 8-8 shows the selection handles around the chart legend.) With some objects, you can use the selection handles to resize or reorient the object.

Figure 8-8:
The Format Legend dialog box appears when you double-click somewhere on the legend in the chart itself.

✔ After selecting some chart objects, you can move them within the chart by positioning the arrowhead pointer in their midst and then dragging their boundary.

✔ To display a chart object's shortcut menu, you Control+click the object and then drag to the desired command on the menu.

✔ To remove the selected part from the chart, press the Delete key.

After you select one object in the chart by clicking it, you can cycle through and select the other objects in the chart by pressing the ↑ and ↓ keys. Pressing → selects the next object; pressing ← selects the previous object.

All the parts of the chart that you can select in a chart window have shortcut menus attached to them. If you know that you want to choose a command from the shortcut menu as soon as you select a part of the chart, you can both select the object and open the shortcut menu by Control+clicking the chart object.

Note that you can move the chart title by dragging it to a new position within the chart. In addition to moving the title, you can also break up the title on several different lines. Then, if you want, you can use options in the Alignment tab of the Format Chart Title dialog box to change the alignment of the broken-up text.

To force part of the title onto a new line, click the insertion point at the place in the text where the line break is to occur. After you position the insertion point in the title, press Return to start a new line.

In addition to changing the way the titles appear in the chart, you can modify the way the data series, legend, and x- and y-axes appear in the chart by opening their shortcut menus and selecting the appropriate commands from them.

Changing the Chart Options

If you find that you need to make some substantial alterations to your chart, you can open the Chart Options dialog box (which contains the same tabs and options as you saw in the Chart Wizard - Step 3 of 4 - Chart Options dialog box when creating the chart — refer to Figure 8-3). You can open this dialog box by clicking somewhere on the chart and then choosing Chart⇨ Chart Options on the menu bar or by Control+clicking somewhere in the chart area (while at the same time avoiding a particular object like a title, axis, data table, legend, and the like) and then choosing Chart Options on the Chart Area's shortcut menu.

The Chart Options dialog box can contain up to six tabs (depending upon the type of chart you've selected — pie charts for instance have only the first three tabs) with options for doing the following stuff:

- ✔ **Titles:** You can use the options on the Titles tab to add or modify the Chart title (that appears at the top of the chart), the Category title (that appears below the x-axis), or the Value title (that appears to the left of the y-axis).

- ✔ **Axes:** You can use the options on the Axes tab to hide or display the tick marks and labels along the Category (x) axis or the Value (y) axis.

- ✔ **Gridlines:** You can use the options on the Gridlines tab to hide or display the major and minor gridlines that appear from the tick marks along the Category (x) axis or the Value (y) axis.

- ✔ **Legend:** You can use the options on the Legend tab to hide or display the legend or to change its placement in relation to the chart area (by choosing the Bottom, Corner, Top, Right, or Left radio button).

- ✔ **Data Labels:** You can use the options on the Data Labels tab to hide or display labels that identify each data series in the chart. You can also specify the appearance of the data label (by choosing the Show value, Show percent, Show label, Show label and percent, or Show bubble sizes radio button).

- ✔ **Data Table:** You can use the options in the Data Table tab to add or remove a data table that shows the worksheet values being charted. (Refer to Figure 8-7 for an example of a chart with a data table.)

Telling all with a text box

Figure 8-9 shows a couple of other changes you can easily make to a chart. In this figure, you see the chart for the Mother Goose Enterprises 1998 first quarter sales (as an Area chart) after adding a text box with an arrow that points out how extraordinary the sales were for the Hickory, Dickory, Dock Clock Repair shops in this quarter and after formatting the values on the y-axis with the Currency number format.

To add a text box to the chart, open the Drawing toolbar by clicking the Drawing button on the Standard toolbar. As you can see in Figure 8-9, the Drawing toolbar automatically docks itself at the bottom of the workbook window. Then click its Text Box button. When you click the Text Box button, Excel changes the mouse pointer to a narrow vertical line with a short cross near the bottom, which you can click at the place where you want the text box drawn or use to draw the text box either in the chart or the worksheet by dragging its outline. When you click this mouse pointer, Excel draws a square text box. When you release the mouse button after dragging this mouse pointer, Excel draws a text box in the shape and size of the outline.

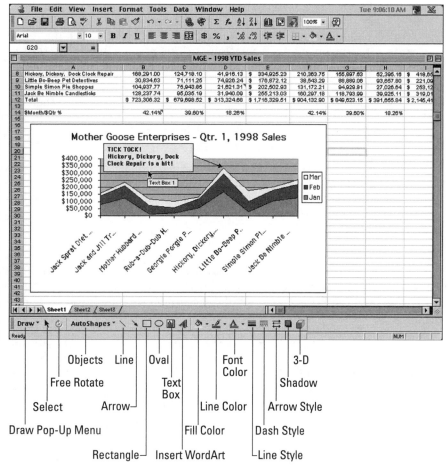

After creating the text box, the program positions the insertion point at the
top, and you can then type the text you want to appear within it. The text
you type appears in the text box and wraps to a new line when you reach
the right edge of the text box. (**Remember:** You can press Return when you
want to force text to appear on a new line.) When you finish entering the
message for your text box, click anywhere outside the box to deselect it.

After adding a text box to a chart (or worksheet), you can edit as follows:

- ✔ You can move the text box to a new location in the chart by dragging it.
- ✔ You can resize the text box by dragging the appropriate selection handle.

✔ Change or remove the border around the text box by opening the Format Text Box dialog box either by choosing Format⇨Text Box (⌘+1) or by choosing the Format Text Box command on the text box shortcut menu and then selecting the Colors and Lines tab in the dialog box. To remove all borders from the text box, select No Line on the Color pop-up menu under Line.

✔ To add the drop-shadow effect, select the text box, then click the Shadow button on the Drawing toolbar (the one with the picture of a drop shadow behind a rectangle), and select the type of drop shadow to apply in the pop-up palette.

✔ To make the text box three-dimensional, select the text box and then click the 3-D button on the Drawing toolbar (the last one with the 3-D rectangle). Finally, select the 3-D box shape you want to apply in the pop-up palette.

When creating a text box, you may want to add an arrow to point directly to the object or part of the chart you're talking about. To add an arrow, click the Arrow button on the Drawing toolbar and then drag the crosshair from the place where the end of the arrow (the one *without* the arrowhead) is to appear to the place where the arrow starts (and the arrowhead appears) and release the mouse button.

Excel then draws a new arrow, which remains selected (with selection handles at the beginning and end of the arrow). You can then modify the arrow as follows:

✔ To move the arrow, drag it into position.

✔ To change the length of the arrow, drag one of the selection handles.

✔ As you change the length, you can also change the direction of the arrow by pivoting the mouse pointer around a stationary selection handle.

✔ If you want to change the shape of the arrowhead or the thickness of the arrow's shaft, select the arrow in the worksheet, click the Arrow Style button on the Drawing toolbar (the one with the three arrows), and choose the type of arrowhead to apply in the pop-up menu. If you want to change the color of the arrow, alter the thickness or style of the line, or create a custom arrowhead, choose the More Arrows command at the bottom of the pop-up menu to open the Format AutoShape dialog box. (You can also open this dialog box by choosing Format⇨ AutoShape on the menu bar or by pressing ⌘+1.)

Formatting the x- or y-axis

When charting a bunch of values, Excel isn't too careful how it formats the values that appear on the y-axis (or the x-axis when using some chart types like the 3-D Column chart or the XY Scatter chart). If you're not happy with the way the values appear on either the x- or y-axis, you can change the formatting as follows:

1. **Double-click the x- or y-axis in the chart or click the axis and then choose Format⇨Selected Axis on the menu bar (or press ⌘+1).**

   Excel opens the Format Axis dialog box containing the following tabs: Patterns, Scale, Font, Number, and Alignment.

2. **To change the appearance of the tick marks along the axis, change the options on the Patterns tab (which is automatically selected when you first open the Format Axis dialog box) as required.**

3. **To change the scale of the selected axis, select the Scale tab and change the Scale options as required.**

4. **To change the font of the labels that appear at the tick marks on the selected axis, select the Font tab and change the Font options as required.**

5. **To change the formatting of the values that appear at the tick marks on the selected axis, select the Number tab; then select the appropriate options in the Category list box, Decimal places text box, and Symbol pop-up menu.**

   For example, to select the Currency format with no decimal places, you select Currency in the Category list box; then type **0** in the Decimal places text box or select 0 with the spinner buttons.

6. **To change the formatting of the orientation of the labels that appear at the tick marks on the selected axis, select the Alignment tab; then indicate the new orientation by clicking it in the Sample text box or by entering the number of degrees (between 180 and –180) in the Degrees text box (or selecting this number with the spinner buttons).**

7. **Click the OK button or press Return to close the Format Axis dialog box.**

As soon as you close the Format Axis box, Excel redraws the axis of the chart according to the new settings. For instance, if you choose a new number format for a chart, Excel immediately formats all the numbers that appear along the selected axis using that format.

Vacillating values mean changing charts

As soon as you finish modifying the objects in a chart, you can deselect the chart and return to the normal worksheet and its cells by clicking the pointer anywhere outside the chart. After a chart is deselected, you can once again move the cell pointer all over the worksheet. Just keep in mind that if you use the arrow keys to move the cell pointer, the cell pointer disappears when you move to a cell in the worksheet that's hidden behind the chart. (Of course, if you try to select a cell covered by a chart by clicking it with the mouse pointer, you'll only succeed in selecting the chart itself.)

Keep in mind that worksheet values represented graphically in the chart remain dynamically linked to the chart so that, should you make a change to one or more of the charted values in the worksheet, Excel automatically updates the chart to suit.

Changing perspectives

Figure 8-10 shows the chart in a chart window in yet another guise: this time, as a 3-D Area chart. When you select this kind of chart (as well as the 3-D Column, 3-D Line, and 3-D Surface charts), Excel draws the chart in perspective view by adding a third axis to the chart. Now you have the category (x) axis with the companies running along the bottom of the closest side, the data series (y) axis with the months running along the bottom of the other side, and the value (z) axis with the dollar amounts running up the left wall.

Figure 8-10: Sales information as an embedded 3-D Area chart.

These three axes form a kind of open box with the category and series axes on the two sides of the floor and the values axis on the left side of the wall of the box. You can modify the view of this type of 3-D-perspective chart by rotating the box, thereby changing the viewing angles of its walls and floor.

To do this, click the chart (double-click if the chart is on a worksheet rather than a chart sheet); then select the frame of the 3-D chart by clicking one of its corners and holding down the mouse button. (If the 3-D chart is on a chart sheet, you can tell when you've clicked a corner because the word *Corners* appears on the formula bar where the current cell address usually appears.) In a second, assuming that you don't let up on the mouse button prematurely and that you have really clicked a corner of the frame and not one of the data series inside the frame, everything disappears from the 3-D chart except for the wire frame representing its orientation.

You can then drag the corner of the wire-frame box around to reorient the entire 3-D chart. When the wire-frame box is positioned the way you want the 3-D chart, release the mouse button. Excel draws the 3-D chart using the new viewing angles. Figure 8-11 shows you how the rotated 3-D Area chart appears after rotating its lower-right corner down and around to the left and then releasing the mouse button.

Figure 8-11:
The 3-D Area chart after rotating it.

Notice how this change to the orientation of the 3-D Area chart causes Excel to flip the category labels with the names of the companies all the way from the lower side of the chart to its right side.

Picture This!

Charts are not the only kind of graphics you can add to a worksheet. Indeed, Excel enables you to spruce up a worksheet with drawings, text boxes, and even graphic images imported from other sources, like scanned images or drawings created in other graphics programs.

To bring in a piece of clip art included with Office 98, you choose the Insert⇨Picture⇨Clip Art command on the menu bar and select the image from the Clip Art tab in the Microsoft Clip Gallery 3.0 dialog box (similar to the one shown in Figure 8-12). To select a clip art image, first select the category of the art image in the left pane of the dialog box and then select the clip art image itself in the right pane before you click the Insert button or press Return.

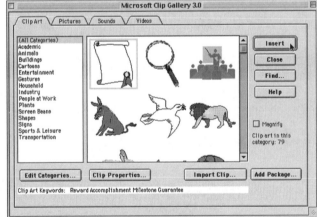

Figure 8-12: The Microsoft Clip Gallery dialog box with the Clip Art tab selected.

If you want to bring in a graphic image created in another program and saved in its own graphics file, choose the Insert⇨Picture⇨From File command and then select the graphic file in the Insert Picture dialog box (which works just like opening an Excel 98 workbook file in the Open dialog box).

If you want to bring in a graphic image created in another graphics program that's not saved in its own file, select the graphic in that program and then copy it to the Clipboard (using ⌘+C or the Edit⇨Copy command on the menu bar) before returning to the Excel worksheet. When you get back to your worksheet, place the cursor where you want the picture to go and then paste the image in place (using ⌘+V or the Edit⇨Paste command).

In addition to ready-made graphics or images drawn in other graphics programs, you can use the tools on the Drawing toolbar to create your own graphics within Excel. The Drawing toolbar contains all sorts of drawing tools that you can use to draw outlined or filled shapes like lines, rectangles, squares, and ovals.

Along with these tools for drawing traditional lines and shapes, the Drawing toolbar contains a new AutoShapes button that gives you access to a whole bunch of ready-made, specialized lines and shapes. To select one of these lines or shapes, you click it on the particular cascading palette that opens when you choose the Lines, Connectors, Basics Shapes, Block Arrows, Flowchart, Stars and Banners, or Callouts pop-up menu that appears when you click the AutoShapes button.

Working with WordArt

If having the specialized lines and shapes available with the AutoShapes button doesn't provide enough variety for jazzing up your worksheet, you may want to try adding some fancy text with the new WordArt button on the Drawing toolbar. You add this kind of text to your worksheet by following these steps:

1. **Select the cell in the area of the worksheet where the WordArt text is to appear.**

   Because WordArt is created as a graphics object on the worksheet, you can size and move the text after you create it just like any other worksheet graphic.

2. **Click the WordArt button (the one with the picture of the letter "A" angled downward) on the Drawing toolbar.**

   When you click the WordArt button, Excel displays the WordArt Gallery dialog box.

3. **Click the picture of the WordArt style you want to use in the WordArt Gallery dialog box and then click OK or press Return.**

   Excel opens the Edit WordArt Text dialog box where you enter the text you want to appear in the worksheet and select its font and font size.

4. **Type the text you want displayed in the worksheet in the Text text box.**

As soon as you start typing, Excel replaces the highlighted "Your Text Here" with the text you want to appear in the worksheet.

5. **Select the font you want to use in the Font pop-up list box and the font size in the Size pop-up list box.**

6. **Click the OK button or press Return.**

Excel draws your WordArt text in the worksheet at the cell pointer's position, while at the same time displaying the floating WordArt toolbar. You can use the buttons on this toolbar to further format the basic WordArt style or to edit the text.

7. **After making any final adjustments to the size, shape, or format of the WordArt text, click a cell somewhere outside of the text to deselect the graphic.**

When you click outside of the WordArt text, Excel deselects the graphic and hides the WordArt toolbar. (If you ever want the toolbar to reappear, all you have to do is click somewhere on the WordArt text to select the graphic.)

QuickTime Anytime

Excel 98 makes adding a regular QuickTime movie (Apple's digital video file format) or QuickTime VR (Virtual Reality) movie to a worksheet as easy as adding a clip art graphic. To insert a QuickTime or QuickTime VR movie in your worksheet, follow these steps:

1. **Open the workbook and select the worksheet where you want to embed the QuickTime movie.**

2. **Choose Insert⇨Movie on the Excel menu bar.**

Excel displays an Open dialog box (shown in Figure 8-13) where you specify the drive and folder containing the QuickTime movie.

Figure 8-13:
Selecting the QuickTime movie to embed in the current worksheet.

Preview	📷 0227~1xl98 ⬍	📡 NT_Server
	🗂 Figs05	Eject
	🗂 Figs06	Desktop
	🗂 Figs07	
	🗂 MGE 98	
	🗂 Mother Goose	Cancel
	📄 PB022.MOV	
Create	📄 seinfeld.53.mov	Open
☑ Show Preview		

3. **Select the drive and folder that contains the QuickTime movie you want to be able to play in your Excel worksheet and then click the name of the QuickTime video file that you want to embed.**

   The Open dialog box contains a Create button and Show Preview check box that enable you to create and display a preview of the QuickTime movie that shows the first frame.

4. **(Optional) To create a preview from the first frame of the QuickTime movie and display this preview in the Preview area to the left of the file list box, click the Show Preview check box and then click the Create button.**

   After verifying that the QuickTime movie is the one you want to embed, you are ready to create a link to it.

5. **Click the Open button or press Return to create a link to the selected QuickTime movie that embeds the video in the current worksheet.**

After you embed a regular QuickTime or QuickTime VR movie in a worksheet, you only have to click the movie's *poster frame* (the picture created from the frame of the video that appears in the worksheet whenever the movie isn't playing) to select it. As soon as you select a QuickTime or QuickTime VR movie, the Movie toolbar (shown in Figure 8-14) appears in the worksheet.

With an embedded QuickTime movie selected, you can move the movie and resize it in the worksheet as you would a still, clip art graphic. To move the QuickTime movie, position the mouse pointer somewhere within its poster frame and then drag its outline with the four-headed arrow to the desired position on the worksheet.

To resize a QuickTime movie, position the mouse pointer on a corner of its poster frame; then drag the outline of its sides with the double-headed arrow until it's the desired size. Keep in mind, however, that resizing a QuickTime movie should be undertaken with great care as you can easily mess up the movie's aspect ratio, which can really take a toll on the video quality and playback speed.

The QuickTime link that binds

When you add a QuickTime movie to a worksheet, you're really adding a link to the original QuickTime movie (which is often quite large) rather than actually adding the movie to the workbook file. This means that you must be careful not to move the QuickTime movie to a new folder after inserting it in the worksheet. Otherwise, you get an error message the next time you open the worksheet and try to play the movie. Also, if you send the worksheet to someone else in the office, you must send the QuickTime movie file along with the original Excel workbook when you want your co-worker to be able to play the QuickTime video.

Show Controller ─ ┌─ Loop
Play ─ ┌─ Set As Poster Frame
Insert Movie ─ ┌─ Format Picture

Figure 8-14:
Selecting an
embedded
QuickTime
movie in the
worksheet
automatically
displays the
Movie
toolbar.

Movie time in the old spreadsheet

To play a regular QuickTime or QuickTime VR movie that you've inserted in a worksheet you have a choice of methods:

- ✔ Double-click somewhere on the poster frame of the QuickTime movie.

- ✔ Click somewhere on the poster frame of the QuickTime movie and then click the Play button on the Movie toolbar.

When you play a regular QuickTime movie, it plays automatically from beginning to end. If you want to pause the movie before it finishes playing, click somewhere within its boundary with the mouse pointer (which automatically changes from an arrowhead to the standard VCR pause button — the two, side-by-side vertical bars thingey). To restart the movie, just click the Play button on the Movie toolbar or double-click the movie. If you want the movie to play continuously until such time as you click within its boundary to pause it, click the Loop button on the Movie toolbar.

If you want, you can display the standard QuickTime movie controller at the bottom of the video and use its buttons to control playback. To display the QuickTime movie controller, click the Show Controller button on the Movie toolbar. This controller contains buttons for adjusting the sound, playing and pausing the movie, and advancing forward and backward a frame at a time. It also contains a slider that you can drag to display a particular frame in the movie.

When you play a QuickTime VR movie, you need to use the mouse or arrow keys to navigate the virtual space. (VR movies usually depict panoramas or spaces that invite exploration.) To move up and down in the virtual space, drag the mouse pointer up and down or press ↑ and ↓. To move left and right in the virtual space, drag the pointer to the left or right or press ← and →. The QuickTime movie lets you know when you can't navigate any further in a particular direction by changing the mouse pointer into an arrow with its arrowhead up against a thick bar (representing a virtual ceiling?).

To zoom in on a particular part of the movie, hold down the Shift key until you're as close as you want to be. To zoom out from a particular part of the movie, you hold down the Control key until you're as far out as you want to be.

Changing the old poster frame

When you first embed a QuickTime movie in a worksheet, Excel uses the movie's very first frame as the *poster frame* (that is, the frame whose picture appears in the worksheet when the movie isn't playing). You can, if you want, easily change the poster frame. For example, if you're working with a movie whose first frame is totally black or otherwise nondescript, you can choose a frame later in the video which better represents the movie's contents and make this frame into the poster frame.

To create a new poster frame for an embedded QuickTime movie, follow these steps:

1. **Click the QuickTime movie whose poster frame you want to change.**

   As soon as you select the QuickTime movie, the Movie toolbar appears in the worksheet.

2. **Double-click the movie or click the movie and then click the Play button on the Movie toolbar to start playing the movie.**

   Next, you play the movie until it reaches a frame that you want to use as the poster frame.

3. **When the movie reaches a frame that you want to make into the poster frame, click somewhere in the movie to pause it.**

   When setting a new poster frame for a QuickTime VR movie, you simply use the mouse or arrow keys to navigate the virtual space until you come upon a view which you want to use as the poster frame.

4. **With the QuickTime movie paused at the frame to be made into the new poster frame, click the Set as Poster Frame button on the Movie toolbar.**

After you make a new poster frame, this frame becomes the placeholder graphic for the movie in the worksheet that appears whenever the movie isn't playing. In the case of regular QuickTime movies, as soon as you start playing the movie, the poster frame is replaced by the very first frame of the movie (and the movie plays through as normal). In the case of QuickTime VR movies, as soon as you start playing the movie, the poster frame is replaced by the very last frame to which you navigated the last time you played the movie.

One on Top of the Other

In case you haven't noticed, graphic objects float on top of the cells of the worksheet. Most of the objects (including charts) are opaque, meaning that they hide (*without* replacing) information in the cells beneath. If you move one opaque graphic on top of another, the one on top hides the one below, just as putting one sheet of paper over another hides the information on the one below. This means that, most of the time, you should make sure that graphic objects don't overlap one another or overlap cells with worksheet information that you want to display.

Sometimes, however, you can create some interesting special effects by placing a transparent graphic object (such as a circle) in front of an opaque one. The only problem you may encounter is if the opaque object gets on top of the transparent one. If this happens, switch their positions by selecting the opaque object and then choosing the Order⇨Send to Back command on the object's shortcut menu. If you ever find a situation where you need to bring up a graphic that's underneath another, click this underlying graphic and then choose the Order⇨Send to Front command on the object's shortcut menu.

Sometimes, you may find that you need to group several objects together so that they act as one unit (like a text box with its arrow). That way, you can move these objects or size them together in one operation. To group objects together, you need to select each object you want to group (by clicking each one as you hold down the Shift key) and then choose the Grouping⇨Group command on the object's shortcut menu. After grouping several objects, whenever you click any part of the mega-object, every part is selected (and selection handles appear only around the perimeter of the combined object).

If you later decide that you need to independently move or size objects that you've grouped together, you can ungroup them by selecting the grouped object and then choosing Grouping⇨Ungroup on the object's shortcut menu.

Graphics: Now You See Them, Now You Don't

Here's something you'll want to know about the graphics you add to a worksheet: how to hide them. You see, adding graphics to a worksheet can appreciably slow down the screen response because Excel has to take the time to redraw each and every little picture in the document window whenever you scroll the view even slightly. To keep this sluggishness from driving you crazy, either hide the display of all the graphics (including charts) while you edit other things in the worksheet, or temporarily replace them with gray rectangles that continue to mark their places in the worksheet but don't take nearly as long to redraw.

To hide all the graphics or replace them with gray placeholders, choose the Tools⇨Preferences command on the menu bar and then select the View tab. Click the Hide all radio button under Objects to get rid of the display of all graphics entirely. Click the Show placeholders radio button to temporarily replace the graphics with shaded rectangles. (This is the safest bet because the placeholders give you a general idea of how changes to the cells of the worksheet impact the graphics.)

Before you print the worksheet, be sure that you redisplay the graphic objects: Open the Options dialog box, select the View tab, and then click the Show all radio button.

Printing Charts Only

Sometimes, you may want to print only a particular chart in the worksheet (independent of the worksheet data it represents or any of the other stuff you've added). To do this, first make sure that the graphic objects are displayed in the worksheet. (For details, see the preceding section.) Click somewhere on the chart area (to display the sizing handles around its perimeter). Next, choose the File⇨Print command on the menu bar (⌘+P) and press Return or simply click the Print tool on the Standard toolbar.

If you choose the File⇨Print command on the menu bar rather than click the Print tool, you can check to be sure that Excel will print your chart correctly. Select the Microsoft Excel option on the Print pop-up list button (the one that says General when you first open the Print dialog box) and make sure that you've selected the Selected Chart radio button under Print area. By default, Excel prints the chart at full-size on the page. This may mean that all of the chart cannot be printed on a single page — be sure to click the Print Preview button to make sure that your entire chart fits on one page.

If you find in Print Preview that you need to change the printed chart size or the orientation of the printing (or both), click the Setup button in the Print Preview window. To change the orientation of the printing (or the paper size), select the Page tab in the Page Setup dialog box and change these options. When everything looks good in the Print Preview window, start printing the chart by clicking the Print button.

Chapter 9

How to Face a Database

*T*he purpose of all the worksheet tables that I've discussed up to this point in the book has been to perform essential calculations (such as to sum monthly or quarterly sales figures) and then present the information in an understandable form. But you can create another kind of worksheet table in Excel: a *database,* which is essentially a list of information. The purpose of a database is not so much to calculate new values but rather to store lots and lots of information in a consistent manner. For example, you can create a database that contains the names and addresses of all your clients, or you can create a database that contains all the essential facts about your employees.

Creating a database is much like creating a list of worksheet data with rows of data beneath a row of column headings. When setting up a database, you start by entering the row of column headings (technically known as *field names* in database parlance) to identify the different kinds of items you need to keep track of (such as First Name, Last Name, Street, City, State, and so on). After you enter the row of field names, you start entering the information for the database in the appropriate columns of the rows immediately below the field names.

As you proceed, notice that each column of the database contains information for a particular item you want to track in the database, such as the client's company name or an employee's telephone extension. Each column is also known as a *field* in the database. In looking back over your work, you see that each row of the database contains complete information about a particular person or thing you're keeping track of in the database, whether it's a company such as Valuerite Reality or a particular employee such as Johnny Hayseed. The individuals or entities described in the rows of the database are also known as the *records* of the database. Each record (row) contains many fields (columns).

Maintaining vast quantities of data in a tabular format is but one small part of the database story in Excel. Excel provides you with very powerful features for organizing the data as well as for displaying just the information you need. For instance, suppose that you entered the clients in a database alphabetically by company name but now want to see them listed alphabetically by company name *and* grouped by states and cities. No problem: You can *sort* the records of the database by their State, City, and then Company fields.

Designing the Data Form

Setting up and maintaining a database is easy with Excel's handy, built-in *data form*. You use the data form to add, delete, or edit records in the database. To create a data form for a new database, you first enter the row of column headings used as field names and one sample record in the following row (check out the client database in Figure 9-1). Then you format each field entry just as you want all subsequent entries in that column of the database to appear. Then position the cell pointer in any one of the cells in these two rows and choose the Data⇨Form command on the menu bar.

As soon as you choose the Data⇨Form command on the menu bar, Excel analyzes the row of field names and entries for the first record and creates a data form that lists the field names down the left side of the form with the entries for the first record in the appropriate text boxes next to them. Figure 9-1 shows the data form for the new Little Bo Peep Pet Detective client database; it looks kind of like a customized dialog box. The data form Excel creates includes the entries you made in the first record. The data form also contains a series of buttons on the right side that you use to add, delete, or find specific records in the database. Right above the first button (New), the data form lists the number of the record you're looking at followed by the total number of records (1 of 1 when you first create the data form).

If you don't format any of the cells in the row of field names or the row with the entries for the first record in some manner beyond the default formatting automatically applied by Excel, the program won't be able to automatically distinguish the row of field names from the row of entries for the first

Figure 9-1:
The data
form for
a new
database
with a row
of field
names
followed by
a single
data record
(row).

database record when you choose the Data➪Form command. In such a case, Excel then displays a nasty-looking alert dialog box indicating that it can't determine which row in your list contains the column labels (that is, the field names). To have Excel use the first row as the field names, click the OK button or choose Return.

To avoid having to deal with this alert dialog box entirely, be sure to add some sort of non-default formatting to one or more of the entries in either the row with the field names or the row with the entries for the first record. To avoid this dialog box, I usually format the cells in the top row with the field names by centering and boldfacing their entries. You can also avoid the alert dialog box by applying a new font or font size to the cells with the field names.

Adding records to the database

After you create the data form with the first record, you can use the form to add the rest of the records to the database. The process is simple. When you click the New button, Excel displays a blank data form (marked New Record at the right side of the data form), which you get to fill in.

Creating a data form from field names alone

You can create a data form for a new database simply by entering a row of field names and selecting them before you choose Data⇨Form on the menu bar. When you do this, Excel displays the alert dialog box indicating that the program can't determine which row in your list contains the column labels (that is, the field names). To have Excel use the selected row as the field names, click OK or press Return. Excel then creates a blank data form listing all the fields down the form in the same order as they appear across the selected row.

Creating a blank data form from field names alone is just fine, provided that your database doesn't contain any calculated fields (that is,

fields whose entries result from a formula's computation rather than from manual entry). If your new database will contain calculated fields, you need to build their formulas in the appropriate fields of the first record. Then select both the row of field names and the first database record with the formulas indicating how the entries are calculated before you choose Form on the Data menu. Excel knows which fields are calculated and which are not. (You can tell that a field is a calculated field in the data form because Excel lists its field name but does not provide a text box for you to enter any information for it.)

After you enter the information for the first field, press the Tab key to advance to the next field in the record.

Whoa! Don't press the Return key to advance to the next field in a record. If you do, you'll insert the new, incomplete record into the database.

Continue entering information for each field and pressing Tab to go to the next field in the database.

  ✔ If you notice that you've made an error and want to edit an entry in a field you already passed, press Shift+Tab to return to that field.

  ✔ To replace the entry, just start typing.

  ✔ To edit some of the characters in the field, press → or click the I-beam pointer in the entry to locate the insertion point; then edit the entry from there.

When entering information in a particular field, you can copy the entry made in that field for the previous record by pressing Control+" (quotation mark). Press Control+", for example, to carry forward the same entry in the State field of each new record when entering a series of records for people who all live in the same state.

When entering dates in a date field, use a consistent date format that Excel knows (for example, enter something like 2/19/93). When entering zip codes that sometimes use leading zeros that you don't want to disappear from the entry (such as zip code 00102), format the first field entry with the Special Zip Code number format. (Refer to "Sorting through the Special number formats" in Chapter 3 for details.) In the case of other numbers that use leading zeros (like part numbers), you can put an ' (apostrophe) before the first 0. The apostrophe tells Excel to treat the number like a text label but doesn't show up in the database itself. (The only place you can see the apostrophe is on the formula bar when the cell pointer's in the cell with the numeric entry.)

Press the ↓ key after you enter all the information for the new record. Instead of the ↓ key, you can press Return or click the New button (see Figure 9-2). Excel inserts the new record as the last record in the database in the worksheet and displays a new blank data form in which you can enter the next record (see Figure 9-3).

When you finish adding records to the database, press the Esc key or click the Close button at the bottom of the dialog box to close the data form. Then save the worksheet with the File⇨Save command on the menu bar or click the Save tool on the Standard toolbar.

Figure 9-2:
Entering information in the data form for the second record.

Figure 9-3:
The
database
after
entering the
second
record.

Calculated field entries

When you want Excel to calculate the entries for a particular field by formula, you need to enter that formula in the correct field in the first record of the database. Then select both the row of field names and the first record when creating the data form, and Excel copies the formula for this calculated field to each new record you add with the data form.

In the Bo Peep clients database, for example, the Total Due field in cell K3 of the first record is calculated by the formula =I3*J3 (cell I3 with the number of case hours and cell J3 with the hourly rate). This formula then computes what the client owes by multiplying the number of case hours by the hourly rate. As you can see, Excel adds the calculated field, Total Due, to the data form but doesn't provide a text box for this field (calculated fields can't be edited). When you enter additional records to the database, Excel calculates the formula for the Total Due field. If you then redisplay the data for these records, you see the calculated value following Total Due (although you won't be able to change it).

Locating, changing, and deleting records

After the database is underway and you're caught up with entering new records, you can start using the data form to perform routine maintenance on the database. For example, you can use the data form to locate a record you want to change and then make the edits to the particular fields. You can also use the data form to find a specific record you want to remove and then delete it from the database.

- ✔ Begin editing by positioning the cell pointer somewhere in the database (either in a cell with one of the database's field names or in a cell that forms a record with a field entry).
- ✔ Locate the record you want to edit in the database by bringing up its data form. (See Table 9-1 and the following two sections "Scrolling the night away!" and "Finders keepers" for hints on locating records.)
- ✔ To edit the fields of the current record, move to that field by pressing Tab or Shift+Tab and replace the entry by typing a new one.
- ✔ Alternatively, press ← or → or click the I-beam cursor to reposition the insertion point and then make your edits.
- ✔ To clear a field entirely, select it and then press the Delete key.

To delete the entire record from the database, click the Delete button. Excel displays an alert box with the following dire warning:

> Displayed record will be permanently deleted

To go ahead and get rid of the record displayed in the data form, click OK. To play it safe and keep the record intact, click Cancel.

Please keep in mind that you *cannot* use the Undo feature to bring back a record you removed with the Delete button! Excel is definitely *not* kidding when it uses words like "permanently deleted." As a precaution, always save a backup version of the worksheet with the database before you start removing old records.

Scrolling the night away!

After you display the data form in the worksheet by positioning the cell pointer somewhere in the database and then choosing the Data⇨Form command from the menu bar, you can use the scroll bar to the right of the list of field names or various keystrokes (both summarized in Table 9-1) to move through the records in the database until you find the one you want to edit or delete.

✔ To move to the data form for the next record in the database: Press ↓, press Return, or click the down scroll arrow at the bottom of the scroll bar.

✔ To move to the data form for the previous record in the database: Press ↑, press Shift+Return, or click the up scroll arrow at the top of the scroll bar.

✔ To move to the data form for the first record in the database: Press Control+↑, press Control+Page Up, or drag the scroll box to the very top of the scroll bar.

✔ To move to the data form for the last record in the database: Press Control+↓, press Control+Page Down, or drag the scroll box to the very bottom of the scroll bar.

Table 9-1	Ways to Get to a Particular Record
Keystrokes or Scroll Bar Technique	*Result*
Press ↓ or Return or click the down scroll arrow or the Find Next button	Moves to the next record in the database and leaves the same field selected
Press ↑ or Shift+Return or click the up scroll arrow or the Find Prev button	Moves to the previous record in the database and leaves the same field selected
Press Page Down	Moves forward ten records in the database
Press Page Up	Moves backward ten records in the database
Press Control+↑ or Control+Page Up or drag the scroll box to the top of the scroll bar	Moves to the first record in the database
Press Control+↓ or Control+Page Down or drag the scroll box to the bottom of the scroll bar	Moves to the last record in the database

Finders keepers

In a really large database, trying to find a particular record by moving from record to record — or even moving ten records at a time with the scroll bar — can take all day. Rather than waste time trying to manually search for a record, you can use the Criteria button in the data form to look it up.

When you click the Criteria button, Excel clears all the field entries in the data form (and replaces the record number with the word *Criteria*) so that you can enter the criteria to search for in the blank text boxes.

For example, suppose that you need to edit Old King Cole's file status. (You've finally located his missing animals!) Unfortunately, his paperwork doesn't include his case number. All you know is that currently his case is open (meaning the Status field for his record contains "Active" rather than "Closed"), and you're pretty sure that he spells his last name with a *C* instead of a *K*.

To find his record, you can at least use the information you have to narrow the search down to all the records where the last name begins with the letter *C* and the Status field contains *Active*. To limit your search in this way, open the data form for the client database, click the Criteria button, and then type the following in the text box for the Last Name field:

C*

Also type the following in the text box for the Status field (see Figure 9-4):

Active

Figure 9-4: The data form after selecting the Criteria button and entering the search criteria in the blank field text boxes.

When you enter search criteria for records in the blank text boxes of the data form, you can use the ? (question mark) and * (asterisk) *wildcard* characters. In Chapter 6, I show you how to use these wildcard characters with the Edit⇨ Find command on the menu bar to locate cells with particular entries.

Now click the Find Next button. Excel displays in the data form the first record in the database where the last name begins with the letter C and the Status field contains *Active*. As shown in Figure 9-5, the first record in this database that meets these criteria is for Eros Cupid. To press on and find our Old King Cole's record, click the Find Next button again. Figure 9-6 shows Old King Cole's record. Having located Cole's record, you can then edit his case status in the text box for the Status field. When you click the Close button, Excel records his new Closed case status in the database.

Figure 9-5: The first record in the database that meets the search criteria.

Figure 9-6: Eureka! The King's long lost record is found.

When you use the Criteria button in the data form to find records, you can include the following operators in the search criteria you enter to locate a specific record in the database:

Operator	Meaning
=	Equal to
>	Greater than
>=	Greater than or equal to
<	Less than
<=	Less than or equal to
<>	Not equal to

For example, to display only those records where a client's total due is greater than or equal to $50,000, type **>=50000** in the text box for the Total Due field before choosing the Find Next button.

When specifying search criteria that fit a number of records, you may have to click the Find Next or Find Prev button several times to locate the record you want. If no record fits the search criteria you enter, the computer beeps at you when you click these buttons.

To change the search criteria, first clear the data form by choosing the Criteria button again and then choosing the Clear button. Then select the appropriate text boxes and clear out the old criteria before you enter the new. (You can just replace the criteria if you're using the same fields.)

To switch back to the current record without using the search criteria you enter, click the Form button. (This button replaces the Criteria button as soon as you click the Criteria button.)

Sorting It All Out

Every database you put together in Excel will have some kind of preferred order for maintaining and viewing the records. Depending on the database, you may want to see the records in alphabetical order by last name. In the case of a database of clients, you may want to see the records arranged alphabetically by company name. In the case of the Little Bo Peep clients database, the preferred order is in numerical order by the case number assigned to each client when he or she hires the agency to find his or her pets.

When you initially enter records for a new database, you no doubt enter them either in the preferred order or the order in which you get a hold of their records. However you start out, as you will soon discover, you don't have the option of adding subsequent records in that preferred order. Whenever you add a new record with the New button in the data form, Excel tacks that record onto the bottom of the database by adding a new row.

This means that if you originally enter all the records in alphabetical order by company (from *Acme Pet Supplies* to *Zastrow and Sons*) and then you add the record for a new client named *Bambi's Pasta Palace,* Excel puts the new record at the bottom of the barrel, in the last row right after *Zastrow and Sons* instead of inserting it in its proper position somewhere after *Acme Pet Supplies* but definitely well ahead of Zastrow and his wonderful boys!

And this is not the only problem you can have with the order used in originally entering records. Even if the records in the database remain fairly stable, the preferred order merely represents the order you use *most* of the time. But what about those times when you need to see the records in another, special order?

For example, although you usually like to work with the clients database in numerical order by case number, you may need to see the records in alphabetical order by the client's last name to quickly locate a client and look up his or her total due in a printout. When using the records to generate mailing labels for a mass-mailing, you want the records in zip-code order. When generating a report for your account representatives that shows which clients are in whose territory, you need the records in alphabetical order by state and maybe even by city.

It seems that flexibility in the record order is exactly what's required to keep up with the different needs you have for the data. This is precisely what the Data⇨Sort command offers you, after you understand how to use it.

To have Excel correctly sort the records in a database, you must specify the fields whose values determine the new order of the records (such fields being technically known as the *sorting keys* in the parlance of the database enthusiast). Further, you must specify what type of order should be created using the information in these fields. You can select from two possible orders: *ascending order,* in which text entries are placed in alphabetical order (A to Z) and values are placed in numerical order (from smallest to largest), and *descending order,* which is the exact reverse of alphabetical order (Z to A) and numerical order (largest to smallest).

When you sort records in a database, you can specify up to three fields on which to sort. (You can also choose between ascending and descending order for each field you specify.) You need to use more than one field only when the first field you use in sorting contains duplicate values and you want a say in how the records with duplicates are arranged. (If you don't specify another field to sort on, Excel just puts the records in the order in which you entered them.)

The best and most common example of when you need more than one field is when you sort a large database alphabetically in last-name order. Say that you have a database that contains several people with the last name Smith, Jones, or Zastrow (as is the case when you work at Zastrow and Sons). If you specify the Last Name field as the only field to sort on (using the default ascending order), all the duplicate Smiths, Joneses, and Zastrows are placed in the order in which their records were originally entered. To better sort these duplicates, you can specify the First Name field as the second field to sort on (again using the default ascending order), making the second field the tie-breaker, so that Ian Smith's record precedes that of Sandra Smith, and Vladimir Zastrow's record comes after that of Mikhail Zastrow.

TIP

Up and down the ascending and descending sort orders

When you use the ascending sort order with a key field that contains many different kinds of entries, Excel places numbers (from smallest to largest) before text entries (in alphabetical order), followed by any logical values (TRUE and FALSE), error values, and finally, blank cells. When you use the descending sort order, Excel arranges the different entries in reverse: FALSE logical values precede TRUE logical values, text entries go from Z to A, and numbers are arranged from largest to smallest.

To sort records in an Excel database, follow these steps:

1. Position the cell pointer in the first field name of the database.

2. Choose Data⇨Sort on the menu bar.

Excel selects all the records of the database (without including the first row of field names) and opens the Sort dialog box shown in Figure 9-7. By default, the first field name appears in the Sort by pop-up list box, and the Ascending radio button is selected at the top of the Sort dialog box.

Figure 9-7:
Setting up the Sort dialog box to sort records alphabetically in last-name/first-name order.

3. Select the name of the field you first want the database records sorted by in the Sort by pop-up list box.

If you want the records arranged in descending order, remember also to choose the Descending radio button to the right.

4. If the first field contains duplicates and you want to specify how these records are sorted, select a second field to sort on in the Then by pop-up list box and select between the Ascending and Descending radio buttons to its right.

5. If necessary, specify a third field to sort the records by, using the second Then by pop-up list box and decide on the sort order to use.

6. Click OK or press Return.

Excel sorts the selected records. If you see that you sorted the database on the wrong fields or in the wrong order, choose the Edit⇨Undo Sort command on the menu bar or press ⌘+Z to immediately restore the database records to their previous order.

Figure 9-7 shows the Sort dialog box after the Last Name field in the Bo Peep clients database is selected as the first field to sort on and the First Name field is selected as the second field on which to sort (these being the records with duplicate entries in the Last Name field). The settings in this dialog box specify that records in the Bo Peep clients database be sorted in alphabetical (ascending) order by last name and then first name. Figure 9-8 shows the clients database right after sorting. (Note how the Harveys — Allison, Christine, and Scott — are now arranged in the proper first name/ last name alphabetical order.)

You can use the Sort Ascending tool (the button with the A above the Z) or the Sort Descending tool (the button with the Z above the A) on the Standard toolbar to sort records in the database on a single field.

- ✔ To sort the database in ascending order by a particular field, position the cell pointer in that field's name at the very top of the database and then click the Sort Ascending button on the Standard toolbar.

- ✔ To sort the database in descending order by a particular field, position the cell pointer in that field's name at the very top of the database and then click the Sort Descending button on the Standard toolbar.

| | File | Edit | View | Insert | Format | Tools | Data | Window | Help | | Wed 10:41:18 AM | |

	A	B	C	D	E	F	G	H	I	J	K	L
1	Little Bo-Peep Pet Detectives – Client List											
2	Case No	Last Name	First Name	Street	City	State	Zip	Status	Hours	Rate	Total Due	Paid
3	101-040	Andersen	Hans	341 The Shadow	Scholar	MN	58764	Closed	175	75.00	$13,125	No
4	103-023	Appleseed	Johnny	6789 Fruitree Tr	Along The Way	SD	66017	Active	321	125.00	$40,125	Yes
5	102-013	Baggins	Bingo	99 Hobbithole	Shire	ME	04047	Active	100	125.00	$12,500	No
6	103-007	Baum	L. Frank	447 Toto Too Rd	Oz	KS	65432	Active	421	125.00	$52,625	No
7	104-026	Brown	Charles	59 Flat Plains	Saltewater	UT	84001	Active	575	125.00	$71,875	No
8	101-001	Bryant	Michael	326 Chef's Lane	Paris	TX	78705	Active	600	100.00	$60,000	Yes
9	101-028	Cassidy	Butch	Sundance Kidde	Hole In Wall	CO	80477	Closed	345.5	75.00	$25,913	No
10	102-006	Cinderella	Poore	8 Lucky Maiden Way	Oxford	TN	07557	Closed	800	75.00	$60,000	No
11	104-055	Cole	Old King	4 Merry Soul	Fiddlers Three	MA	1824	Active	180	120.00	$21,600	Yes
12	103-004	Cupid	Eros	97 Mount Olympus	Greece	CT	03331	Active	123.5	75.00	$9,263	No
13	103-022	Dragon	Kai	2 Pleistocene Era	Ann's World	ID	00001	Active	450.2	75.00	$33,765	No
14	104-031	Eaters	Big	444 Big Pigs Court	Dogtown	AZ	85257	Closed	780	125.00	$97,500	Yes
15	106-022	Foliage	Red	49 Maple Syrup	Waffle	VT	05452	Active	205	125.00	$25,625	Yes
16	102-020	Franklin	Ben	1789 Constitution	Jefferson	WV	20178	Active	189.5	75.00	$14,213	Yes
17	104-019	Fudde	Elmer	8 Warner Way	Hollywood	CA	33461	Active	463.5	125.00	$57,938	Yes
18	102-002	Gearing	Shane	1 Gunfighter's End	LaLa Land	CA	90069	Active	902.5	125.00	$112,813	Yes
19	102-012	Gondor	Aragorn	2956 Gandalf	Midearth	WY	80342	Closed	157	125.00	$19,625	Yes
20	104-005	Gookin	Polly	4 Feathertop Hill	Hawthorne	MA	01824	Active	169.5	125.00	$21,188	Yes
21	101-014	Harvey	Allison	231 Rue de la Paie	Sorbonne	AZ	53912	Closed	175	75.00	$13,125	No
22	105-008	Harvey	Christine	660 MTV Drive	New York	NY	10032	Active	226.5	125.00	$28,313	No
23	101-920	Harvey	Scott	12 Elm Street	Scholar	MN	58764	Active	250	75.00	$18,750	Yes
24	106-021	Horse	Seabisquit	First Place Finish	Raceway	KY	23986	Active	300	125.00	$37,500	No
25	101-015	Humperdinck	Engelbert	6 Hansel+Gretel Tr	Gingerbread	MD	20815	Active	705.5	125.00	$88,188	Yes
26	103-017	Jacken	Jill	Up the Hill	Pail of Water	OK	45678	Closed	200	75.00	$15,000	No
27	105-027	Laurel	Stan	2 Oliver Hardy	Celluloyde	NM	82128	Closed	352	125.00	$44,000	No
28	101-030	Liberty	Statuesque	31 Gotham Centre	Big Apple	NY	10011	Active	236.5	125.00	$29,563	No
29	103-016	Oakenshield	Rex	Mines of Goblins	Everest	NJ	07639	Closed	400	125.00	$50,000	No
30	103-024	Oakley	Anney	Six Shooter Path	Target	ND	66540	Active	502.5	125.00	$62,813	No
31	101-029	Oow	Lu	888 Sandy Beach	Honolulu	HI	99909	Active	732	125.00	$91,500	No
32	104-018	Ridinghoode	Crimson	232 Cottage Path	Wulfen	PA	15201	Active	125.5	125.00	$15,688	Yes

Figure 9-8:
The clients
database
sorted in
alphabetical
order by
last name
and then by
first name.

TIP

Sorting something besides a database

The Sort command is not just for sorting records in the database. You can use it to sort financial data or text headings in the spreadsheets you build as well. When sorting regular worksheet tables, just be sure to select all the cells with data to be sorted (and only those with the data to be sorted) before you choose Data⇨Sort command on the menu bar.

Also note that Excel automatically excludes the first row of the cell selection from the sort (on the assumption that this row is a header row containing field names that shouldn't be included). To include the first row of the cell selection in the sort, be sure to select the No Header Row radio button in the My List Has section before you click the OK button to begin sorting.

You AutoFilter the Database to See the Records You Want

Excel's AutoFilter feature makes it a breeze to hide everything in a database except the records you want to see. All you have to do to filter a database with this incredibly nifty feature is position the cell pointer somewhere in the database before you choose Data⇨Filter⇨AutoFilter on the menu bar. When you choose the AutoFilter command, Excel adds pop-up list buttons to every cell with a field name in that row (like those shown in Figure 9-9).

To filter the database to just those records that contain a particular value, you then click the appropriate field's pop-up list button to open a list box containing all the entries made in that field and select the one you want to use as a filter. Excel then displays only those records that contain the value you selected in that field. (All other records are temporarily hidden.)

For example, in Figure 9-9, I filtered the Little Bo Peep clients database to display only those records where the State field contains AZ (for Arizona) by clicking the State's pop-up list button and then clicking AZ in the pop-up list box. (It was as simple as that.)

Figure 9-9:
The clients database after filtering out all records except those where the State is AZ.

After you filter a database so that only the records you want to work with are displayed, you can copy those records to another part of the worksheet to the right of the database (or better yet, another worksheet in the workbook). Simply select the cells and then choose Edit⇨Copy on the menu bar (⌘+C), move the cell pointer to the first cell where the copied records are to appear, and press Return. After copying the filtered records, you can then redisplay all the records in the database or apply a slightly different filter.

If you find that filtering the database by selecting a single value in a field pop-up list box gives you more records than you really want to contend with, you can further filter the database by selecting another value in a second field's pop-up list box. For example, say that you select CA as the filter value in the State field's pop-up list box and end up with hundreds of California records still displayed in the worksheet. To reduce the number of California records to a more manageable number, you can then select a value like San Francisco in the City field's pop-up list box to further filter the database and reduce the records you have to work with on-screen. When you finish working with the San Francisco, California, records, you can display another set by choosing the City field's pop-up list box again and changing the filter value from San Francisco to some other city (such as Los Angeles).

When you're ready to once again display all the records in the database, choose Data⇨Filter⇨Show All on the menu bar. You can also remove a filter from a particular field by selecting its pop-up list button and then selecting the (All) option at the top of the pop-up list.

Note that if you've only applied a single field filter to the database, selecting the (All) option is tantamount to choosing the Data⇨Filter⇨Show All command on the menu bar.

Viewing the top ten records

Excel 98 contains an AutoFilter option called Top 10. You can use this option on a numerical field to show only a certain number of records (like the ones with the ten highest or lowest values in that field or those in the ten highest or lowest percent in that field). To use the Top 10 option to filter a database, follow these steps:

1. **Choose Data⇨Filter⇨AutoFilter on the menu bar.**

2. **Click the pop-up list button in the field that you want to use in filtering the database records.**

3. **Select the (Top 10) option in the pop-up list box.**

   Excel opens the Top 10 AutoFilter dialog box, similar to the one shown in Figure 9-10.

Figure 9-10:
The Top 10
AutoFilter
dialog box.

By default, the Top 10 AutoFilter chooses to show the top ten items in the selected field. You can, however, change these default settings before filtering the database.

4. **To show only the bottom ten records, change Top to Bottom in the pop-up list box.**

5. **To show more than the top or bottom ten records, enter the new value in the text box that currently holds 10 or select a new value using the spinner buttons.**

6. **To show those records that fall into the top or bottom 10 (or whatever)** *percent,* **change Items to Percent in its pop-up list box.**

7. **Click OK or press Return to filter the database using your Top 10 settings.**

Getting creative with custom AutoFilters

In addition to filtering a database to records that contain a particular field entry (such as *Newark* as the City or *CA* as the State), you can create custom AutoFilters that enable you to filter the database to records that meet less-exacting criteria (such as last names starting with the letter M) or ranges of values (such as salaries between $25,000 and $35,000 per year).

To create a custom filter for a field, click the field's pop-up list button and then select the (Custom) option at the top of the pop-up list box — between (Top 10) and the first field entry in the list box. When you select the (Custom) option, Excel displays the Custom AutoFilter dialog box, similar to the one shown in Figure 9-11.

In this dialog box, you first select the operator that you want to use in the first pop-up list box (=, >, <, >=, <=, or <> — see Table 9-2 for details) and then enter the value (be it text or numbers) that should be met, exceeded, fallen below, or not found in the records of the database in the text box to the right. Note that you can select any of the entries made in that field of the database by clicking the pop-up list button and selecting the entry in the pop-up list box (much like you do when selecting an AutoFilter value in the database itself).

Figure 9-11:
Custom
AutoFilter
where the
Total Due is
greater
than or
equal to
$25,000 or
less than or
equal to
$50,000.

Table 9-2   Operators Used in Creating Custom AutoFilters

Operator	Meaning	Example	What It Locates in the Database
=	Equal to	Last Name=D*	Records where the last name starts with the letter D
>	Greater than	ZIP>42500	Records where the number in the ZIP field comes after 42,500
<	Less than	Salary<25000	Records where the value in the Salary field is less than 25,000 per year
>=	Greater than	Hired>=1/11/92	Records where the date in or equal to the Hired field is on or after January 11, 1992
<=	Less than	Joined<=2/15/91	Records where the date in the or equal to Joined field is on or before February 15, 1991
<>	Not equal to	State<>NY	Records where the entry in the State field is not NY (New York)

If you only want to filter records where a particular field entry matches, exceeds, falls below, or simply is not the same as the one you enter in the text box, you then click OK or press Return to apply this filter to the database. However, you can use the Custom AutoFilter dialog box to filter the database to records with field entries that fall within a range of values or meet either one of two criteria.

To set up a range of values, you select the > or >= operator for the top operator and then enter or select the lowest (or first) value in the range. Then make sure that the And radio button is selected and select < or <= as the bottom operator and enter the highest (or last) value in the range.

Figure 9-11 illustrates how to filter the records in the clients database so that only those records where Total Due amounts are between 25,000 and 50,000 are displayed. As shown in Figure 9-11, you set up this range of values as the filter by first selecting >= as the operator and 25000 as the lower value of the range. Then, with the And radio button selected, you select <= as the operator and 50000 as the upper value of the range.

To set up an either/or condition in the Custom AutoFilter dialog box, you normally choose between the = (equal) and <> (unequal) operators (which-ever is appropriate) and then enter or select the first value that must be met or must not be equaled. Then you click the Or radio button and select whichever operator is appropriate and enter or select the second value that must be met or must not be equaled.

For example, if you want to filter the database so that only records where the state is WA (Washington) or OR (Oregon) are displayed, you select = as the first operator and then select or enter WA as the first entry. Next, you click the Or radio button, select = as the second operator, and then select or enter OR as the second entry. When you then filter the database by clicking OK or pressing Return, Excel displays only those records where either WA or OR is entered as the code in the State field.

Chapter 10

Of Hyperlinks and HTML

● ●

In This Chapter

▶ Creating a hyperlink to another Office document, Excel workbook, worksheet, or cell range

▶ Creating a hyperlink to a Web page

▶ Changing the Hyperlink and Followed Hyperlink styles

▶ Converting an Excel data table into an HTML table

▶ Viewing your HTML table with your Web browser

▶ Publishing your worksheet data on the World Wide Web

● ●

*N*ow that everyone and his brother seems to have Internet fever and the World Wide Web has become the greatest thing since sliced bread, it should come as no surprise to learn that Excel 98 has added a whole bunch of exciting Web-related features. Chief among these features are the ability to add hyperlinks to the cells of your worksheet and the ability to convert your worksheet data into HTML (*H*ypertext *M*arkup *L*anguage) tables and your charts into GIF (Graphics Interchange Format) images.

Hyperlinks in a worksheet make the opening of other Office documents, Excel workbooks and worksheets (whether these documents are located on your hard disk, a server on your LAN [Local Area Network], or Web pages on the Internet or the company's intranet) just a mouse click away. HTML tables enable you to publish your worksheet data and charts on your Web pages (on your company's intranet or a Web site on the Internet) so that your data can be viewed more or less as you formatted it with Excel 98.

Adding Hyperlinks to a Worksheet

The hyperlinks that you add to your Excel worksheets can be of these types: hypertext that normally appears in the cell as underlined blue text, graphics from files that you've inserted into the worksheet, or graphics that you've drawn with the tools on the Drawing toolbar — in effect turning the graphic images into buttons.

When adding a hyperlink of either text or graphics, you can link it to an external file or Internet URL (*U*niform *R*esource *L*ocator) or to a named location in the worksheet. The named location can be a cell reference or named cell range (see Chapter 6 for details on naming cell ranges) in a particular worksheet.

To create the text in a cell to which the hyperlink is to be attached, follow these steps:

1. **Select the cell in the worksheet of the workbook that is to contain the hyperlink.**

2. **Enter the text for the hyperlink in the cell; then click the Return button on the formula bar.**

To insert a graphics file into the worksheet to whose image the hyperlink is to be attached, follow these steps:

1. **Choose Insert⇨Picture⇨From File; then select the file with the image you want to use in the Insert Picture dialog box and click the Insert button or press Return.**

   Excel inserts the graphic image into your worksheet. This graphic is selected (as evidenced by the sizing handles around the boundary box that surrounds it).

2. **Use the sizing handles to size the graphic image and then drag it to the place in the worksheet where you want the hyperlinked image to appear.**

To link the text or graphic image to another file, Web site, or named location in the workbook, follow these steps:

1. **Select the cell with the text or click the graphic to be linked.**

2. **Choose Insert⇨Hyperlink on the menu bar or click the Insert Hyperlink button (the one with the picture of a piece of chain link in front of the globe) on the Standard toolbar.**

   Excel opens the Insert Hyperlink dialog box (similar to the one shown in Figure 10-1) where you indicate the file, the Web address (URL), or the named location in the workbook.

3a. **To open another document, a Web page on the company's intranet, or a Web site on the Internet, enter the directory path to the document in the Link to file or URL text box.**

   If the document you want to link to is located on your hard disk or a hard disk that is mapped on your computer, click the Select button and select its file in the Link to file dialog box (which works just like the Select a document dialog box that I describe in Chapter 2) before you click OK.

Figure 10-1:
The Insert
Hyperlink
dialog box.

If the document you want to link to is located on a Web site, enter its Web address (the `http://www.dummies.com/excel98.html`-like thing) by typing the entire thing into the Link to file or URL text box.

3b. **To move the cell pointer to another cell or cell range in the same workbook, select the Named location in file (optional) text box and enter the sheet name followed by the cell address or the defined range name.**

The easiest way to enter the worksheet name and cell address or range name is to click the Select button and then select the sheet name and cell reference or the defined range name in the Browse Excel Workbook dialog box (similar to the one shown in Figure 10-2). To select a cell reference in a worksheet, click the Sheet Name radio button, select the worksheet name in the list box, and then enter the cell reference in the Reference text box before you click OK. To select a range name, click the Defined Name radio button; then select the range name in the list box before you click OK.

4. **Click the OK button or press Return to close the Insert Hyperlink dialog box.**

Follow those hyperlinks!

After you create a hyperlink in a worksheet, you can follow it to whatever external document, Web page, or cell range within the same workbook that is associated with the hyperlink. To follow a hyperlink, position the mouse pointer over the underlined blue text (if you assigned the hyperlink to text in a cell) or the graphic image (if you assigned the hyperlink to a graphic inserted in the worksheet). When the mouse pointer changes to a hand with the index finger pointing upward, click the hypertext or graphic image, and Excel 98 makes the jump to the designated external document, Web page, or cell within the workbook. What happens when you make the jump depends on the destination of the hyperlink as follows:

Figure 10-2:
Selecting
the
worksheet
name and
cell
reference
for a local
hyperlink in
the Browse
Excel
Workbook
dialog box.

- ✓ **Hyperlinks to external documents:** Excel opens the document in its own window. If the program that created the document (like Word 98 or PowerPoint 98) is not already running, the Macintosh OS launches the program at the same time it opens the target document.

- ✓ **Hyperlinks to Web pages:** Excel opens the Web page in its own Web browser window. If you are not online at the time you click this hyperlink, the Macintosh OS connects you to the Internet via your modem (and, if necessary, launches your Web browser) prior to opening the Web page whose URL address is listed in the hyperlink.

- ✓ **Hyperlinks to cell ranges within the same workbook:** Excel activates the worksheet and selects the cell or cells whose sheet and cell range address is listed in the hyperlink.

After you follow a hypertext link to its destination, the color of its text changes from the traditional blue to a dark shade of purple (without affecting its underlining). This color change indicates that you've used the hyperlink. (Note, however, that graphic hyperlinks do not show any change in color after you follow them.) Excel automatically restores the hypertext links that you've followed in a worksheet to their original blue text color the next time you open its workbook.

Figures 10-3 through 10-5 illustrate how you can use hyperlinks to jump to different parts of the same workbook. Figure 10-3 shows a worksheet that contains an interactive table of contents to all the Profit and Loss data tables and charts in this workbook. This interactive table of contents consists of a list of the data tables and charts contained in the workbook. A hypertext link to the appropriate worksheet and cell range has been added to each entry of this list in the cell range B4:B15 (I removed the gridlines from this worksheet to make it easier to see and use the hyperlinks).

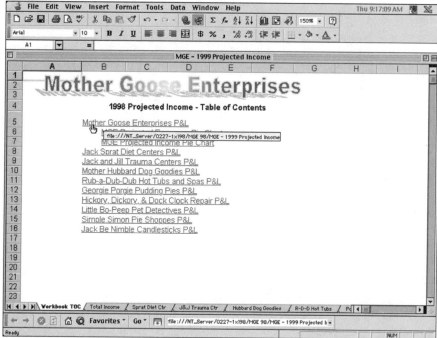

Figure 10-3:
An inter-
active table
of contents
with
hypertext
links to
sheets with
P&L data
and pie
charts.

Figure 10-4 shows what happens when I click the <u>Mother Goose Enterprises P&L</u> hyperlink. Excel immediately takes me to cell A1 of the Total Income worksheet. In this worksheet, the graphic image of a sign post (inserted from the Microsoft Clip Art Gallery 3.0) appears to the right of the worksheet title over the cell range D1:D7. This graphic contains a hyperlink that, when clicked, takes me to cell A1 of the Workbook TOC worksheet (the one shown in Figure 10-3).

Figure 10-5 shows what happens when I click the <u>MGE Projected Expenses Pie Chart</u> hypertext link. This hyperlink is attached to the named cell range, Exp_Pie. This cell range encompasses the cells A28:D45 in the Total Income worksheet. Note that clicking this hypertext link selects all cells in this named cell range, which just happen to be the ones that lie under the 3-D pie chart that shows the breakdown of the projected expenses anticipated in 1998. Because there is no way to attach a hyperlink directly to a chart that you add to a worksheet, you have to resort to selecting the underlying cells when you want a hyperlink to display a particular chart that's been added to a worksheet.

To the right of the MGE Projected 1998 Expenses pie chart, you see a star burst graphic (that I created with the Drawing toolbar, using the Stars and Banners option on the AutoShapes pop-up menu). This handmade graphic image contains the same hyperlink as the house clip art graphic (shown in Figure 10-4) so that, when clicked, it too takes me back to cell A1 of the Workbook TOC worksheet.

Editing and formatting hypertext links

The contents of cells that contain hypertext links are formatted according to the settings contained in two built-in workbook styles: Hyperlink and Followed. The Hyperlink style is applied to all new hypertext links you set up in a worksheet that you haven't yet used. The Followed Hyperlink is applied to all hypertext links that you used. If you want to change the way used and unused hypertext appears in the workbook, you need to change the formatting used in Followed Hyperlink and Hyperlink styles respectively. (Refer to "Showing Off in Styles" in Chapter 3 for information on modifying styles.)

If you need to edit the contents of a cell containing a hypertext link, you must be careful that, while getting Excel 98 into Edit mode so that you can change the text, you don't inadvertently follow the link. This means that under no circumstances can you click the cell with the hypertext link with the (primary) mouse button because that's the way you follow the hypertext link to your destination! The best way to get around this problem, if you're used to selecting cells by clicking them, is by doing the following:

1. **Click a cell right next door to the one with the hypertext link (above, below, right, or left), provided that this neighboring cell doesn't contain its own hyperlink.**

2. **Press the appropriate arrow key to then select the cell with the hypertext link to be edited (↓, ↑, →, or ←).**

3. **Press ⌘+U to put Excel 98 into Edit mode.**

4. **Make your changes to the contents of the hypertext in the cell; then click the Enter button on the formula bar or press Return to complete your edits.**

If you need to edit the destination of a hypertext link (as opposed to contents of the cell to which the link is attached), you need to select the cell with the arrow keys and then choose Insert⇨Hyperlink on the menu bar or Control+click the cell with the link to open the cell's shortcut menu (and avoid following the hyperlink) and then choose the Hyperlink⇨Edit Hyperlink command on this menu. Doing this opens the Edit Hyperlink dialog box (which looks suspiciously like the Insert Hyperlink dialog shown in Figure 10-1 after you fill it in) where you can change either the type and/or the location of the hyperlink.

To remove a hyperlink from a cell without otherwise changing its contents, click the Remove Link button at the bottom of the Edit Hyperlink dialog box. At the time you remove the hyperlink from a cell, Excel also automatically removes the formatting that's part of the Hyperlink style (the underlining and blue color).

To copy a hyperlink from one cell to another, you need to Control+click the cell (be sure that the Control key is down before you click it or else Excel will follow the hyperlink) and then choose Hyperlink⇨Copy Hyperlink commands on the cell's shortcut menu. Excel then places a marquee around the cell, and you can paste the copied hyperlink in a new cell by selecting the new cell and then pressing the Enter key on the numeric keypad or clicking the Paste button on the Standard toolbar (just as you would when copying the contents of the cell).

Note that if you copy a hyperlink to an empty cell in the workbook, the directory path or URL address of the destination appears in the cell. Then, when you enter data in that cell, the hyperlink destination disappears, and the data entry appears in the Hyperlink cell style.

If you want to remove the cell entry along with the hypertext link and Hyperlink style formatting from a cell, you choose Edit⇨Clear⇨All on the menu bar. If you try deleting a hypertext link by selecting the cell and pressing the Delete key, you succeed only in removing the cell entry and its underlying hyperlink without getting rid of the Hyperlink style. This means that any text you then enter in the cell will appear underlined in blue (although clicking its cell will *no* longer take you anywhere else).

Editing and formatting graphics with hyperlinks

When editing the graphics images to which you assign hyperlinks, you can edit the graphic image by Control+clicking the graphic and then choosing Format Picture on the graphic's shortcut menu. Doing this opens the Format Picture dialog box where you can modify various and sundry attributes of the image such as its color, fill, brightness and contrast, how it's cropped, and whether or not the image moves and is resized when you edit the underlying cells.

If you want to manually resize the graphic image or move it to a new place in the worksheet, you need to Control+click the graphic to select it and open its shortcut menu. Then click the image again to close its shortcut menu (without deselecting the graphic).

With the graphic image selected and the shortcut menu closed, you can then manipulate its size and/or position with the mouse. To resize the graphic image, you drag the appropriate sizing handles. To relocate the graphic image, you drag the graphic (when the mouse pointer changes to an arrowhead pointing to two double-headed arrows in the form of a cross) to its new position in the worksheet.

To copy a graphic image along with its hyperlink, Control+click the image, then choose the Copy command on the graphic's shortcut menu. Next, click somewhere outside of the graphic and choose Edit⇨Paste on the menu bar, click the Paste button on the Standard buttons bar, or press ⌘+V to paste a copy of the image in the worksheet. The copy of the image that you paste remains selected in the worksheet so that you can still reposition and resize the image before finally deselecting it.

To delete a graphic image and at the same time remove its hyperlink, Control+click the graphic then choose the Cut command on the graphic's shortcut menu.

Excel 98 Web Toolbar at Your Service

Figure 10-6 shows the tools on the Web toolbar. You can use these tools to follow hyperlinks in your worksheets or even to surf the Internet from within Excel even when your worksheet doesn't contain Web site hyperlinks. To display the Web toolbar, click the Web Toolbar button on the Standard toolbar or choose View⇨Toolbars⇨Web on the menu bar.

Figure 10-6: The Web toolbar.

Start Page
Search The Web
Forward
Favorites Pop-Up Menu
Backward
Show Only Web Toolbar

Go Pop-Up Menu
Address
Refresh Current Page
Stop Current Jump

You can temporarily remove all toolbars from the worksheet display except for the Web toolbar itself by clicking its Show Only Web Toolbar button (located to the immediate left of the Address bar).

By following spreadsheet hyperlinks with the Web toolbar displayed, you can use the toolbar's Forward and Back buttons to jump back and forth between the current worksheet and other worksheets within the same Excel workbook, worksheets in other workbooks, and even other kinds of Office documents to which the hyperlinks are tied.

After following a worksheet hyperlink to another document or another sheet within the same document, you can return to that original worksheet by clicking the Back button on the Web toolbar. After returning to the original worksheet, you can then return to the other document or sheet you just came from by clicking the Forward button.

If you are able to go online, you can surf the Internet from the Web toolbar by doing any the following things:

✔ Click the Start button to visit the Web page designated as the Home page for your Web browser.

✔ Click the Search the Web button to go to the microsoft.com Search Wizard page where you can search for Web sites in various categories or perform a full-site Web search.

✔ Click the Favorites button and then choose a page on its pop-up menu to visit of the Web pages you've bookmarked with your Web browser.

✔ Enter the URL of the Web page you want to visit in the Address bar (as in `http://www.dummies.com` to visit the Dummies Web site) and press Return.

After you have your fill of surfing the Internet, you can return to the Excel worksheet by closing your Web browser (⌘+Q).

Spreadsheets on the Web?

Actually, the concept of publishing Excel spreadsheet data on the World Wide Web makes a heck of a lot of sense, both from the standpoint of the worksheet's tabular layout and the worksheet's calculated contents. As anyone who's tried to code an HTML table will tell you, this is one of the nastiest jobs a person can perform. Even creating the simplest HTML table is a pain because you have to use <TH> and </TH> tags to set up the column headings in the table along with <TR> and </TR> tags to set up the rows of the table and <TD> and </TD> tags to define the number and width of the columns as well as what data goes in each cell of the table.

Even when using an HTML authoring tool that doesn't make you go through this kind of brute-force table making with the objectionable HTML table tags (like Word 98, which enables you to set up and fill in an HTML table from the menu bar just like you would in creating a regular Word table), you don't end up with a fancy table with sculpted borders between the cells, and you still don't have the luxury of performing calculations between data in the table cells like you do when using the Internet Assistant for Excel to convert your worksheet data tables.

By using the Internet Assistant Wizard in Excel 98, you get the best of both worlds: You can use all Excel's calculation power, while at the same time automatically generating very fancy-looking HTML tables for your Web pages.

Converting worksheet data into an HTML table

The Internet Assistant Wizard walks you through the steps (which are really quite straightforward) for converting your data table in the current worksheet into an HTML table. During this procedure, you can either choose to have the HTML table placed in a brand new HTML document or into an existing HTML document.

Creating a table in a new HTML document

To convert Excel worksheet data to an HTML table in a new HTML document, follow these steps:

1. **Open the workbook with the data to be converted; then activate its worksheet and select the cells as a range.**

2. **Choose File⇨Save as HTML on the menu bar.**

   Doing this opens the Internet Assistant Wizard - Step 1 of 4 dialog box (similar to the one shown in Figure 10-7).

3a. **(Optional) To add other data ranges to be included in the HTML document, click the Add button; then type in the address of the new cell range or select its cells in the worksheet and click OK or press Return.**

3b. **(Optional) To change the order in which the data ranges and charts appear in the HTML document, click the name of the range or chart in the Ranges or charts to convert list box; then click the appropriate Move arrow button. (Clicking the one pointing up moves the selected range or chart up one position in the list, and clicking the one pointing down moves the selected range or chart down one position in the list.)**

Figure 10-7:
The Internet
Assistant
Wizard -
Step 1 of 4
dialog box.

3c. (Optional) To remove a data range or chart listed in the Ranges and charts to convert list box from the HTML document, select its name in this list box and then click the Remove button.

4. When the Ranges and charts to convert list box contains the data ranges and charts you want included in the correct order, click the Next button or press Return.

When you click Next, Excel displays the Internet Assistant Wizard - Step 2 of 4 dialog box (similar to the one shown in Figure 10-8).

Figure 10-8:
The Internet
Assistant
Wizard -
Step 2 of 4
dialog box.

5. By default, the Internet Assistant Wizard creates a new HTML document that contains the converted worksheet and chart data along with a header and footer so that you just need to click the Next button or press Return to move on to the Step 3 dialog box.

When you click Next, the Internet Assistant Wizard displays the Internet Assistant Wizard - Step 3 of 4 dialog box (similar to the one shown in Figure 10-9).

Figure 10-9:
The Internet
Assistant
Wizard -
Step 3 of 4
dialog box.

6. **When creating a new HTML document, you can enter the text to be displayed as the document's title; header; description below the header; and a footer with the date last updated, name, and e-mail address. You can also have the Internet Assistant insert a horizontal rule above and below the HTML table. When you finish making your choices in this dialog box, click Next or press Return to move to the next dialog box.**

The Internet Assistant Wizard - Step 4 of 4 dialog box (shown in Figure 10-10) then appears, where you indicate the path and filename for the new HTML document.

Figure 10-10:
The Internet
Assistant
Wizard -
Step 4 of 4
dialog box.

7. **Edit the path and filename in the File path text box in the Step 4 dialog box or use the Select button to open the destination folder and to enter the new filename before you click the Finish button or press Return.**

When you click the Finish button, the Internet Assistant Wizard creates a new HTML document with a table containing the selected worksheet and chart data.

8. **Deselect the data in the Excel worksheet.**

Creating a table in an existing HTML document

Many times you will want to add a table of worksheet data or a chart to an existing HTML document. To insert the data and charts into an existing HTML document, you must have already indicated the place in this HTML document where the converted data are to appear. To do this, you enter this weird-looking comment tag:

```
<!--##Table##-->
```

on its own line in the HTML document where you want to insert the converted HTML tables and charts. To do this, you can simply open the HTML document with your favorite HTML authoring tool (like Adobe PageMill). If you don't have a favorite HTML authoring tool, you can always open up and edit the HTML document with the SimpleText program that comes installed on your Macintosh as part of the System software.

After you insert this comment tag into the existing HTML document, you follow the same first four steps for saving the data in an HTML document as outlined in the earlier section, "Creating a table in a new HTML document." Then, with the Internet Assistant Wizard - Step 2 dialog box (refer to Figure 10-8) open, take these new steps:

1. **Select the Insert the converted data into an existing HTML file (just the table will be created) radio button in the Internet Assistant Wizard - Step 2 dialog box.**

2. **Click the Next> button or press Return.**

When you click Next, Excel displays the Internet Assistant Wizard - Step 3 of 4 dialog box (similar to the one shown in Figure 10-11).

3. **Enter the path and name of the HTML document into which the new table is to be inserted in the Path of the existing file text box or use the Select button to open its folder and select the file before you click Next or press Return.**

The Internet Assistant Wizard then checks the specified HTML file for the `<--##Table##-->` comment tag indicating where the new table is to be inserted. If this tag is not found in the specified HTML file, Excel 98 displays an alert box (as shown in Figure 10-12) indicating that you

Figure 10-11:
The HTML
Wizard -
Step 3 of 4
dialog box
when
inserting the
table into an
existing
HTML file.

need to use your Web browser or a text editor to add this string to the
HTML document. At that point, you must click OK or press Return to
close the alert box; then open the designated HTML file, add this tag,
and save the document before you return to Internet Assistant Wizard
in Excel 98, where you can try clicking the Next button again.

Assuming that the Table comment code is found when you click Next,
the Internet Assistant Wizard - Step 4 of 4 dialog box then appears
where you can edit the file and/or path for the HTML document to
which your worksheet data (and, perhaps, selected charts) are to be
inserted.

Figure 10-12:
An alert box
indicating
that the
Internet
Assistant
Wizard has
not found
the <!--
##Table##-->
tag in your
HTML file.

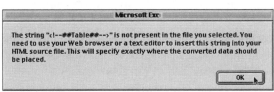

4. **(Optional) If you want to create a new HTML document (rather than
   replace the existing one), edit the path and filename in the File path
   text box in the Step 4 dialog box or use the Select button to open the
   new destination folder.**

5. **To save a revised version of the HTML document with the selected
   worksheet data and/or charts, click the Finish button or press Return.**

When you click the Finish button, the Internet Assistant Wizard creates a new a HTML table containing the selected worksheet data and adds it along with any charts that you've selected as GIF to the existing HTML document you specified.

Checking your HTML table with your Web browser

After the HTML table has been created from your Excel worksheet data, you will want to check out the results with your Web browser. You can do this locally on your computer's hard disk before you (or your company's Web master) download or copy the HTML document to your Web server. Just follow these steps:

1. **If you use Internet Explorer as your Web browser, choose Microsoft Internet Explorer on the Office Manager menu on the menu bar. If you use Netscape Navigator, return to the Finder and then double-click the Netscape Navigator program icon (or alias, if you've made one).**

   Doing this opens the PPP (Point-to-Point Protocol) Status dialog box, which connects you to your Internet Service Provider. (You know, that ISP thing.)

2. **If you use a dial-up account to access the Internet, click the Cancel button in the PPP Status dialog box that appears.**

   Clicking the Cancel button generates an Internet Explorer or Netscape Navigator alert dialog box with an error message telling you that the Home site or server at the address shown in the Address or Location text box could not be located.

3. **If an alert box telling you that the address indicated in the Address or Location text box could not be located, click OK or press Return to get rid of the alert dialog box.**

4. **Choose File⇨Open File on the Web browser's menu bar or press ⌘+O.**

   Doing this opens an Open Local File dialog box where you can specify the folder and name of the HTML file that contains the HTML table that you want to check.

5. **Select the folder in the folder pop-up menu and then select the file in the list box. After designating the folder and file in this dialog box, click the Open button or press Return to open the HTML file in the Web browsing window.**

After you complete these steps, your Web browser loads the HTML document, displaying its data tables and charts exactly as they will appear to other users who visit your Web site when you (or your Web master) put the document up with the other Web pages.

Figure 10-13 shows you the top part of the HTML table created from sample worksheet data when viewed in Microsoft's Internet Explorer 4. (The process of creating this table in a new HTML document is outlined in Figures 10-7 through 10-10 in the section "Creating a table in a new HTML document.") Figure 10-14 shows the very bottom part of this same HTML table when viewed with Netscape Communicator 4.

Note how the information entered into the Internet Assistant Wizard - Step 3 dialog box (shown back in Figure 10-9) appears in the final HTML document shown in these two figures. The Title information appears centered on the title bar of Internet Explorer (Figure 10-13) and Netscape Communicator (Figure 10-14). The Header and Description below header information appear in Figure 10-13 above the first rows of the HTML table separated by a rule (the horizontal line). The Last Update, By (my name) and Email information appear in Figure 10-14 below the last rows of the HTML table separated by a second rule. Note that the Email information near the bottom of Figure 10-14 is a live hypertext link. If you wanted to send me a message, all you have to do is click the hypertext gharvey@mindovermedia.com, and your Web browser opens a brand new e-mail message form that you can fill in and then send to me by clicking its Send Now button.

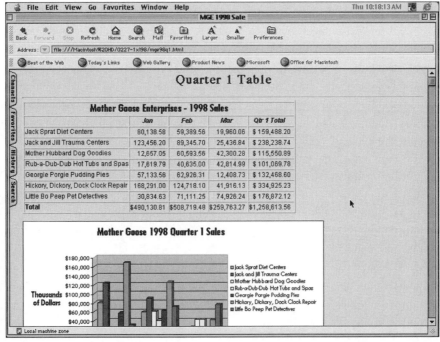

Figure 10-13:
The top part of the HTML table created from the worksheet data shown in Microsoft's Internet Explorer 4 browser.

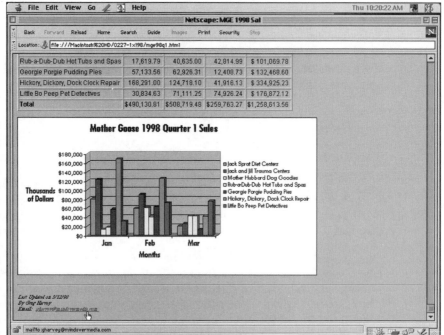

Rub-a-Dub-Dub Hot Tubs and Spas	17,619.79	40,635.00	42,814.99	$ 101,069.78
Georgie Porgie Pudding Pies	57,133.56	62,926.31	12,408.73	$ 132,468.60
Hickory, Dickory, Dock Clock Repair	168,291.00	124,718.10	41,916.13	$ 334,925.23
Little Bo Peep Pet Detectives	30,834.63	71,111.25	74,926.24	$ 176,872.12
Total	$490,130.81	$508,719.48	$259,763.27	$1,258,613.56

Figure 10-14:
The bottom
part of the
HTML table
created
from the
worksheet
data shown
in the
Netscape
Communi-
cator 4
browser.

Part V
Doing a Custom Job

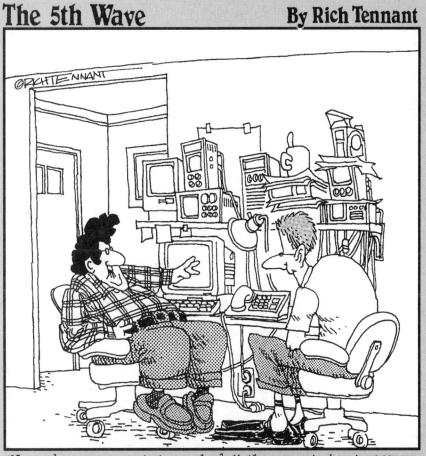

The 5th Wave   By Rich Tennant

"Now, when someone rings my doorbell, the current goes to a scanner that digitizes the audio impulses and sends the image to the Mac where it's converted to a Pict file. The image is then animated, compressed, and sent via high-speed modem to an automated phone service that sends an e-mail message back to tell me someone was at my door 40 minutes ago."

In this part . . .

*I*n case you haven't noticed, one of the biggest problems with computers is how rigid they are, working for
you only when you do exactly what they want you to do,
right when they want you to do it. And, like it or not, software programs like Excel 98 are no different with their
demanding command sequences and inflexible procedures.

Having seen how Excel 98 wants things done, I say it's
high time to turn the tables and find out how to make the
program work the way you want it to. To that end, Part V
concentrates on all the areas that you can customize.
This includes streamlining routine procedures with
macros in Chapter 11 and creating tailor-made toolbars in
Chapter 12.

Chapter 11

Macros Like Your Mother Used to Make

. . . .

In This Chapter

▶ Recording macros that perform common tasks

▶ Playing your macros

▶ Editing macros

▶ Adding macros to Excel toolbars

. . . .

Macros! Just hearing the word can be enough to make you want to head for the hills. But rather than think of this term as so much techno-babble, keep in mind that "macro" is short for "macro instruction" and that the word "macro" refers to the BIG picture. A *macro* (at least, at the level of this book) is nothing more than a way to record the actions you take to get a particular task done (such as to enter a company name in a worksheet, save and print a worksheet, or format row headings) and have Excel 98 play those actions back for you.

Using a macro to perform a routine task instead of doing it by hand has some definite advantages. First, Excel can execute the commands involved much faster than you can (no matter how good you are at the keyboard or how familiar you are with Excel). Also, Excel performs the task flawlessly each and every time (because the macro plays back your actions exactly as recorded, you only have to worry that you record them correctly). Besides, you can even streamline the playback process by assigning keystroke shortcuts to your favorite macros, essentially reducing to just two key-strokes common tasks that otherwise require quite a few steps.

Recording Macros

The process of recording a macro is surprisingly straightforward:

1. **Open the Record New Macro dialog box to turn on the macro recorder by choosing Tools⇨Macro⇨Record New Macro.**

2. **Name the macro and (optionally) assign it a keystroke.**

3. **Perform the sequence of actions you want recorded in the macro just as you normally do in Excel.**

   You can choose commands from the pull-down or shortcut menus, click tools in the toolbars, or use shortcut keystrokes.

4. **Turn off the macro recorder when you're finished by clicking the Stop Recording button that appears in the tiny Stop Recording toolbar as soon as you start recording.**

   You can also turn off the macro recorder by choosing Tools⇨Macro⇨ Stop Recording.

5. **Perform the task anytime you want simply by double-clicking the macro name in the Macro dialog box (opened by choosing Tools⇨ Macro⇨Macros or pressing Option+F8) or by selecting the macro name and then clicking the Run button.**

   Alternately, if you bothered to assign a keystroke shortcut to the macro when you recorded it, you can run the macro by pressing the keystroke shortcut.

You'll be happy to know that, when recording your actions, Excel doesn't record mistakes. (Don't you wish everyone else was so forgiving?) In other words, if you're entering the heading "January" in the macro and you type **Janaury** by mistake and then correct your error, Excel does not record your pressing of the Backspace key to delete the characters "aury" and then typing **uary**. The only thing the macro records is the final, corrected result of **January**!

To record your actions, Excel 98 uses a language called *Visual Basic* (a language, by the way, that you don't need to know diddly about in order to create and use *simple* macros — the only kind you're going to get involved with in this book). Visual Basic commands are recorded in a separate module sheet. (A *module sheet* is just a fancy name for a worksheet that doesn't use cells and therefore looks more like a typical page on a word processor screen.)

Personally Speaking

Excel automatically assumes that you want to record your macro as part of the current workbook. Recording the macro as part of the workbook means that you can run the macro only when this workbook is open. You may want to have access to some of the macros that you create any old time you're using Excel, regardless of whether the workbook that happened to be current when you originally recorded the macro is now open or whether you're creating a new workbook or editing an existing one.

To record a macro so that it's universally available for use anytime, any-where in Excel 98, you must record the macro in the Personal Macro Work-book rather than in the current workbook. Because the Personal Macro Workbook is automatically opened whenever you start up Excel (although it remains hidden at all times), you can run any of its macros no matter what workbook or workbooks are open at the time.

To record a macro in the Personal Macro Workbook, follow these steps:

1. **Choose Tools⇨Macro⇨Record New Macro to open the Record Macro dialog box.**

2. **Choose the Personal Macro Workbook in the Store macro in pop-up menu in the Record Macro dialog box.**

3. **Name your macro and (optionally) assign it a keystroke shortcut before you click OK and start recording the new macro.**

Excel doesn't actually create a Personal Macro Workbook for you until you take the trouble to record your first macro in that location and then save the macro in this workbook when you exit the program (no sense creating something you're never gonna use). After creating your first macro(s) in the Personal Macro Workbook and saving your changes, Excel 98 creates the Personal Macro Workbook inside the Excel folder, which itself is located within the Startup folder inside the Office folder on your hard disk. After that, Excel automatically opens this Personal Macro Workbook (thereby making its macros available) each and every time you launch Excel 98, while at the same time hiding the workbook.

A Macro a Day

The best way to get a feel for how easy it is to record and play back a simple macro is to follow along with the steps for creating a couple of them. The first sample macro enters and formats a company name in a cell. In these steps, you turn on the macro to record as you enter the company name, such as **Mother Goose Enterprises,** and change the font to 18-point, bold Palatino. If you're actually following along at your computer as you read these steps, be sure to adapt the basic macro so that it enters the name of *your* company in the font and type size *you* want to use.

The very first thing you need is a place in which to perform the actions you're going to have Excel record in the macro. For this example, open a new worksheet (although you can also use a blank cell in an existing worksheet). Then follow these steps:

1. **Position the pointer in the cell where you want to enter the company name.**

For this example, position the pointer in cell A1 in a blank worksheet in the current workbook. If necessary, choose a new blank worksheet by selecting the next sheet tab or pressing Control+Page Down.

2. Choose Tools⇨Macro⇨Record New Macro on the menu bar.

The Record Macro dialog box, similar to the one shown in Figure 11-1, appears.

Record Macro

Macro name:
Company_Name

Shortcut key: Store macro in:
Option+Cmd+ c   Personal Macro Workbook

Description:
Macro recorded 3/12/98 by Greg Harvey for entering the
Company Name in a cell

Cancel   OK

3. Replace the temporary macro name, Macro1, in the Macro name text box with a more descriptive macro name of your own.

When naming a macro, follow the same guidelines as when naming ranges (refer to Chapter 6); that is, start the name with a letter (not a number), don't use spaces (tie the parts of the name together with an underscore created by pressing Shift+hyphen), and don't use weird punctuation in the name.

For this example, in place of Macro1, type Company_Name.

4. (Optional) To assign a shortcut key to play your macro, click the Shortcut key text box and then enter a letter from A to z (in upper- or lowercase) or a number between 0 and 9 in its text box below.

The number or letter you enter is the key you use (in combination with the ⌘+Option or the ⌘+Option+Shift keys) to run the macro.

5. (Optional) To store your macro in your Personal Macro Workbook, choose Personal Macro Workbook on the Store macro in pop-up menu.

If you want to save the macro in a module sheet in a brand new workbook (which you can save later after recording the macro) rather than in either the current workbook (in which you will perform the actions recorded in the new macro) or in the Personal Macro Workbook, choose New Workbook on the Store macro in pop-up menu.

6. (Optional) Edit or annotate the macro description in the Description text box that appears beneath the Macro name text box.

This is a good place to describe briefly the purpose of the macro you're creating. (You *do* know what this thing is supposed to do, don't you? Enter the name of your company, that's what.)

Figure 11-1 shows the Record Macro dialog box just before closing the dialog box to record the macro. As you can see, the shortcut keystroke will be ⌘+Option+c (for Company). Also, because you so often add the company name to new workbooks, Personal Macro Workbook is selected in the Store macro in text box so that this macro is available anytime you're using Excel 98.

7. **Click OK or press Return to start recording your macro.**

   The Record Macro dialog box closes, and Excel shows you that the macro recorder is turned on by displaying the message, "Recording," on the status line and by displaying the Stop Recording toolbar (which consists of just two buttons, Stop Recording and Relative Reference).

8. **Perform the task you want to record.**

   For the Company_Name sample macro, you enter the company name in cell A1. Next, select the new font (Palatino in this case) from the Font drop-down list box and the font size (18 points) from the Font Size drop-down list box, and then click the Bold button.

9. **When you finish recording all the actions you want your macro to perform, turn off the macro recorder by clicking the Stop Recording button either in its own toolbar (shown in Figure 11-2) or by choosing Tools⇨Macro⇨Stop Recording on the menu bar.**

Figure 11-2:
Recording
the
Company_
Name
macro.

As soon as you stop recording a macro, the Recording message disappears from the status bar, and the Stop Recording toolbar disappears.

It's playback time!

After you turn off the macro recorder, you are ready to test the macro. If your macro enters new text or deletes some text as part of its actions, be very careful where you test it out. Be sure that the cell pointer is in a part of the worksheet where existing cell entries won't be trashed when you play back the macro. When you're ready to test the macro, you can do any of the following:

- ✔ The easiest way to play back a macro is to press the shortcut key-strokes (⌘+Option+C for the sample Company Name macro), assuming that you assigned a shortcut to your macro.

- ✔ You can choose Tools⇨Macro⇨Macros on the menu bar or press Option+F8 and then double-click the macro's name in the Macro dialog box or select the name and click the Run button. (This method works for any macro whether or not you assigned shortcut keys.)

If, when you play back the macro, you find it running amok in your work-sheet, press Esc to stop the macro prematurely. Excel displays a macro error dialog box indicating the point at which the macro was interrupted. Click the Halt button in this dialog box to shut the macro down.

Where Excel saves your macro depends on how you created the macro in the first place:

- ✔ If you created the macro as part of the current workbook, Excel places the macro in a hidden module sheet (called something like Module1, Module2, and so on) that is added to the workbook. To see the contents of the macro on this hidden module sheet, you need to press Option+F8 or choose Tools⇨Macro⇨Macros, select the macro in the Macro name text box, and then click the Edit button.

- ✔ If you created the macro as part of the Personal Macro Workbook, Excel places the macro in a hidden module sheet (called something like Module1, Module2, and so on) in the hidden workbook called Personal Macro Workbook. To see the contents of the macro on this hidden module sheet, you first need to choose Window⇨Unhide and then select Personal Macro Workbook in the Unhide workbook list box before you click OK or press Return. When the Personal Macro Work-book is open, you need to press Option+F8 or choose Tools⇨Macro⇨ Macros, select the macro in the Macro name text box, and then click the Edit button.

- ✔ If you saved the macro as part of a new workbook, Excel puts the macro in a hidden module sheet (called something like Module1, Module2, and so on) that is added to a new workbook (and given a temporary file-name like Workbook1, Workbook2, or whatever the next available number is). To see the contents of the macro on this hidden module sheet, you need to press Option+F8 or choose Tools⇨Macro⇨Macros, select the macro in the Macro name text box, and then click the Edit button.

When you save the current workbook or the new workbook, the macros in its hidden module sheets are saved as part of the files. In the case of the hidden Personal Macro Workbook, when you exit Excel, the program asks whether you want to save changes to this macro workbook. Be sure to click the Yes button so that you can still use the macros you've placed there the next time you work in Excel 98.

A macro for all months

The second sample macro enters the 12 months of the year (from January to December) across a single row of a worksheet. This macro enters the names of the months, makes them bold and italic, and then widens their columns with the best-fit feature.

As with the first macro, first find a place in a worksheet where you can enter and format the names. For this macro, you can select a new worksheet in your workbook or use a region of an existing worksheet that has 12 unused columns so that existing cell entries don't skew how wide the best-fit feature makes the columns. (You want the length of the name of the month to determine how wide to make each column.)

Figure 11-3 shows the Record Macro dialog box for this macro. Its name, appropriately enough, is Months_of_the_Year, and its shortcut keystroke is ⌘+Option+M.

Figure 11-3:
The Record
Macro
dialog box.

> **Record Macro**
> Macro name:
> Months_of_the_Year
> Shortcut key: Store macro in:
>   Option+Cmd+ [m]   [Personal Macro Workbook ⬍]
> Description:
> Macro recorded 3/12/98 by Greg Harvey for entering the
> 12 months across a row of cells
>   [Cancel] [OK]

To create this macro (or one like it), follow these steps:

1. **Position the cell pointer in cell A1 and choose Tools⇨Macro⇨Record New Macro.**

2. **Type Months_of_the_Year in the Macro name text box in the Record Macro dialog box.**

3. **(Optional) Click the Shortcut key check box and enter a letter in its text box.**

   In this example, I assign the macro the shortcut key, ⌘+Option+M.

4. **Indicate where to locate the macro in the Store macro in pop-up list box.**

   If you want to be able to use this macro in any worksheet you build (which would make the most sense), you need to choose Personal Macro Workbook in the pop-up list.

5. **(Optional) Enter a description of the macro in the Description text box.**

6. **Click OK or press Return to begin recording the macro.**

7. **Type January in cell A1, click the Enter button on the formula bar, and then use the AutoFill handle to select through cell L1 (until the screen tip says "December").**

   You didn't think that you were going to have to type out all those months, did you?

8. **Click the Bold and Italic tools on the Formatting toolbar.**

   This step adds these enhancements to the entries (the cell range A1:L1 with the month names is still selected).

9. **Choose 12 on the Font Size pop-up button on the Formatting toolbar.**

10. **With the range of columns containing the months (Columns A through L) still selected, choose Format⇨Column⇨AutoFit Selection on the menu bar.**

11. **Select the first cell, A1, to deselect the cell range with the names of the months.**

12. **Click the Stop Recording button on the Stop Recording toolbar or choose Tools⇨Macro⇨Stop Recording on the menu bar to stop recording.**

After turning off the macro recorder, you're ready to test your Months_of_the_Year macro. To adequately test the macro, use some new columns to the right. For example, I tested this macro on the virgin columns N through Y in Sheet2 by placing the cell pointer in cell N1 and then pressing ⌘+Option+M.

If you play this macro where I did, you get a rather rude Microsoft Visual Basic error dialog box indicating that

```
Run-time error '1004,'
AutoFill method of Range of class failed
```

occurred. (Is that English?!) This Microsoft Visual Basic error dialog box gives you a choice between ending the macro playback right there with the End button and debugging the macro (yeah, right!) with the Debug button. All this because I didn't play this macro when the cell pointer was in cell A1, where it was recorded.

Relative macro recording

What, you may ask, causes the Months_of_the_Year macro to screw up so that it displays a Macro Error dialog box with the Run-time error '1004' when you play it back from cell N1? Chapter 4 explains the differences between copying a formula with *relative cell references* and one with *absolute cell references.* In that chapter, I explain that Excel adjusts cell references in copies of a formula unless you take steps to convert them to *absolute* (or unchanging) references.

When recording macros, just the opposite is true: When you select a cell range (or a range of columns in this case), Excel records the cell references as absolute references rather than relative ones. This is the reason that the Months_of_the_Year macro only works properly when you run it with the cell pointer in cell A1. Excel keeps wanting to apply AutoFill to the cell range A1:L1 when cell A1 is the active cell. When cell A1 isn't active, the Visual Basic AutoFill command can't be completed, and you end up with this lovely

```
Run-time error '1004,'
AutoFill method of Range of class failed
```

message in a Microsoft Visual Basic dialog box.

Rerecording a macro

To change the Months_of_the_Year macro so that it works correctly from any cell in the worksheet and not just in cell A1, you have to rerecord it, this time using relative cell references (something that should have been done when the macro was originally recorded). To do this, follow these steps:

1. **Open up a new worksheet where you can perform the actions to be recorded.**

2. **Choose the Tools⇨Macro⇨Record New Macro on the menu bar.**

3. **Set up the Record Macro dialog box the same way you did when you first created the macro and then click OK or press Return.**

4. **Click the Yes button when Excel prompts whether you want to replace the existing macro.**

5. **Click the Relative Reference button in the Stop Recording toolbar before you start recording the macro steps.**

6. **Perform all the actions to be rerecorded (typing** January, **using AutoFill to generate the rest of the months, applying bold and italics to the cell range, changing the font size to 12 points, and then selecting their columns and adjusting their widths with the Format⇨ Column⇨AutoFit Selection command as outlined earlier in the steps in the section called "A macro for all months").**

7. **Click the Stop Recording button in the Stop Recording toolbar or choose Tools⇨Macro⇨Stop Recording on the menu bar to stop recording.**

   This time, Excel records the command for AutoFilling the months of the year with relative column references so that the AutoFilling is always relative to the cell where the macro enters January.

After stopping the macro, test it in a new worksheet, starting in a cell other than cell A1. Now, no matter where you position the cell pointer when you run the macro, Excel is able to fill in the names of the months with AutoFill without so much as a Run-time error '1,' let alone '1004'!

Chapter 12

Button Up That Toolbar!

*A*ll of the preceding chapters have shown you how to use the tools on the various built-in toolbars (from the Standard toolbar all the way to the Stop Recording macro toolbar) exactly as they are configured when they come with Excel 98. In this chapter, you find out how to customize the existing toolbars so that they contain only the tools you need, and you also discover how to create toolbars of your own.

As you soon discover when you read this chapter, the tools found on the built-in toolbars represent just a small part of the total number of tools supplied with Excel. You can add unused tools to any of the existing toolbars or combine them to create new toolbars of your own design.

Not only can you customize Excel toolbars by creating new combinations of various built-in buttons, but you can also customize toolbars by assigning the macros that you've recorded (see Chapter 11 for details) to any of the custom buttons that come with Excel 98. Further, if none of the pictures used on the custom buttons suits the function of the macro that you're adding to a toolbar, you can use a graphic created in another program (such as a clip-art image or one that you create yourself with another graphics program).

Toolbars — Now You See 'em, Now You Don't

As you discover in previous chapters, if not in practice, Excel 98 comes with a whole truckload of built-in toolbars. Each toolbar consists of a group of buttons that the program designers thought would be most helpful in getting particular tasks done. As you know, the Standard and Formatting toolbars that are automatically displayed at the top of the screen when you start Excel contain a wide variety of tools useful for creating, formatting, and printing documents.

Although the arrangements on most of the built-in toolbars may satisfy your needs, you can easily modify the arrangement of any of them. For example, if there are tools you seldom or never use, you can replace them with ones more useful for the type of work you do. If you use a tool quite often but are not happy with its position in the toolbar — or even the toolbar it's on — you can move it to a more convenient position.

To display a new toolbar on-screen (or hide one that's already displayed), you choose View⇨Toolbars and then choose the name of the toolbar (Chart, Drawing, and so on) on the cascading menu that appears. You can also shorten this process by Control+clicking one of the displayed toolbars and clicking the name of the toolbar you want to display.

You can also display (or hide) a toolbar in the Excel program window from the Toolbars tab in the Customize dialog box. To open this dialog box (shown in Figure 12-1), you choose View⇨Toolbars⇨Customize on the menu bar or choose Customize on one of the toolbar's shortcut menus. After the Toolbars tab is displayed in the open Customize dialog box, you select the toolbar's check box in the Toolbars list box to display the toolbar on the screen (or hide the toolbar if its check box is already selected).

If you click the Options tab in the Customize dialog box, you see two check boxes whose settings affect all the toolbars displayed in Excel:

- ✔ **Large icons:** Normally, Excel uses small icons in displaying the buttons on the toolbars. Select this check box to increase the size of the icons and, consequently, the size of the buttons. (This feature is especially helpful when you're running Excel on a computer with a really small screen, such as a PowerBook.)

- ✔ **Show ScreenTips on toolbars:** Normally, Excel shows you the name of each button on a toolbar when you position the mouse pointer on it without clicking the mouse button, the column letter or row number where you'd end up when using the scroll bars, and the address of the

Figure 12-1:
The
Toolbars
tab in the
Customize
dialog box.

cell range where your cell selection will be moved or copied to when using drag and drop. (Microsoft refers to these descriptions as ScreenTips.) If you no longer want to see these types of indicators, you can remove the display of all ScreenTips from the program display by deselecting this check box.

Customizing the Built-In Toolbars

To modify the contents of a particular toolbar from the Customize dialog box, you must either already have that toolbar displayed on-screen, or you must select it on the Toolbars tab of the Customize dialog box. Remember that you can select as many toolbars as you want in this list box, should you feel up to modifying more than one toolbar at a time.

After selecting the toolbar(s) that you want to modify, choose the Commands tab in the Customize dialog box (shown in Figure 12-2).

Figure 12-2:
The
Commands
tab in the
Customize
dialog box.

Adding buttons from the Customize dialog box

When you click the Commands tab in the Customize dialog box, Excel displays a Categories list box with all the groups of buttons available (File through New Menu) followed by a Commands list box that actually displays the command names alone or the command names with their icons in each group. To display a new group of commands in the Commands list box, you need only select its category name in the Categories list box. After the Commands tab of the Customize dialog box displays the commands for a particular category, you can then select individual commands just as you would any graphic object in a worksheet window.

To add one of the commands shown in the Commands list box to one of the toolbars displayed on the Excel 98 screen, you drag the command name or command name-plus-icon from the Commands list box in the Customize dialog box to its new position on the toolbar and release the mouse button.

As you drag, an icon of a generic button (representing the selected command) appears at the tip of the arrowhead mouse pointer, and a tiny box appears at the bottom of the arrowhead and slightly to the right. As long as you have the mouse pointer over a part of the screen where you can't add the button for the selected command, this tiny box at the bottom of the mouse pointer contains an **x** in it. When you finally move the mouse pointer over some place on a toolbar where you can insert the button, the **x** in this tiny box changes to the + sign. The plus sign is your signal that the toolbar will accept the button if you release the mouse button.

To let you know where the new button will be inserted in a toolbar, Excel displays a heavy I-beam (something like one that appears when inserting cells into an existing range with drag and drop — see "Insertions courtesy of drag and drop" in Chapter 4) in the toolbar at the tip of the arrowhead mouse pointer. The I-beam shape indicates where on the toolbar the new button for the command you're adding will be inserted. When positioning the new button on the toolbar, you can insert it in front of or between any of the existing buttons.

Note that you can always find out what a particular command does by choosing its name or name-plus-icon in the Commands list box and then clicking the Description button at the bottom of the dialog box. When you click the Description button, Excel 98 displays a text box with a short description of the selected command's function. To get rid of the text box, just click anywhere on the Customize dialog box outside of the confines of the text box describing the function of the selected command or move the mouse pointer outside of the text box and wait until the box disappears. (Clicking is definitely faster.)

Removing buttons from a toolbar

When the Customize dialog box is open, you can not only add new buttons to a displayed toolbar but also get rid of existing buttons by literally dragging them off the toolbar. To junk a button that you don't need, select it on the toolbar and then drag the icon of the button until it's off the toolbar before you release the mouse button. As soon as you release the mouse button, the toolbar button disappears, and Excel closes up the gap on the toolbar.

Playing musical chairs with buttons

When customizing a toolbar, you may only want to reposition the buttons or move or copy them to one of the other toolbars that are displayed.

- ✔ To reposition a button on the same toolbar, drag its button icon until the I-beam indicator is positioned slightly in front of the button it is to precede and release the mouse button.

- ✔ To move a button to a different toolbar, drag its button icon to the desired position on the new toolbar and then release the mouse button.

- ✔ To copy a button to a different toolbar, hold down the Option key as you drag its button icon to the new toolbar. (The plus sign appears in the tiny little box attached to the arrowhead pointer when you position the mouse pointer over any of the toolbars displayed on the screen.)

What a bunch of spaced-out buttons!

You may have noticed how buttons on various built-in toolbars are grouped together with little gray vertical bars appearing before and after the group of buttons. You too can group various buttons when customizing a toolbar.

To insert a vertical bar on the left or right side of a button to separate it from other buttons, drag the button slightly in the opposite direction of where you want the vertical bar to appear (to the right to insert a space on its left side and to the left to insert a space on its right side) and release the mouse button. Excel inserts a vertical bar before or after the button you just dragged.

To delete a vertical bar in front of or after a button so that the button abuts — or touches — the one next to it, drag the button in the appropriate direction until it touches or slightly overlaps the neighboring button and then release the mouse button. Excel redraws the toolbar to remove the space from the button you just dragged.

It's not my default!

Sometimes, you may make changes to a built-in toolbar and then decide that you don't want to keep those changes. No matter what wild changes you make to a built-in toolbar, you can always restore the toolbar to its original form by opening the Customize dialog box (by choosing View⇨Toolbars⇨ Customize on the menu bar or choosing the Customize command on a toolbar shortcut menu) and then selecting the toolbar's name in the Toolbars list box and clicking the Reset button.

Designing Your Own Toolbars

You are by no means limited to the built-in toolbars that come with Excel. You can create your own toolbars to combine any of the available buttons: those that are used in the built-in toolbars as well as those that are not.

To create a toolbar of your very own, follow these steps:

1. **Choose Tools⇨Toolbars⇨Customize on the menu bar to open the Customize dialog box.**

2. **If it's not already selected, select the Toolbars tab in the Customize dialog box and then click the New button.**

   The New Toolbar dialog box opens where you name the new toolbar.

3. **Enter a name for the new toolbar in the Toolbar name text box and then click OK or press Return.**

   Excel closes the New Toolbar dialog box and adds the name of your new toolbar to the bottom of the Toolbars list in the Customize dialog box. The program also opens a tiny, floating toolbar (similar to the one shown in Figure 12-3) with just enough room on it for a single button and with none of the toolbar's name showing in the title bar.

4. **Select the Commands tab in the Customize dialog box and then choose the category containing the command for the first button you want to add to the new toolbar from the Categories list box.**

5. **Drag the button icon for the command from the Commands list box in the Customize dialog box to the tiny toolbar dialog box in the upper-left corner of the document window; then release the mouse button.**

6. **Repeat Steps 4 and 5 until you have added all the buttons you want to the new toolbar.**

   After the buttons are on the new toolbar, you can rearrange and space them out as you want.

Figure 12-3:
The new Greg's Cool Tools toolbar before the buttons are added.

7. Click the Close button or press Return to close the Customize dialog box.

As you add buttons to the new toolbar, Excel automatically widens the toolbar dialog box. When the dialog box is wide enough, the name you assigned to the toolbar appears in the title bar. If the toolbar dialog box starts running into the Customize dialog box, just drag the new toolbar down by its title bar until it's entirely clear of the Customize dialog box.

Figures 12-3 and 12-4 show the process of creating a new toolbar (called, modestly enough, Greg's Cool Tools). Figure 12-3 shows the Customize dialog box after naming the new toolbar in the New Toolbar dialog box and adding its name to the bottom of the Toolbars list box. Figure 12-4 shows Greg's Cool Tools toolbar after I added the following thirteen buttons: Clear Contents, Clear Formatting, Comments, Delete Comment, AutoFormat, Merge Cells, Unmerge Cells, Rotate Text Up, Rotate Text Down, Angle Text Downward, Angle Text Upward, Page Break Preview, and Normal.

Note how I used the vertical bars in the custom toolbar to create five groups of buttons. Each group contains buttons that perform a similar function (be it erasing, formatting, previewing, merging, or rotating text).

Figure 12-4:
The
completed
Greg's Cool
Tools
toolbar.

After creating a new toolbar, you can display, hide, move, resize, and dock it just like you do any of the built-in toolbars. If you don't want to keep a toolbar you've created, delete it by opening the Toolbars tab in the Customize dialog box and selecting the toolbar name in the Toolbars list box (so that it appears highlighted).

As soon as you select the name of a toolbar that you created, the Delete button becomes available. (This button remains grayed out and unavailable when you select any of the built-in toolbars.) When you click Delete, Excel displays an alert dialog box, in which you confirm the deletion by clicking OK or pressing Return.

Adding buttons that play macros

As I hinted earlier in this chapter, you can assign macros that you've recorded (covered back in Chapter 12) to tools and then place these tools on toolbars (either on one of the built-ins or on one of your own creation). That way, you can play back a macro by clicking its button. This feature is particularly helpful when you've assigned all 26 letters (A through Z) and 10 numbers (0 through 9) as shortcut keystrokes in a particular macro sheet.

Excel 98 doesn't offer much in the way of variety when it comes to custom buttons (see Figure 12-5) to which you can assign macros. You've got a

Figure 12-5:
The
Commands
tab of the
Customize
dialog box
after
selecting
the Macros
category.

choice between a happy-face button and a happy-face button (it keeps those macros smiling).

To assign a macro to a custom button, follow these steps:

1. **If the macro you want to assign to a toolbar button is attached to a particular workbook rather than to your Personal Macro Workbook, make sure that the workbook is open. If the workbook is not open, you need to open it with the Open tool on the Standard toolbar or the File⇨Open command on the menu bar.**

   Remember, Excel opens your Personal Macro Workbook each time you start the program, making its macros available anywhere and anytime in the program. Macros saved as part of a particular workbook, however, are only available when that workbook is open.

2. **Choose View⇨Toolbars⇨Customize on the menu bar to open the Customize dialog box.**

3. **If the toolbar to which you want to add the macro is not already displayed, select its check box in the Toolbars list box on the Toolbars tab.**

4. **Select the Commands tab and then select Macros in the Categories list box and Custom Button (the one with the Happy Face icon) in the Commands list box.**

5. Drag the Happy Face icon from the Commands list box to the place on the toolbar where you want the macro button to appear; then release the mouse button.

6. (Optional) To assign your own name (which appears as the button's tooltip when you position the mouse pointer over it), Control+click the button; then choose Name on the shortcut menu, type the new button name in its text box, and then press Return.

7. (Optional) To change the icon to something besides that ridiculous Happy Face, Control+click the macro button; then choose Change Button Image on its shortcut menu and click the new icon you want to use in the pop-up palette that appears.

Note that even here you don't get much a selection in the way of custom icons. See the "Cute as a button" section that follows for a way to draw your own icons.

8. To assign the macro to the macro button, Control+click its button; then choose Assign Macro on the shortcut menu.

Excel opens the Assign Macro dialog box (see Figure 12-6).

Figure 12-6: The Assign Macro dialog box.

9. **Select or record the macro that you want to assign to the tool.**

   To assign an existing macro to the selected tool, double-click the macro name in the Macro Name list box or select the macro name and click OK or press Return.

   To record a new macro for the tool, click the Record button and record a macro just as you would record any other (see Chapter 11).

10. **Repeat Steps 5 through 9 for every macro you want to assign to a custom button.**

11. **Click the Close button or press Return to close the Customize dialog box.**

Cute as a button

Fortunately, you aren't stuck with button images that have pictures of smiley faces, hearts, and coffee mugs. You can copy an image from another button, or, if you're an artist, you can use the Button Editor to create your own image.

To paste a picture from one button to another, follow these steps:

1. **Open the Customize dialog box by choosing View⇨Toolbars⇨ Customize on the menu bar or by choosing the Customize command on a toolbar shortcut menu.**

2. **If it's not already displayed, open the toolbar that contains the button image you want to copy by selecting its check box in the Toolbars list box on the Toolbars tab.**

3. **Control+click the button you want to copy; then choose Copy Button Image on its shortcut menu to copy this image to the Clipboard.**

4. **Control+click the button onto which you want to copy the image that's in the Clipboard; then choose Paste Button Image on its short- cut menu.**

That's all there is to it. Excel replaces the face of the selected tool with the picture stored in the Clipboard.

If you'd prefer to create your own masterpiece rather than steal one of the existing button images (which may already be associated with a particular action if it appears on another toolbar that you use), you can edit an image with the new Button Editor. To open the Button Editor (shown in Figure 12-7), you open the Customize dialog box and, if necessary, display the toolbar; then select Edit Button Image on the button's shortcut menu.

To edit the button's icon, click the color you want to use and then click the squares (called pixels) in the Picture area to paint with the color. If you make a mistake, you can click the pixel a second time to restore it to its

Figure 12-7:
Customizing
the Happy
Face icon
in the
Button
Editor.

original color. If you want to draw a picture from scratch rather than edit the one you selected, you need to click the Clear button before you start drawing. If you want to erase part of the image, click the Erase box in the Colors area and then click the pixels that you want to erase in the picture.

Figure 12-7 shows my artwork after editing that silly Happy Face icon in the Button Editor so that it looks more like my silly dog Spike. Figure 12-8 shows my custom toolbar after replacing the button with the image of the Happy Face with Spike's image and assigning to it the Company Name macro created in Chapter 11. Refer to "A Macro a Day" for details.

Figure 12-8:
Greg's Cool
Tools
custom
toolbar
after
editing that
horrible
Happy Face
button.

Part VI
The Part of Tens

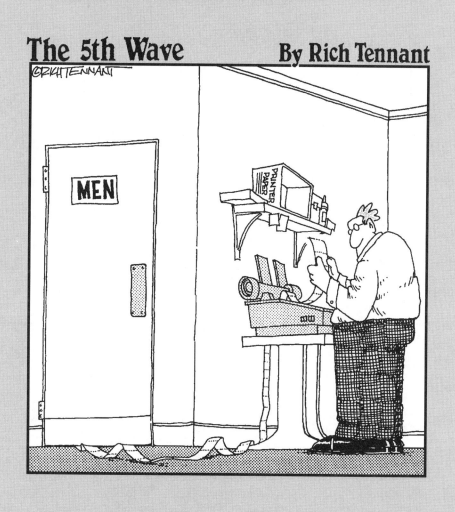

The 5th Wave   By Rich Tennant

MEN

PRINTER PAPER

In this part . . .

Finally, you come to the fun part of Excel 98, the Part of Tens, where the chapters all consist of lists with the top ten Excel tips on this, that, and everything in between. In homage to David Letterman (Indiana's favorite son), you'll find a chapter on the top ten new features in Excel 98, top ten things in Excel that always trip you up, top ten ways to impress your boss, as well as the top ten thousand (or so it seems) keystroke shortcuts included in this baby. And, in homage to Cecil B. deMille, Moses, and a much higher power, we've even included a chapter with the Ten Commandments of Excel 98 that, although not written in stone, when followed faithfully, are guaranteed to give you heavenly results.

Chapter 13
Top Ten New Features in Excel 98

*I*f you're looking for a quick rundown on what's new in Excel 98, look no further! Here it is, my official Top Ten New Features list. Just a cursory glance down the list tells you that the thrust of the new features is auto this 'n' that, such 'n' such tips, and so 'n' so Wizards.

And just in case you're interested in more than just a cursory feature description, I've included a cross-reference with chapter and verse to the place in this book where I cover the feature in more detail.

10. **QuickTime and QuickTime VR movies:** This new Insert⇨Movie feature lets you add links to QuickTime and QuickTime VR movies to your spreadsheets the same way you add clip art. You can then use the new Movie toolbar to playback the movies that you add. (See "QuickTime Anytime" in Chapter 8.)

9. **Edit Formula button:** This new formula bar feature makes it easy to modify the formulas and functions you enter into a cell. (See "Editing a function with the Edit Formula button" in Chapter 2.)

8. **Natural formulas:** This dandy new feature lets you use column and row headings that you've entered in a table of data instead of cell addresses in the formulas that you create to calculate totals, averages, and so on — all without having to assign a single range name. (See "Naming formulas with data table headings" in Chapter 6.)

7. **Screentips:** This feature employs tiny, pop-up notes that appear at the tip of your mouse pointer as you pass over particular objects or use the mouse in certain drag operations. Screentips identify the different buttons on toolbars as well as keep you informed of your progress in the worksheet. In addition to appearing when you move over the buttons on the various Excel toolbars, Screentips appear when using the scroll bars to scroll to new cells, when using the Fill handle to fill in a series of data entries, and when moving and copying cell selections in a worksheet, keeping you informed of your current position. (See "The secrets of scrolling" in Chapter 1, "Fill 'er up with AutoFill" in Chapter 2, and "Insertions courtesy of drag and drop" in Chapter 4.)

6. **Save As HTML:** This command opens the Internet Assistant Wizard, which walks you through the steps for converting worksheet data to an HTML table that you can publish in Web pages for the Internet or your company's intranet. (See "Converting worksheet data into an HTML table" in Chapter 10.)

5. **Hyperlinks:** This features makes it a snap to add links to cell entries or graphic images added to a worksheet. When you click a hyperlink, the link can take you to another document or workbook, another worksheet within the same workbook, or a Web page on the Internet or your company's intranet. (See "Adding Hyperlinks to a Worksheet" in Chapter 10.)

4. **Page Break preview:** This brand-new preview feature not only gives you an overview of the page breaks prior to printing your report but lets you modify them. (See "When Ya Gonna Give Your Page a Break?" in Chapter 5.)

3. **Conditional formatting:** This new formatting feature lets you set up the conditions under which certain cell formats are to be applied to a cell selection. (See "Conditional Formatting" in Chapter 3.)

2. **Office Assistant:** In an attempt to enliven the online help, Microsoft has come up with the Office Assistant — your personal aide-de-camp who is ready to answer any of your questions about using Excel 98 as well as to suggest better ways to get things done. When you first use the Office Assistant, he takes the persona of Max, a rather animated Macintosh computer. If, however, you find that Max doesn't suit your personality, you can select any one of the eight other available characters. (See "Conferring with your Office Assistant" in Chapter 1.)

1. **New and improved cell formatting:** Excel 98 incorporates a whole bunch of really great, new cell-formatting features, including automatically widening columns to accommodate the number format you apply to cells, merging cells together, indenting entries within their cells, rotating cell entry text anywhere from −90 to +90 degrees, and shrinking the font in cells to suit the current column width. (See "Look Ma, no more format overflow!," "Altering the Alignment," "Intent on Indents," "Reordering the orientation," and "Shrink to Fit" in Chapter 3.)

Chapter 14
Top Ten Beginner Basics

● ●

*1*f these ten items are all you ever really master in Excel 98, you'll still be way ahead of the competition. When all is said and done, this top ten list lays out all the fundamental skills required to successfully use Excel 98:

10. To start Excel 98 from the Office Manager pop-menu, click the Microsoft Office icon on the menu bar and then choose Microsoft Excel on the menu. Excel 98 launches with a new, blank workbook that you can begin using.

9. To open an Excel workbook for editing at the same time you start Excel 98, locate and open the folder containing the workbook in the Finder. Then, double-click the workbook's icon.

8. To locate a part of a worksheet that you cannot see on-screen, use the scroll bars at the right and bottom of the workbook window to bring new parts of the worksheet into view. When scrolling, the CellTips indicator on the scroll bar shows the letter of the column or the number of the row that will appear in the upper-left corner of the worksheet upon releasing the mouse button.

7. To start a new workbook (containing three blank worksheets), click the New tool on the Standard toolbar (or choose File⇨New or press ⌘+N). To insert a new worksheet in a workbook (should you need more than three), choose Insert⇨Worksheet from the menu bar.

6. To activate an open workbook and display it on-screen (in front of any others you have open), open the Window menu and select the name or number of the workbook you want. To locate a particular worksheet in the active workbook, select that worksheet's sheet tab at the bottom of the workbook document window. To display more sheet tabs, click the sheet scrolling arrows on the left side of the bottom of the workbook window.

5. To enter stuff in a worksheet, select the cell where the information should appear; then begin typing. When you're finished, click the Enter button on the formula bar or press Tab, Return, or one of the arrow keys.

4. To edit the stuff you've already entered into a cell, double-click the cell or position the cell pointer in the cell and press ⌘+U. Excel then locates the insertion point at the end of the cell entry. When you finish correcting the entry, click the Enter button on the formula bar or press Tab or Return.

3. To choose one of the many commands from the menus on the menu bar, choose the menu name (on the menu bar) to open the menu and then choose the command name on the pull-down menu. To choose a command on a shortcut menu, Control+click the object (cell, sheet tab, toolbar, chart, and so on).

2. To save a copy of your workbook on disk the first time around, choose File⇨Save or File⇨Save As from the menu bar (or click the Save button on the Standard toolbar or press ⌘+S); then designate the drive and folder where the file should be located and replace the temporary Workbook1 filename in the File name text box with your own filename. To save changes to the workbook thereafter, click the Save tool on the Standard toolbar (or choose File⇨Save or press ⌘+S).

1. To quit Excel when you're done working with the program, choose the File⇨Quit command on the menu bar or click the program's close box or press ⌘+Q. If the workbook you have open contains unsaved changes, Excel 98 asks whether you want to save the workbook before closing Excel. Before you shut off your computer, be sure to use the Special⇨Shut Down command on the menu bar to shut down your Macintosh.

Chapter 15

The Ten Commandments of Excel 98

● ●

*I*n working with Excel 98, you're likely to discover certain dos and don'ts that, if followed religiously, can make using this program just heavenly. Lo and behold, the following Excel ten commandments contain just such precepts for eternal Excel bliss:

10. Thou shalt commit thy work to disk by saving thy changes often (File⇨Save or ⌘+S).

9. Thou shalt nameth thy workbooks when saving them the first time with meaningful filenames, including spaces and all manner of weird signs and symbols. So, too, shalt thou mark well into which folder thou savest thy file lest thou thinkest in error that thy workbook be lost when next thou hast need of it.

8. Thou shalt not spread wide the data in thy worksheet, but rather shalt thou gather together thy tables and avoideth skipping columns and rows unless this is necessary to make thy data intelligible. All this shalt thou do in order that thou mightest conserve the memory of thy computer.

7. Thou shalt begin all thy Excel 98 formulas with = (equal) as the sign of computation. If, however, ye be formerly of the Lotus 1-2-3 tribe, thou shalt haveth special dispensation and canst commence thy formulas with the + sign and thy functions with the @ sign.

6. Thou shalt select thy cells before thou bringeth any Excel command to bear upon them, just as surely as thou doest sow before thou reapest.

5. Thou shalt useth the Undo feature (Edit⇨Undo or ⌘+Z) immediately upon committing any transgression in thy worksheet so that thou mayest clean up thy mess. Should thou forgeteth to useth thy Undo straightway, thou must select the action that thou wouldst undo from the pop-up menu attached to the Undo button that thou findest on the Standard toolbar. Note well that any action that thou selectest from this menu will undo not only that action but all actions that proceedeth it on this menu.

4. Thou shalt not delete, neither shalt thou insert, columns and rows in a worksheet lest thou hath first verified that no part as yet uncovered of thy worksheet will thereby be wiped out or otherwise displaced.

3. Thou shalt not print thy worksheet lest thou hath first previewed the printing (File⇨Print Preview) and art satisfied that all of thy pages are upright in the sight of the printer.

2. Thou shalt changeth the manner of recalculation of thy workbooks from automatic to manual (Tools⇨Preferences⇨Calculation tab⇨Manual) when thy workbook groweth so great in size that Excel sloweth down to a camel crawl whenever thou doest anything in any one of its worksheets. Woe to thee, however, should thou also removest the check mark from the Recalculate before Save check box when thou setteth up manual calculation or should thou ignorest the Calculate message on the status bar and not presseth the Calc Now button on the Calculation tab of thy Preferences dialog box or ⌘+= before such time as thou mayest print any of thy workbook data.

1. Thou shalt protecteth thy completed workbook and all of its worksheets from corruption and inequities at the hands of others (Tools⇨Protection⇨Protect Sheet or Protect Workbook). And if thou be brazen enough to addeth a password to thy workbook protection, beware lest thou forgeteth thy password in any part. For verily I say unto to thee, on the day that thou knowest not thy password, that day shalt be the last upon which thou lookest upon thy workbook in any way.

Chapter 16

Top Ten Things in Excel 98 That Can Trip You Up

The following "welcome warnings" point out the most common pitfalls that get beginning Excel users. Avoid these pitfalls like the plague, and I promise that you'll be a lot happier using Excel 98:

10. If you introduce a space into an otherwise completely numeric entry, Excel categorizes the entry as text (indicated by its alignment at the left edge of the cell). If you feed that entry into a formula, the text classification completely throws off the answer because text entries are treated like zeros (0) in a formula.

9. When nesting parentheses in a formula, pair them properly so that you have a right parenthesis for every left parenthesis in the formula. If you do not include a right parenthesis for every left one, Excel 98 displays an alert dialog box, suggesting how the program "thinks" the parentheses should balance out. If you agree with Excel's solution to the parentheses problem, click the Yes button in this alert box.

8. You can re-enter edited cell contents by clicking the Enter box on the formula bar or by pressing Tab, Return, or Enter, but you can't use the arrow keys. When you're editing a cell entry, the arrow keys only move the insertion point through the entry.

7. Be sure that you don't press one of the arrow keys to complete a cell entry within a preselected cell range instead of clicking the Enter box on the formula bar or pressing Return (to move down a row) or Enter (to move right one column). Pressing an arrow key deselects the range of cells when Excel moves the cell pointer.

6. When you know that you're going to want to do something more after entering data in a cell (like add some formatting or a hyperlink to it), be sure to complete the entry by pressing the Enter key on the numeric keypad rather than the Return key on the regular keyboard. Pressing the Enter key leaves the cell pointer in the cell with the new entry, whereas pressing the Return key moves the cell pointer down one row.

5. The Edit⇨Undo command changes in response to whatever action you just took. Because it keeps changing after each action, you'd do best to remember to strike when the iron is hot, so to speak, by using the Undo

feature to restore the worksheet to its previous state *before* you choose another command. However, if you do forget, you can undo multiple actions by selecting the last action you want undone in the pop-up menu attached to the Undo button on the Standard toolbar.

4. Deleting entire columns and rows from a worksheet is risky business unless you're sure that the columns and rows in question contain nothing of value. Remember, when you delete an entire row from the worksheet, you delete *all information from Column A through IV* in that row (and you can see only very few columns in this row). Likewise, when you delete an entire column from the worksheet, you delete *all information from Row 1 through 65,536* in that column.

3. Be careful with global search-and-replace operations; they can really mess up a worksheet in a hurry if you inadvertently replace values, parts of formulas, or characters in titles and headings that you hadn't intended to change. As a precaution, *never undertake a global search-and-replace operation on an unsaved worksheet.*

   Also, verify whether or not the Find entire cells only check box is selected before you begin. You can end up with a lot of unwanted replacements if you leave this check box unselected when you really only want to replace entire cell entries (rather than matching parts in cell entries). If you do make a mess, choose the Edit⇨Undo Replace command (⌘+Z) to restore the worksheet. If you don't discover the problem in time to use Undo, close the messed-up worksheet without saving the changes and open the unreplaced version that you saved — thanks to reading this warning!

2. To make it impossible to remove protection from a particular worksheet in a workbook or an entire workbook and all its worksheets unless you know the password, enter a password in the Password (Optional) text box of the Protect Sheet or Protect Workbook dialog box (Tools⇨Protection⇨Protect Sheet or Protect Workbook). Excel masks each character you type in this text box with an asterisk. After you click OK, Excel makes you re-enter the password before protecting the worksheet or workbook. From then on, you can remove protection from the worksheet or workbook only if you can reproduce the password exactly as you assigned it (including any case differences). Be very careful with passwords. If you forget the password, you cannot change any locked cells, and you cannot unlock any more cells in the particular worksheet or, in the case of a workbook, any of its worksheets!

1. You *cannot* use the Undo feature to bring back a database record you removed with the Delete button in the data form! Excel is definitely *not* kidding when it uses words like "deleted permanently." As a precaution, always save a backup version of the worksheet with the database before you start removing old records.

Chapter 17

Top Ten Ways to Impress the Boss

*T*he ten little tips contained in this chapter are worth their weight in
Motorola PowerPC 750 (G3) chips (gold is out this season). Please keep
them in mind as you work with Excel 98. After all, who wants computing to
be any harder than it has to be?

10. Watch the Office Assistant or the Office Assistant button on the Stan-
    dard toolbar if the Office Assistant isn't open. When a yellow light bulb
    appears in the Office Assistant button or the Office Assistant window
    (assuming that you have this window open), you know that Excel has
    some tidbits of wisdom to dispense to you based on the things you
    were just doing in the workbook.

    If the Office Assistant window isn't open, click the Office Assistant
    button on the Standard toolbar to open it. Then click the light bulb on
    the Office Assistant window to display a balloon with the latest tip.
    When you finish reading the tip, click the Close button in the balloon to
    make it disappear.

9. Name any often-used cell range in a worksheet by selecting the cell or
   cells in the worksheet, clicking the Name box on the formula, typing the
   new range name in this box, and then pressing Return. After naming a
   cell or cell range in this manner, you can then use its name to move to
   it, select its cells, or print it. Remember, you can select a range name
   from the pop-up menu on the Name box or by pressing the Go To key
   (F5) and then selecting the range name in the Go To dialog box. When
   you click OK, Excel not only moves you to the first cell in that range but
   selects all its cells as well.

8. Don't waste all day scrolling through a seemingly endless table of data.
   Instead, use the ⌘+arrow key (or End and then arrow key) combination
   to jump from one edge of the table to another edge or to jump from the
   edge of one table to another.

7. If you find yourself continually entering the same list of items over and
   over again in new worksheets, create a custom list of items and then
   enter the entire list by typing just the first item in the series and then
   dragging out the rest of the series with the AutoFill handle. (See "Creating custom lists for AutoFill" in Chapter 2 for a refresher course on how
   to create a custom series.)

6. Lose the graphics in a workbook worksheet by replacing them on-screen with placeholders (Tools⇨Preferences⇨View tab⇨Show Place-holders) when you find that Excel just can't keep up with your movements in a particular worksheet. Screen response time is greatly improved by this trick — just don't forget to put the graphics back before you print the worksheet or you'll end up with shaded rectangles where the pictures ought to be!

5. When making editing and formatting changes in your Excel workbooks, don't overlook the shortcut menus attached to the things that need fixing (opened by Control+clicking the object). Shortcut menus can save a lot of time that you would otherwise waste searching the menus on the menu bar to find the editing or formatting command you need. Also, don't forget how much time you can save by using the tools on the Standard and Formatting toolbars to get things done!

4. Before making changes to an unfamiliar worksheet, use the Zoom button on the Standard toolbar to zoom out to 50% or 25% so that you can get a good idea of how the information is laid out. When inserting or deleting cells in an unfamiliar worksheet, resist the temptation to insert or remove entire columns and rows, which can damage unseen tables of data. Instead, just insert or cut out the cell ranges in the region you're working in — you know, think globally, but act locally!

3. To maximize the number of worksheet cells displayed on-screen at one time without having to resort to changing the magnification with the Zoom feature, choose View⇨Full Screen. This makes the formula bar, the Standard and Formatting toolbars, and the status bar all go away, leaving only the menu bar and scroll bars in addition to the cells in the current worksheet (giving you a view of some 42 full rows rather than the normal thirty something). When you're ready to return to the normal (rather cramped) screen display, click the Close Full Screen button in the floating Full Screen toolbar (which automatically appears whenever you choose View⇨Full Screen) or, if this toolbar is hidden, choose View⇨Full Screen a second time.

2. Give yourself a break and record a macro for doing those little tasks that you end up doing over and over and over again (choose Tools⇨Macro⇨Record New Macro). Using macros to get things done not only alleviates the boredom but also frees you up to do truly important things (like surfing the World Wide Wait — er, Web!).

1. Name each worksheet that you use in a workbook with some intelligible English name like Invoice or Price List (by double-clicking the sheet tab, entering a new name on the tab, and then pressing Enter) rather than leave them with their normally indecipherable names like Sheet1 and Sheet2. That way, you not only know which sheets in your workbook you've already used, but you also have a fair idea of what they contain and when you should select them.

Chapter 18

Top Ten Thousand Keystroke Shortcuts

● ●

*I*f you like using keystroke shortcuts on your computer, have I got great news for you — Excel is loaded with them. There are keystroke shortcuts for doing just about everything you'd probably be tempted to do with the program. In the tables in this chapter, I've brought together the most popular of these keystroke shortcuts and arranged them alphabetically by the feature or the type of work they do.

AutoFilter Shortcuts

Press	To
Option+↓	Open the AutoFilter list
↓	Select next item in AutoFilter list
↑	Select previous item in AutoFilter list
Home	Select first item (All) in the AutoFilter list
End	Select last item in the AutoFilter list
Return	Filter the list using the item selected in the AutoFilter list

Calculation Shortcuts

Press	To
Control+=(equal sign)	Calculate all open worksheets
Shift+F9	Calculate active worksheet

Cell Selection Shortcuts

Press	*To*
Control+Shift+* (asterisk)	Select current region (the area with the cell pointer enclosed by blank rows and columns)
Control+Spacebar	Select entire column
Shift+Spacebar	Select entire row
⌘+A	Select entire worksheet
⌘+Shift+O (letter O)	Select all cells with comments
Control+] (close square bracket)	Select cells directly referred to in the formula in the active cell
Control+Shift+} (close curly brace)	Select cells directly or indirectly referred to in the formula in the active cell
Control+[(open square bracket)	Select cells directly referred to in the formula(s) in the current cell selection
Control+Shift+{ (open curly brace)	Select cells directly or indirectly referred to in formula(s) in the current cell selection
⌘+Shift+Z	Select visible cells in the current cell selection

Data Entry Shortcuts

Press	*To*
Esc	Cancel cell entry
⌘+Y	Repeat last action
Control+Option+Return	Start new line in same cell
Delete	Delete selection or character to left of insertion point
Del	Delete selection or character to right of insertion point
Control+Del	Delete to end of line
↑, ↓, ←, →	Move one character up, down, left, or right
Shift+F2	Edit cell comment
Control+Shift+F3	Create names from row and column labels
Control+D	Fill down
Control+R	Fill right
Control+Return	Fill selected range with current entry
Return	Complete cell entry and move one cell down

Press	*To*
Enter	Complete cell entry and leave cell pointer in active cell
Shift+Return	Complete cell entry and move one cell up
Tab	Complete cell entry and move one cell to the right
Shift+Tab	Complete cell entry and move one cell to the left
↑, ↓, ←, →	Complete cell entry and move up, down, left, or right one cell
Home	Complete cell entry and move to cell at beginning of row

Data Form Shortcuts

Press	*To*
Tab	Move to the next field you can edit in the record
Shift+Tab	Move to the previous field you can edit in the record
↓	Move to the same field in the next record
↑	Move to the same field in the previous record
Return	Move to the first field of the next record
Shift+Return	Move to the first field of the previous record
Page Down	Move to the same field ten records ahead
Page Up	Move to the same field ten records back
Control+Page Down	Move to a new record
Control+Page Up	Move to the first record
Home	Move to the beginning of a field entry
End	Move to the end of a field entry

Data Formatting Shortcuts

Press	*To*
⌘+1	Format dialog box
⌘+Shift+L	Style dialog box
Control+Shift+~ (tilde)	General number format
Control+Shift+$	Currency number format
Control+Shift+%	Percentage number format

(continued)

Data Formatting Shortcuts *(continued)*

Press	To
Control+Shift+^	Exponential number format
Control+Shift+#	Date number format with day, month, year
Control+Shift+@	Time number format with hour, minute, AM/PM
⌘+Option+0 (zero)	Apply outline border to cell selection
⌘+Option+- (hyphen)	Remove all borders from cell selection
⌘+Option+arrow key	Apply/remove outline border from edge of cell selection in arrow's direction
Control+B	Apply/remove bold to text
Control+I	Apply/remove italics to text
Control+U	Apply/remove underlining to text
⌘+Shift+_ (underline)	Apply/remove strikethrough effect to text
⌘+Shift+W	Apply/remove shadow effect to text
⌘+Shift+D	Apply/remove outline effect to text
Control+9	Hide rows
Control+Shift+(	Unhide rows
Control+0 (zero)	Hide columns
Control+Shift+)	Unhide columns

Editing Shortcuts

Press	To
⌘+C	Copy the selection
⌘+V	Paste the selection
⌘+X	Cut the selection
Delete	Clear the contents of the selection
Control+Shift+Plus Sign (+)	Insert (dialog box)
Control+- (hyphen)	Delete the selection
⌘+Z	Undo last action
⌘+Y	Redo last action
⌘+K	Delete (dialog box)
⌘+F	Find (dialog box)
F7	Spell check worksheet

File Shortcuts

Press	To
⌘+N	New workbook file
⌘+O	Open workbook file
⌘+W	Close workbook file
⌘+S	Save workbook file

Formula Bar Shortcuts

Press	To
= (equal sign)	Start a formula
Return	Complete entry
Esc	Cancel entry
⌘+U	Edit active cell
⌘+Shift+T	AutoSum formula
Control+; (semicolon)	Current date
Control+Shift+: (colon)	Current time
Control+K	Insert hyperlink
Control+Shift+" (quotation mark)	Copy value from cell above
Control+' (apostrophe)	Copy formula from cell above
Control+` (accent grave)	Switch between value and formula display

Menu Bar Shortcuts

Press	To
F10	Activate menu bar
Shift+F10	Show shortcut menu
↓ or ↑	Next or previous menu option
← or →	Switch between main and submenu

Navigation Shortcuts

Press	To
↑, ↓, ←, →	Move one cell in the direction of the arrow
Control+arrow key or End, arrow key	Move to the end of the current data region in the direction of arrow key
Home	Move to the beginning of the row
Control+Home	Move to the first cell (A1) of the worksheet
Control+End or End, Home	Move to the last active cell of the worksheet (cell at the intersection of the last occupied row and column)
End, Return	Move to the right to the last nonblank cell in row
Page Up	Move up one screen
Page Down	Move down one screen
Option+Page Up	Move one screen to the left
Option+Page Down	Move one screen to the right
Control+Page Up	Move to the previous worksheet in workbook
Control+Page Down	Move to the next worksheet in workbook
Control+F6 or Control+Tab	Move to next workbook window
Control+Shift+F6 or Control+Shift+Tab	Move the previous workbook window
F6	Move to the next pane in worksheet
Shift+F6	Move to the previous pane in worksheet
Control+Delete	Scroll to display the active cell

Office Assistant Shortcuts

Press	To
Help	Open Office Assistant dialog box
Esc	Close Office Assistant or Tip message
⌘+topic number	Select Help topic from Office Assistant message (where 1 is first topic, 2 is second topic, etc.)
⌘+N	Next tip in Tip message
⌘+B	Previous tip in Tip message

Print and Print Preview Shortcuts

Press	To
⌘+P	Print dialog box
↑, ↓, ←, →	Move around preview page when zoomed in
Control+↑ or Control+←	Move to first page when zoomed out
Control+↓ or Control+→	Move to the first page when zoomed out
Page Up	Move to previous page when zoomed out
Page Down	Move to the next page when zoomed out

Toolbar Shortcuts

Press	To
Option+F10	Activate toolbar
Control+Tab	Next toolbar
Control+Shift+Tab	Previous toolbar
Tab	Next toolbar button or menu
Shift+Tab	Previous toolbar button or menu
Return	Open menu or perform button's action

Window and Dialog Box Shortcuts

Press	To
⌘+W	Close active workbook window
⌘+F6	Switch to the next workbook window
⌘+Shift+F6	Switch to the previous workbook window
Control+Tab or Control+Page Down	Switch to the next tab in dialog box
Control+Shift+Tab or Control+Page Up	Switch to the previous tab in dialog box
Tab	Move to the next text box in dialog box
Shift+Tab	Move the previous text box in dialog box
Esc	Cancel changes and close dialog box
Return	Affirm changes and close dialog box
↑, ↓, ←, →	Move between options in pop-up menu or group of options
First letter of option name	Select option in open pop-up menu

Index

(continued)

YOUR ONLINE RESOURCE

WWW.DUMMIES.COM

Discover Dummies Online!

The Dummies Web Site is your fun and friendly online resource for the latest information about ...*For Dummies*® books and your favorite topics. The Web site is the place to communicate with us, exchange ideas with other ...*For Dummies* readers, chat with authors, and have fun!

Ten Fun and Useful Things You Can Do at www.dummies.com

1. Win free ...*For Dummies* books and more!
2. Register your book and be entered in a prize drawing.
3. Meet your favorite authors through the IDG Books Author Chat Series.
4. Exchange helpful information with other ...*For Dummies* readers.
5. Discover other great ...*For Dummies* books you must have!
6. Purchase Dummieswear™ exclusively from our Web site.
7. Buy ...*For Dummies* books online.
8. Talk to us. Make comments, ask questions, get answers!
9. Download free software.
10. Find additional useful resources from authors.

Link directly to these ten fun and useful things at
http://www.dummies.com/10useful

For other technology titles from IDG Books Worldwide, go to
www.idgbooks.com

Not on the Web yet? It's easy to get started with *Dummies 101*®: *The Internet For Windows*®*95* or *The Internet For Dummies*®, 5th Edition, at local retailers everywhere.

IDG BOOKS WORLDWIDE

Find other ...*For Dummies* books on these topics:

Business • Career • Databases • Food & Beverage • Games • Gardening • Graphics • Hardware
Health & Fitness • Internet and the World Wide Web • Networking • Office Suites
Operating Systems • Personal Finance • Pets • Programming • Recreation • Sports
Spreadsheets • Teacher Resources • Test Prep • Word Processing

IDG BOOKS WORLDWIDE BOOK REGISTRATION

Register This Book and Win!

We want to hear from you!

Visit **http://my2cents.dummies.com** to register this book and tell us how you liked it!

- Get entered in our monthly prize giveaway.

- Give us feedback about this book — tell us what you like best, what you like least, or maybe what you'd like to ask the author and us to change!

- Let us know any other ...*For Dummies*® topics that interest you.

Your feedback helps us determine what books to publish, tells us what coverage to add as we revise our books, and lets us know whether we're meeting your needs as a ...*For Dummies* reader. You're our most valuable resource, and what you have to say is important to us!

Not on the Web yet? It's easy to get started with *Dummies 101*®: *The Internet For Windows*® *95* or *The Internet For Dummies*®, 5th Edition, at local retailers everywhere.

Or let us know what you think by sending us a letter at the following address:

...*For Dummies* Book Registration
Dummies Press
7260 Shadeland Station, Suite 100
Indianapolis, IN 46256-3945
Fax 317-596-5498

BUSINESS AND
GENERAL
REFERENCE
BOOK SERIES
FROM IDG

COMPUTER
BOOK SERIES
FROM IDG